The Big Book of Coding Interviews

(in Python)

Interview Druid

Third Edition: 2018

The Big Book of Coding Interviews (in Python)

By Interview Druid

© Interview Druid, Parineeth M. R. All Rights reserved. No part of this book may be reproduced in any form, mimeograph or any other means, without permission in writing from the copyright owners.

If you spot any mistakes in the book, please e-mail them to interviewdruid@gmail.com

Contents

1. Data Structures 1
    1.1 Linked Lists 6
    1.2 Stacks and Queues 33
    1.3 Trees 49
    1.4 Lists 97
    1.5 Strings 131
    1.6 Bitmaps 159
    1.7 Application of Data Structures 176
2. Sorting and Searching 183
    2.1 Searching 185
    2.2 Sorting 213
3. Algorithms 230
    3.1 Greedy Algorithms 231
    3.2 Dynamic Programming 239
    3.3 Miscellaneous Algorithms 268
4. Math 303
5. Design 331
6. Python 345
7. Computer Science Concepts 367
8. Puzzles 382
    8.1 Arithmetic Puzzles 383
    8.2 Measurement Puzzles 391
    8.3 Probability Puzzles 400
    8.4 Lateral Thinking Puzzles 409
    8.5 Logic Puzzles 417
    8.6 Classic Puzzles 424

9. Personality..440

List of Coding Problems

1.1 Linked Lists

1. Reverse a linked list — 6
2. Reverse every K nodes — 8
3. Find the Kth node from the end — 10
4. Swap K^{th} node from beginning and end — 11
5. Delete a node given a reference to it — 13
6. Remove duplicates — 14
7. Rotate a linked list — 15
8. Find where two linked lists merge — 17
9. Find if a linked list has a cycle — 19
10. Interleave linked lists — 22
11. Merge two sorted linked lists — 23
12. Copy a linked list having a reference to a random node — 24
13. Is linked list a palindrome — 27
14. Add linked lists — 29
15. Multiply linked lists — 31

1.2 Stacks and Queues

1. Queue using stacks — 33
2. Stack using queues — 36
3. N stacks using lists — 39
4. Circular queue — 41
5. Get minimum in stack — 43

6. Sort the stack	45
7. Check nesting of parenthesis, brackets, braces	47

1.3 Trees

1. Mirror image of binary tree	49
2. Is binary tree symmetric	50
3. Is binary tree balanced	51
4. Is binary tree a binary search tree	52
5. Print binary tree in level order	53
6. Print binary tree in spiral (zigzag) order	55
7. Find least common ancestor in binary tree	58
8. Convert list to binary search tree	60
9. Convert doubly linked list to binary search tree	62
10. Convert binary search tree to doubly linked list	64
11. Find previous and next nodes in binary search tree	66
12. Find K^{th} largest node in binary search tree	69
13. Find the node pairs that sum to K in binary search tree	70
14. Store the sum of nodes that are greater than current node	72
15. Vertical sum of binary tree	74
16. K-heavy path	77
17. Find diameter of binary tree	79
18. Construct binary tree using in-order and pre-order	81
19. Serialize and deserialize a binary tree	83
20. Print the border nodes of a binary tree	85
21. Print the right view of a binary tree	87

List of Coding Problems

1.1 Linked Lists

1. Reverse a linked list	6
2. Reverse every K nodes	8
3. Find the Kth node from the end	10
4. Swap K^{th} node from beginning and end	11
5. Delete a node given a reference to it	13
6. Remove duplicates	14
7. Rotate a linked list	15
8. Find where two linked lists merge	17
9. Find if a linked list has a cycle	19
10. Interleave linked lists	22
11. Merge two sorted linked lists	23
12. Copy a linked list having a reference to a random node	24
13. Is linked list a palindrome	27
14. Add linked lists	29
15. Multiply linked lists	31

1.2 Stacks and Queues

1. Queue using stacks	33
2. Stack using queues	36
3. N stacks using lists	39
4. Circular queue	41
5. Get minimum in stack	43

    6. Sort the stack   45

    7. Check nesting of parenthesis, brackets, braces   47

1.3 Trees

    1. Mirror image of binary tree   49

    2. Is binary tree symmetric   50

    3. Is binary tree balanced   51

    4. Is binary tree a binary search tree   52

    5. Print binary tree in level order   53

    6. Print binary tree in spiral (zigzag) order   55

    7. Find least common ancestor in binary tree   58

    8. Convert list to binary search tree   60

    9. Convert doubly linked list to binary search tree   62

    10. Convert binary search tree to doubly linked list   64

    11. Find previous and next nodes in binary search tree   66

    12. Find K^{th} largest node in binary search tree   69

    13. Find the node pairs that sum to K in binary search tree   70

    14. Store the sum of nodes that are greater than current node   72

    15. Vertical sum of binary tree   74

    16. K-heavy path   77

    17. Find diameter of binary tree   79

    18. Construct binary tree using in-order and pre-order   81

    19. Serialize and deserialize a binary tree   83

    20. Print the border nodes of a binary tree   85

    21. Print the right view of a binary tree   87

22. Find if one tree is sub-tree of another tree — 88

23. Correct binary search tree where two nodes have been swapped — 90

24. In-order traversal without recursion — 92

25. Morris traversal — 93

26. Merge two binary search trees — 96

4. Lists

1. Find next greatest — 97

2. Remove element — 97

3. Remove duplicates — 99

4. Move zeroes to one end — 100

5. Rotate list — 101

6. Large number subtraction — 103

7. Generate power set — 105

8. Generate all subsets of size R — 106

9. Union and intersection — 107

10. Find most frequently occurring element — 110

11. Find the lowest absolute difference between elements — 112

12. Find 3 elements that sum to S — 113

13. Find maximum product of 3 elements — 115

14. Find product of all other elements except self — 116

15. Find the equilibrium point — 117

16. Find largest sub-list of equal 0's and 1's — 118

17. Matrix rotation — 121

18. Print matrix in spiral order — 124

19. If M[i][j] is 1, then all cells in row i and column j should be set to 1	126
20. Find number of paths in matrix	129

5. Strings

1. Find if two strings are anagrams	131
2. Count number of words in a string	132
3. Convert string to integer	133
4. Convert number to words	134
5. Convert Roman numeral to integer	136
6. Run length encoding	137
7. Remove duplicate characters	138
8. Replace space with "%20"	139
9. Find if one string is rotation of another	140
10. Reverse the words in a string	142
11. Find first non-repeating character in a string	144
12. Find first non-repeating character in a stream	145
13. Find the longest palindrome	147
14. Is any permutation of a word a palindrome	149
15. Generate all substrings of a string	150
16. Generate all permutations of a string	151
17. Scrabble words	152
18. Interleave two strings	153
19. Generate all words for a telephone number	155
20. Generate all permutations of parenthesis, brackets, braces	157

1.6 Bitwise operations

1. Bit set, reset, toggle	159
2. Count the number of bits set	159
3. Find if a number is a power of 2	160
4. Reverse the bits in an integer	160
5. Find the number of different bits between two integers	161
6. Swap bits in an integer	162
7. Compute parity bit	163
8. Copy bits	164
9. Circular bit shift	166
10. Find maximum integer without comparison operators	167
11. Add two numbers without using + operator	168
12. Subtract two numbers without using – operator	170
13. Multiply two numbers without using * operator	171
14. Divide two numbers without using / operator	172
15. Find the number that occurs odd number of times	173
16. Find two numbers that occur odd number of times	174

1.7 Application of Data Structures

1. Priority Queues	176
2. Dictionary	177
3. Insert, delete, fetch and get_random in O(1)	178
4. Implement LRU cache	179
5. Facebook/LinkedIn data structure	182

2.1 Searching

1. Find smallest and second smallest — 185
2. Find max and min using least number of comparisons — 186
3. Find the first occurrence of an element in sorted list — 187
4. Find first element greater than K in sorted list — 188
5. Search a sorted list with interspersed empty slots — 189
6. Search a sorted list of unknown length — 191
7. Find the row in matrix with maximum number of 1's — 193
8. Search a matrix whose rows and columns are sorted — 195
9. Find max in a list whose values first increase and then decrease — 197
10. Find max in a sorted list that has been rotated — 199
11. Search an element in a sorted list that has been rotated — 202
12. Find the largest K numbers in a trillion numbers — 204
13. Find the max in each window of size K — 207
14. Find the median in a stream — 210

2.2 Sorting

1. Wave sort — 213
2. Merge small and large sorted lists — 214
3. Merge M sorted lists — 215
4. Simple linked list sort — 217
5. Linked list sort — 219
6. Dutch National Flag Problem — 221
7. Find the Kth smallest in a sorted list — 223
8. Sort an almost sorted list — 225

9. Sort words so that anagrams occur together — 227

3.1 Greedy Algorithms

1. Stock sale for max profit — 231
2. Activity selection problem — 233
3. Find the least number of train platforms needed — 234
4. N Gas stations problem — 236

3.2 Dynamic Programming

1. Max continuous sum — 239
2. Coin change problem — 241
3. Longest increasing sub-sequence — 244
4. Snake and ladders problem — 246
5. Thief stealing from neighboring houses problem — 248
6. Minimum number of list jumps — 250
7. Number of unique binary search trees — 251
8. Rod cutting problem — 253
9. Maximum sum sub-matrix — 255
10. Minimum path sum in a 2-D matrix — 258
11. Egg break problem — 260
12. Word break problem — 263
13. Box stacking problem — 266

3.3 Miscellaneous Algorithms

1. Match nuts and bolts — 268
2. N queens problem — 269
3. Complete the equation — 271

4. Sudoku solver	272
5. Longest compound word	274
6. Correct the travel itinerary	275
7. Find the number of islands in a matrix	277
8. Find the number of inversions	280
9. Water trapped in histogram	283
10. Area of largest rectangle in histogram	285
11. Expression evaluation	289
12. Connected components in an undirected graph	292
13. Find if cycle is present in directed graph	294
14. Topological sort	297
15. Word transformation	301

4. Math

1. Greatest Common Divisor	304
2. Swap two variables without using temporary variable	305
3. Find missing number	306
4. Find two missing numbers	307
5. Generate primes	309
6. Compute x^y	310
7. Generate random numbers from 1 to 7 using rand5()	311
8. Generate random numbers from 1 to 5 using rand7()	312
9. Perfect card shuffle	313
10. Pick m random values in a list	316
11. Obtain fair coin using an unfair coin	317

12. Generate random numbers using binary random function   318

13. Compute square root   319

14. Number of ways to climb steps   320

15. Find if lines intersect   322

16. Find if two rectangles overlap   323

17. Find the rectangle overlap area   325

18. Card deck encoding   327

19. Ant collision probability   328

20. Probability of forming triangle from broken stick   329

List of Puzzles

8.1 Arithmetic Puzzles

1. Sugar syrup evaporation	383
2. Car average speed	383
3. Number of squares on a chess board	384
4. Number of rectangles on a chess board	385
5. Number of painted cubes	386
6. Angle between hour hand and minute hand in a clock	387
7. Number of times hour and minute hand are aligned in a clock	387
8. Number of matches in a tournament	389
9. Maximum square tile in a rectangular floor	389
10. Handshake puzzle	390

8.2 Measurement Puzzles

1. Measure 4 gallons using a 3 gallon and 5 gallon jug	391
2. Measure 6 gallons using a 7 gallon and 4 gallon jug	392
3. Measure 6 gallons using a 4 gallon and 9 gallon jug	392
4. Measure a single gallon using co-prime jugs	393
5. Measure 15 minutes using a 7 minute and 11 minute sandglass	394
6. Measure 9 minutes using a 7 minute and 4 minute sandglass	394
7. Rope burning puzzle	395
8. Find the heavy marble	395
9. Find box with bad oranges	396
10. Find all boxes with bad oranges	397

11. Weigh scale puzzle	398
12. Find the least number of weights needed	398

8.3 Probability Puzzles

1. Draw socks from drawers	400
2. Black and white marble puzzle	401
3. Red and Blue marble mixing puzzle	402
4. Increase chance of selecting blue marble in jars	403
5. Dice marking puzzle	403
6. Monty Hall problem	404
7. Birthday paradox	404
8. Girl child, boy child puzzle	405
9. Airplane seating puzzle	406
10. Two dogs with same number of hair	408

8.4 Lateral thinking

1. Cut a cake into 8 pieces with 3 cuts	409
2. Crescent moon partitioning	410
3. Calendar on cubes puzzle	410
4. Arrange 10 trees in 5 rows of 4 each	411
5. Arrange 9 trees in 9 rows of 3 each	412
6. Can 4 trees be equidistant on a farm	412
7. Shortest path in the cube	413
8. Age of old man's daughter	413
9. Three light bulbs puzzle	415
10. Camel racing puzzle	415

8.5 Logic

1. Incorrect fruit labelling puzzle	417
2. Gold, silver chest puzzle	418
3. Gold, silver, bronze chest puzzle	418
4. Number of true statements	420
5. Safe path in forest puzzle-1	421
6. Safe path in forest puzzle-2	422
7. Black hat, white hat puzzle	422

8.6 Classic Puzzles

1. Bridge crossing	424
2. Missionaries and Cannibals	425
3. Average salary of 3 people	426
4. Find the poisoned barrel	427
5. Pay the worker using a silver bar	428
6. Coin partitioning	429
7. Dropped pill puzzle	430
8. Coin placing game on circular table	431
9. First to call 50 game	432
10. Cake fair sharing	433
11. Divide a cuboid cake from which a piece has been cut	434
12. Number of horse races needed	435
13. Guess color of hat puzzle	436
14. Prison switch toggling puzzle	438
15. Door toggling puzzle	438

Preface

Dear reader,

This book is a collection of interesting programming interview questions. All aspects and elements of programming interviews including data structures, searching and sorting, algorithms, math, object design, programming language concepts, computer science concepts, puzzles and personality have been exhaustively covered.

Frankly, there is no limit to the number of questions that an interviewer can choose from in an interview. However, some questions are asked more frequently than others. So questions in this book have been carefully chosen after analyzing several interviews so that they represent the frequently asked interview questions.

To make this book a delectable treat to read, I have added plenty of examples, diagrams and tables to help you figure out the solutions.

There are bound to be areas for improvement. Please send me your invaluable feedback to interviewdruid@gmail.com. I will try my best to incorporate your feedback into the subsequent revisions of the book. **If you liked reading the book, I beg you to PLEASE, PLEASE, PLEASE give your review comments on Amazon.**

The link to the github project is

https://github.com/parineeth/tbboci-3rd-edition-python

The complete source code for the coding problems is available at the following URLs

https://goo.gl/qXe5HE

https://goo.gl/2eEbmf

http://www.interviewdruid.com/3rd-edition-python.zip

https://www.dropbox.com/s/k4j31q5zc86s4ib/3rd-edition-python.zip

I hope you enjoy reading this book and successfully crack the coding interviews ahead of you!

Preface

Dear reader,

This book is a collection of interesting programming interview questions. All aspects and elements of programming interviews including data structures, searching and sorting, algorithms, math, object design, programming language concepts, computer science concepts, puzzles and personality have been exhaustively covered.

Frankly, there is no limit to the number of questions that an interviewer can choose from in an interview. However, some questions are asked more frequently than others. So questions in this book have been carefully chosen after analyzing several interviews so that they represent the frequently asked interview questions.

To make this book a delectable treat to read, I have added plenty of examples, diagrams and tables to help you figure out the solutions.

There are bound to be areas for improvement. Please send me your invaluable feedback to interviewdruid@gmail.com. I will try my best to incorporate your feedback into the subsequent revisions of the book. **If you liked reading the book, I beg you to PLEASE, PLEASE, PLEASE give your review comments on Amazon.**

The link to the github project is

https://github.com/parineeth/tbboci-3rd-edition-python

The complete source code for the coding problems is available at the following URLs

https://goo.gl/qXe5HE

https://goo.gl/2eEbmf

http://www.interviewdruid.com/3rd-edition-python.zip

https://www.dropbox.com/s/k4j31q5zc86s4ib/3rd-edition-python.zip

I hope you enjoy reading this book and successfully crack the coding interviews ahead of you!

Preliminaries

1. The link to the github project is

https://github.com/parineeth/tbboci-3rd-edition-python

The complete source code for the coding problems is available at the following URLs

https://goo.gl/qXe5HE

https://goo.gl/2eEbmf

http://www.interviewdruid.com/3rd-edition-python.zip

https://www.dropbox.com/s/k4j31q5zc86s4ib/3rd-edition-python.zip

2. We are using // for integer division to be consistent with different versions of Python

3. We are using range() always in the code since the code will be portable across different versions of Python. If you are using Python 2.x, then you may want to use xrange() instead of range()

4. Queue in Python 2.7 has been renamed to queue in Python 3.x. So to handle this in a portable way, we do the following:

```
try:
    import queue
except ImportError:
    import Queue as queue
```

5. In Python, the stack is implemented using a FIFO Queue. The Python Queue doesn't have the peek function. So to mimic the peek function we make use of the following function

```
def peek(stack):
    result = stack.get()
    stack.put(result)
    return result
```

6. Non-decreasing order indicates that the elements will be arranged from smallest to biggest and there can be repetition of elements in the input. For instance [1, 2, 2, 3, 5] is in non-decreasing order.

Non-increasing order indicates that the elements will be arranged from biggest to smallest and there can be repetition of elements in the input. For instance [5, 5, 4, 2, 1] is in non-increasing order.

1. Data Structures

A linked list is a sequence of nodes, where each node is linked to its neighboring node.

In a singly linked list, a node is linked to only one of its neighbors. The nodes can be traversed in one direction only. In a circular linked list, the last node in the linked list is linked with the first node in the linked list. By making the linked list circular, it is possible to reach any node in the linked list from any starting node. The circular linked list is still traversed in one direction only. In a doubly linked list, each node is linked to its previous neighbor and its next neighbor. The nodes in the doubly linked list can be traversed in both directions.

The advantage of linked lists over lists is that insertion and deletion operations on linked lists are inexpensive. Insertion and deletion operations using lists on the other hand require moving the list elements and are significantly more expensive. If the number of elements is not known before hand in a list, when the list becomes full the entire list will have to be resized which is a costly operation.

The main drawback of linked lists is that they don't provide random access to elements whereas lists provide random access. Also additional memory is consumed by linked lists compared to lists since each node in the linked list will have to maintain the reference to the neighbor.

A linked list can have different types of nodes in it. Also the same node can be a part of many linked lists.

Stack is a data structure with the Last In First Out (LIFO) semantics. The stack can be implemented as a list or a linked list. The main operations on a stack are push, pop and peek. All operations on a stack happen at only one end of the stack – at the top of the stack.

Queue is a data structure with the First In First Out (FIFO) semantics. Queue can also be implemented as a list or a linked list. When using lists, queues are implemented using circular lists. Elements are inserted at the rear end of the queue (enqueue) and removed from the front end of the queue (dequeue).

Tree is a connected acyclic graph. The two most commonly used techniques to traverse a tree are depth first search and breadth first search. Depth First Search can be implemented by placing the nodes of the tree in a stack. Breadth First Search can be implemented by placing the nodes of the tree in a queue.

A binary tree is a tree where each node has at most two child nodes. A balanced binary tree is a binary tree where for each node, the depth of its left sub-tree and the depth of right sub-tree differ by at most 1 node. By maintaining a balanced binary tree, the depth of the tree is minimized. Two of the most popular data structures for maintaining balanced binary trees are Red Black trees and AVL trees

A binary search tree is a binary tree where for each node X in the tree, the nodes in the left sub-tree of X store elements less than the element stored in X and the nodes in the right sub-tree of X store elements greater than the element stored in X.

A binary tree can be traversed using pre-order, in-order or post-order traversal techniques. In pre-order traversal, the root is first processed, followed by the left sub-tree and then the right sub-tree. In in-order traversal, the left sub-tree is first processed, followed by the root and then the right sub-tree. In post-order traversal, the left sub-tree is first processed, followed by the right sub-tree and then the root. It is important to note that in-order traversal can be ambiguous. For instance, although the two trees below are different, they have the same in-order result BAC.

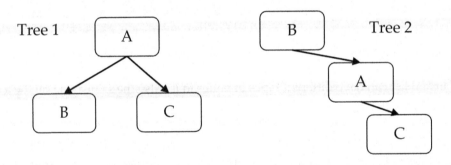

A list is a collection of similar objects which are stored in a set of contiguous memory locations. An element of the list is accessed using the element's index in the list. Both sequential and random access of elements is possible using a list. Lists may be one-dimensional (if they use a single index) or multi-dimensional (if they use more than one index).

Strings are a collection of characters. Searching for a sub-string (pattern) in a long string (text) is commonly encountered in strings. This is also referred to as searching for a needle in a haystack. A brute force approach has a time complexity of O(nm) where n is the length of pattern and m is the length of the text. To speed up string searching, algorithms try to skip characters in the text. The main approaches for solving the exact string match problem are Knuth Morris Pratt algorithm and the Boyer Moore Algorithm.

In the Knuth Morris Pratt algorithm, the pattern is compared with the text from left to right. A lookup table is pre-computed on the pattern which indicates by how many characters the pattern can be advanced if there is a mismatch. The worst case time complexity is O(n+m)

In the Boyer Moore algorithm, the pattern is compared with the text from right to left. This helps speed up the algorithm since many more characters in the text can be skipped when a mismatch occurs. The algorithm uses two rules: the bad character rule and the good suffix rule, to advance the search. The worst case time complexity is O(nm). However in most practical cases Boyer Moore runs faster than Knuth Morris Pratt algorithm. So Boyer Moore algorithm is preferred to the Knuth Morris Pratt algorithm. If the pattern is very long, Boyer Moyer algorithm is most likely to be the most efficient exact string match algorithm

A dictionary (also called hash table) maps a key to a value using a hash function as shown.

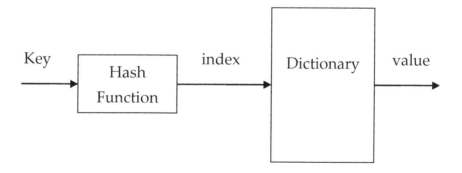

Different kinds of hash functions can be used to generate the index from the key. For instance, a commonly used hash function divides the numeric key value with a prime number and the resulting remainder forms the index (index = key mod prime number). The prime number should preferably not be close to a power of 2. Cyclic Redundancy Check (CRC) functions are also good hash functions

An ideal hash function should map each key to a unique index. In practice, ideal hash functions are rare. An overflow can occur if two keys are mapped to the same index. One of the techniques used to handle overflows is to maintain a linked list for all the keys that are mapped to the same index.

For an ideal dictionary, the time complexity is listed below

Insert time complexity: O(1)

Delete time complexity: O(1)

Search time complexity: O(1)

Heap is a complete binary tree (every node other than the leaves have 2 children). There are two types of heaps: a max-heap and a min-heap. In a max heap, each parent node is >= any of its children. In a min-heap, each parent node is <= any of its children. A max-heap is shown below

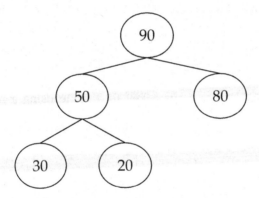

Heaps are generally represented using simple lists. If the parent node is stored at index i, then the left child is stored at index 2*i and the right child is stored at index (2*i)+1.

Using a heap the maximum or minimum element can be easily identified since it will be at the root of the heap. A heap does not maintain all the elements in the sorted order.

The time complexity of different operations on a heap is given below

Insert operation - O(log n)

Delete min/max - O(log n)

Find minimum or maximum - O(1)

1.1 Linked Lists

1. Reverse a linked list

A linked list can be reversed without using recursion by maintaining 3 nodes: prev_node, cur_node and next_node. As we traverse the linked list, we update the 3 nodes and the links in the linked list are reversed. The time complexity is O(n).

```python
#Reverses the linked list without using recursion
#head: first node in the original linked list
#Return value: the first node of the reversed linked list
@staticmethod
def reverse(head):
    cur_node = head
    prev_node = None

    while (cur_node):
        #Store the next node in a temporary variable
        next_node = cur_node.next

        #Reverse the link
        cur_node.next = prev_node

        #Update the previous node to the current node
        prev_node = cur_node

        #Proceed to the next node in the original linked list
        cur_node = next_node

    #Once the linked list has been reversed, prev_node will be
    #referring to the new head. So return it
    return prev_node
```

The linked list can also be reversed using recursion. However this approach takes up additional memory that is proportional to the size of the linked list and so is not preferred. Sometimes interviewers explicitly ask for a recursive solution to reverse a linked list. So we are discussing the recursive solution also. Given the head node in a linked list consisting of n nodes, to reverse it using recursion, we first reverse the remaining n-1 nodes in the list recursively and then connect up the head node to the end of the reversed list. The steps are shown in the diagrams below:

1.1 Linked Lists

1. Initially cur_node refers to the head of the list

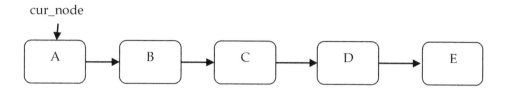

2. Recursively reverse the remaining list (BCDE becomes EDCB)

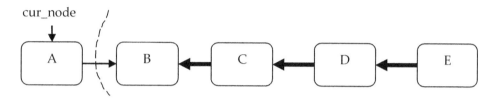

3. Set cur_node.next.next = cur_node. Here cur_node = A.
So A.next.next = A. But A.next is B. So B.next = A. So B now points to A.
Then set cur_node.next = None. So A.next = None

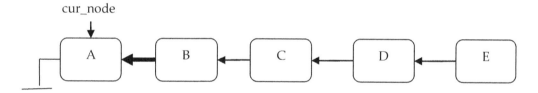

```
#Recursively reverses the linked list
#cur_node: current node of the linked list being processed
#Return value: first node of the reversed linked list
@staticmethod
def reverse_r(cur_node):
    if (not cur_node or not cur_node.next):
        return cur_node #Return last node in original linked list as new head

    #Recursively reverses the remaining nodes in the linked list
    new_head = LinkedListNode.reverse_r(cur_node.next)

    #connect up the current node to the reversed linked list
    cur_node.next.next = cur_node
    cur_node.next = None

    return new_head
```

The Big Book of Coding Interviews

2. Reverse every k nodes in a linked list. So if the input is A->B->C->D->E->F->G->H and k is 3, then the output should be C->B->A->F->E->D->H->G

Both recursive and non-recursive solutions exist to reverse every k nodes with O(n) time complexity. Although the recursive solution takes more space, we will use it here since it is simpler. If there are n nodes in the linked list, we reverse the first k nodes and then recursively process the remaining n - k nodes. Let the linked list be A->B->C->D->E->F->G->H and k = 3. The diagram below illustrates the technique.

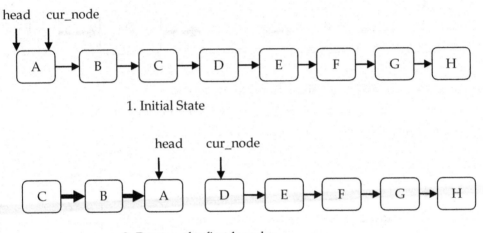

1. Initial State

2. Reverse the first k nodes

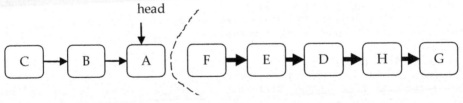

3. Recursively reverse the remaining nodes

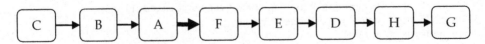

4. Connect the two linked lists

1.1 Linked Lists

```python
#head: first node of the linked list
#k: how many nodes should be reversed
#Return value: first node of the new linked list after reversing every k nodes
@staticmethod
def  k_reverse(head, k):
    if (not head or k == 0):
        return head

    cur_node = head
    prev_node = None
    i = 0
    while (cur_node and i < k):
        #Store the next node in a temporary variable
        temp_node = cur_node.next

        #Reverse the link
        cur_node.next = prev_node

        #Update the previous node to the current node
        prev_node = cur_node

        #Proceed to the next node in the original linked list
        cur_node = temp_node

        i += 1

    #We have reversed k nodes. So cur_node refers to the (k+1)th node
    #and head refers to the kth node.
    #Now recursively reverse the remaining nodes from cur_node onwards
    #and assign the result to head.next.
    if (cur_node):
        head.next = LinkedListNode.k_reverse(cur_node, k)

    #prev_node will refer to first node in the linked list after reversal
    return prev_node
```

3. Find the kth node from the end of a linked list

We can treat the last node in the linked list as either the 0th node from the end or we can treat the last node as the 1st node from the end. So k can begin from 0 or 1. In the function below, we are treating the last node as the 1st node from the end. To find the kth node from the end, we first find the length of the linked list. Then we again traverse through the linked list to find the (length – k +1)th node from the beginning which corresponds to the kth node from the end. If the length of the linked list is n, then in the worst case we will access 2n nodes. The time complexity is O(n)

```python
#head: the first node of the linked list
#k: node position from the end. k starts from 1 onwards
#Return value: kth node from end if it exists, None otherwise
@staticmethod
def find_kth_node_from_end(head, k):
    length = 0
    n1 = head
    while (n1):
        length += 1
        n1 = n1.next

    n1 = head
    for i in range(1, length + 1):
        if (i == length - k + 1):
            return n1     #n1 is the kth node from end. So return it

        n1 = n1.next

    #k value passed doesn't match with the linked list. So return None
    return None
```

1.1 Linked Lists

```python
#head: first node of the linked list
#k: how many nodes should be reversed
#Return value: first node of the new linked list after reversing every k nodes
@staticmethod
def  k_reverse(head, k):
    if (not head or k == 0):
        return head

    cur_node = head
    prev_node = None
    i = 0
    while (cur_node and i < k):
        #Store the next node in a temporary variable
        temp_node = cur_node.next

        #Reverse the link
        cur_node.next = prev_node

        #Update the previous node to the current node
        prev_node = cur_node

        #Proceed to the next node in the original linked list
        cur_node = temp_node

        i += 1

    #We have reversed k nodes. So cur_node refers to the (k+1)th node
    #and head refers to the kth node.
    #Now recursively reverse the remaining nodes from cur_node onwards
    #and assign the result to head.next.
    if (cur_node):
        head.next = LinkedListNode.k_reverse(cur_node, k)

    #prev_node will refer to first node in the linked list after reversal
    return prev_node
```

3. Find the kth node from the end of a linked list

We can treat the last node in the linked list as either the 0th node from the end or we can treat the last node as the 1st node from the end. So k can begin from 0 or 1. In the function below, we are treating the last node as the 1st node from the end. To find the kth node from the end, we first find the length of the linked list. Then we again traverse through the linked list to find the (length – k +1)th node from the beginning which corresponds to the kth node from the end. If the length of the linked list is n, then in the worst case we will access 2n nodes. The time complexity is O(n)

```
#head: the first node of the linked list
#k: node position from the end. k starts from 1 onwards
#Return value: kth node from end if it exists, None otherwise
@staticmethod
def find_kth_node_from_end(head, k):
    length = 0
    n1 = head
    while (n1):
        length += 1
        n1 = n1.next

    n1 = head
    for i in range(1, length + 1):
        if (i == length - k + 1):
            return n1      #n1 is the kth node from end. So return it

        n1 = n1.next

    #k value passed doesn't match with the linked list. So return None
    return None
```

1.1 Linked Lists

4. Swap the kth node from the end with the kth node from the beginning of a linked list

---

If the length of the linked list is n, then k can take values from 1 to n. We can solve the problem in O(n) using the following steps:

1. Find the kth node from the start of the linked list (k1) and its previous node (prev1).

2. Find the kth node from the end of the linked list (k2) and its previous node (prev2).

3. Swap k1 and k2. While swapping we have to handle three possible cases:

- k1 and k2 are identical. In this case we don't have to swap
- k1 and k2 are neighbors (either k1.next = k2 or k2.next = k1)
- k1 and k2 are not neighbors

Note that if k is 1, then we have to swap the head of the linked list with the tail of the linked list. In this case, the head of the linked list will change. Also note that the node k1 may lie before or after k2. For instance, if linked list length is 10 and k = 3, then k1 is before k2. But if linked list length is 10 and k = 9, then k1 is after k2.

```
#Helper function which swaps two neighbors n1 and n2
#head: first node in the linked list
#prev: node previous to n1
#n1: first node to be swapped
#n2: second node to be swapped. n2 occurs immediately after n1
#Return value: head of the result linked list after swapping neighbors
@staticmethod
def swap_neighbors(head, prev, n1, n2):
    #Swap n1 and n2
    n1.next = n2.next
    n2.next = n1

    if (prev):
        prev.next = n2
    else:
        head = n2 #If prev doesn't exist, update head to n2

    return head
```

```python
#Main function for swapping the kth node from beginning and end
#head: first node in the linked list.
#k: which node in the linked list should be swapped
#length: number of nodes in the linked list
#Return value: head of the result linked list on success, None on error
@staticmethod
def swap_kth_node(head, k, length):
    if (not head or k < 1 or k > length):
        return None

    #k1 is the kth node from begining and prev1 is previous to k1
    k1, prev1 = LinkedListNode.find_kth_node_from_begin(head, k)

    #k2 is the kth node from end and prev2 is previous to k2
    k2, prev2 = LinkedListNode.find_kth_node_from_end(head, k)

    if (not k1 or not k2):
        return None #the k value is incorrect

    if (k1 == k2):
        return head #both nodes are the same. So no need to swap

    #If k1 and k2 are neighbors, then handle this case and return
    if (k1.next == k2):
        return LinkedListNode.swap_neighbors(head, prev1, k1, k2)

    if (k2.next == k1):
        return LinkedListNode.swap_neighbors(head, prev2, k2, k1)

    #k1 and k2 are not neighbors. So swap k1.next with k2.next
    k1.next, k2.next = k2.next, k1.next

    if (prev1):
        prev1.next = k2
    else:
        head = k2 #After swap, k2 becomes new head

    if (prev2):
        prev2.next = k1
    else:
        head = k1 #After swap, k1 becomes new head

    return head
```

5. Delete a node in a linked list given only a reference to that node

Let us say that we are given only a reference to the node n1 that needs to be deleted. We don't know the node previous to n1. If we delete the node that n1 refers to, then we can't update the next field of the node preceding n1. So we can't directly delete n1, but we have to employ a trick to do the job.

To solve the problem, let n2 be the reference to the node next to n1. We copy n2.data into n1.data. We also copy n2.next into n1.next. Now n1 points to a node that is exactly identical to the node pointed by n2. Now instead of deleting n1, we delete n2. This achieves the required result.

This solution will not work if the node being deleted is the last node in the linked list and the last node points to None. One possible approach to make this solution work for all nodes in the linked list is to use a circular linked list.

```
#n1: the node to be deleted
#Return value: True on success, False on failure
@staticmethod
def delete_node(n1):
    if (n1.next):
        #Get the next node
        n2 = n1.next

        #Copy the contents of the next node into the current node
        n1.data = n2.data
        n1.next = n2.next

        #Return indicating the operation is successful
        return True

    #return indicating the operation failed
    return False
```

6. Remove duplicates from a linked list

For removing duplicates, we can try two approaches

1. Use brute force. Pick each node (let's call it current node) in the linked list, then check the nodes that occur after the current node and remove those nodes that are identical to the current node. The time complexity is $O(n^2)$. We don't need additional memory.

2. Use a dictionary. As we traverse the linked list, we store the data of the nodes in the dictionary. If the data of a node has already been stored in the dictionary, then it is a duplicate and we delete the node from the linked list. The time complexity is $O(n)$ but we will use additional memory because of the dictionary.

The code for the brute force approach is given below

```
#head: first node in the linked list
@staticmethod
def remove_duplicates(head):
    #If there are 0 or 1 nodes in linked list, then simply return
    if (not head or not head.next):
        return

    cur_node = head
    while (cur_node) :
        #Iterate from node after cur_node to the end of the linked list
        iter_node = cur_node.next
        prev_node = cur_node

        while (iter_node) :
            if (cur_node.data == iter_node.data) :
                #iter_node is a duplicate of cur_node. so
                #remove it
                prev_node.next = iter_node.next
                iter_node = iter_node.next
            else :
                prev_node = iter_node
                iter_node = iter_node.next

        cur_node = cur_node.next
```

7. Rotate a linked list by k positions

Consider the linked list A->B->C->D->E. If we rotate the linked list by k = 2 positions, then the linked list will become D->E->A->B->C. To perform the rotation we do the following:

1. Locate the kth node from the end (let's call this node the pivot). If k = 2, we have to locate the second last node which in this case is D.

2. Make the node previous to the pivot point to None. So in this case C will point to None.

3. Traverse until the end of the linked list and make the last node point to the head of the linked list. So the last node E will point to the head A.

4. Make the pivot the head of the new linked list. So D will now become the new head.

Note that if k = length of linked list, then after rotation we end up with the original linked list. So we apply the formula, k = k % length to figure out the actual rotation required.

```
#head: first node of the linked list
#k: by how many positions the linked list should be rotated
#length: number of nodes in the linked list
#Return value: first node of the rotated linked list
@staticmethod
def rotate(head, k, length):
    #If there are 0 or 1 nodes in the linked list, then simply return
    if (length < 2):
        return head

    #If we shift by k times, then we get back the same linked list.
    #So we just have to shift k % length times
    k = k % length

    #If k is 0, then no need to shift
    if (k == 0):
        return head

    #Find the kth node from the end. If k = 1, then pivot will have
    #the last node and prev will be the node previous to last node
    pivot, prev = LinkedListNode.find_kth_node_from_end(head, k, length)

    #Find the last node in the linked list
    last = pivot
    while (last.next):
```

```
        last = last.next

    #Make the last node point to head and the node previous to pivot
    #point to None
    last.next = head
    prev.next = None

    #pivot will be the new head
    return pivot
```

1.1 Linked Lists

8. Two linked lists merge at a common node. Given the heads of the two linked lists, find the node where the linked lists merge. In the diagram below, the two linked lists ABCXYZ and PQXYZ merge at node X.

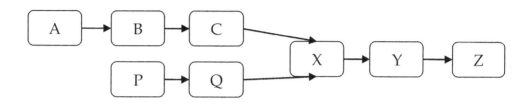

Using a brute force approach, we can pick each node in the first linked list and compare it with every node in the second linked list in sequential order. If we get a match, then we have found the first common node between the two linked lists. If one linked list has m nodes and the other has n nodes, this takes O(mn) time.

However there are better techniques to solve the problem. Two approaches which can perform better than the brute force approach are described below

Approach 1: Marking the nodes

An extra field is maintained in each node to indicate if the node has been visited or not. Initially the nodes in both linked lists have the field set to False indicating that they have not yet been visited. The nodes of the first linked list are then traversed and the visited field in the first linked list nodes is set to True indicating that they have been visited. Then the nodes of the second linked list are traversed in sequential order. As soon as we encounter a node in the second linked list with the visited field set to True, we have found the first node that is common to both the linked lists. The time taken by this approach is O(m+n) and it requires additional space in each node to store the visited field

Approach 2: Counting

The lengths of the two linked lists are first computed. Let m be the number of nodes in the longer linked list and n be the number of nodes in the shorter linked list. n1 is made to point to the head of the longer linked list and n2 is made to point to the head of the shorter linked list. The absolute difference in the lengths of the two linked lists m-n is then computed. n1 is advanced in the longer linked list by m-n nodes. Now the number of remaining nodes starting from n1 in the longer linked list is equal to the number of nodes in the shorter linked list. If n1 and n2 point to the same node, we have found the first common node. If not, we advance n1 and n2 by one node in their respective linked lists and compare them. This process is repeated until we get a match or we reach the end of the linked lists. The time taken by this approach is also O(m+n) and requires no additional space. So this approach is the preferred solution and is given below.

```python
#head1: first node of linked list1
#head2: first node of linked list2
#Return value: first common node between the two linked lists
@staticmethod
def find_intersection_node(head1, head2):
    #Find the length of the two linked lists
    length1 = LinkedListNode.find_length(head1)
    length2 = LinkedListNode.find_length(head2)

    #store head of the longer linked list in n1 and head of
    #shorter linked list in n2
    if (length1 >= length2) :
        n1 = head1
        n2 = head2
    else :
        n1 = head2
        n2 = head1

    #Find the difference in length of the two linked lists. Then advance
    #n1 by the difference
    diff = abs(length1 - length2)
    while (diff > 0) :
        n1 = n1.next
        diff -= 1

    #Go on comparing the nodes in linked list1 starting from n1 and
    #linked list2 starting from n2 till n1 and n2 match
    while (n1 and n2 and n1 != n2) :
        n1 = n1.next
        n2 = n2.next

    #n1 will have the common node if it exists, otherwise n1 will be None
    return n1
```

1.1 Linked Lists

9. Find out if there is a cycle in a linked list. Also find the node where the cycle begins

We can maintain the is_visited field in each node. Initially the is_visited field in all the nodes is set to False. When a node is traversed in the linked list, the is_visited field is changed from False to True. While traversing the linked list, the moment we encounter a node whose is_visited field is already True, we know that there is a cycle in the linked list and the cycle begins at this node. The drawback of this approach is that it uses additional memory.

To solve the problem without using additional memory, we use the following idea. Suppose two runners take part in a race, one of them being faster than the other, the faster runner will overtake the slower runner as soon as the race starts. If the race track is a loop, then later in the race, the faster runner will again meet the slower runner and overtake him. Similarly, we can traverse the linked list using a fast reference and a slow reference. At each step, the fast reference is moved ahead by 2 nodes, whereas the slow reference is moved ahead by 1 node. If there is a loop in the linked list, the two references will meet at a common node.

To find where the loop starts, we need to do the following: Let n1 be the fast reference and n2 be the slow reference. When n1 and n2 meet, initialize a third reference n3 to refer to the beginning of the linked list. So n1 is ahead of n3 in the linked list. Now ignore n2 and advance n1 and n3 one node at a time. The node where n1 and n3 meet is where the loop starts. The proof for this is given below

<u>Proof:</u>

Finding the node where the loop starts requires some mathematical jugglery. You can skip this portion if you want to. Let n1 be the faster reference and n2 be the slower reference. Initially both references point to the beginning of the linked list. n1 is two times faster than n2. So in each step, n1 advances by 2 nodes and n2 advances by 1 node. Let the number of nodes from the beginning of the linked list (node A) to the node where the loop starts (node B) be K. Let the length of the loop (BCDB) be L.

The Big Book of Coding Interviews

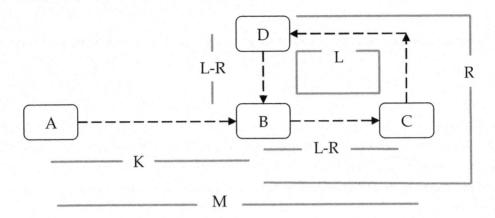

When n2 reaches the start of the loop (node B), n2 has traversed K nodes. Since n1 is twice as fast as n2, n1 has traversed 2K nodes and reached node D. The first K nodes that n1 has traversed are the nodes before the loop whereas the next K nodes that n1 has traversed are nodes inside the loop. The K nodes that n1 has traversed inside the loop can be written as K = nL + R where n indicates the number of times n1 has completed the loop and R indicates by how many nodes n1 is ahead of n2 inside the loop.

So inside the loop, n1 is R nodes ahead of n2. Since we are dealing with a loop, we can instead view the same information as n1 is behind n2 by L-R nodes inside the loop. If n1 is behind n2 by X nodes, then by the time n2 advances by X nodes, n1 will advance by 2X nodes, make up for the lost ground and meet exactly with n2. Now since n1 is behind n2 by L-R nodes, by the time n2 advances by L-R nodes and reaches node C, n1 will advance 2(L-R) nodes and both will meet exactly at node C. Let the number of nodes from the beginning of the loop (node A) to the node where n1 and n2 meet (node C) be M.

M = K + (L-R)

But we already have K = nL + R. Substituting for K, we have

M = n*L + R + L- R

M = (n+1)L

So M is a multiple of the length of the loop.

So to find the node where the loop starts, when n2 and n1 meet at node C, initialize a third reference n3 to point to the beginning of the linked list. n1 is M nodes ahead of n3. Now ignore n2 and advance n1 and n3 one node at a time. By the time n3 traverses K nodes and reaches node B at the beginning of the loop, n1 also traverses K nodes and n1

1.1 Linked Lists

is still M nodes ahead of n3. But M is a multiple of the loop length. So if n3 is at node B, M nodes ahead of B corresponds to node B itself. So n1 is also at B. So n1 and n3 meet at node B exactly where the loop starts.

```
#head: first node of the linked list
#Return value: first node in loop if loop exists, None otherwise
@staticmethod
def find_loop(head):
    n1 = n2 = head
    found_loop = False

    #n1 moves fast. So advance it by two steps
    #n2 is slow. So advance it by one step
    while (n1):
        n1 = n1.next
        if (n1):
            n1 = n1.next
            n2 = n2.next

        #If n1 and n2 meet then there is a loop in the linked list
        if (n1 == n2):
            found_loop = True
            break

    if (not found_loop):
        return None

    #Find the beginning of the loop
    n3 = head
    while (n1 != n3):
        n1 = n1.next
        n3 = n3.next

    return n1
```

10. Interleave two linked lists

Let's consider two linked lists, L1 having the members A->B->C->D and L2 having the members X->Y->Z. Interleaving the two linked lists will result in the single linked list A->X->B->Y->C->Z->D, wherein the first node of L2 is placed next to the first node of L1, second node of L2 is placed next to second node of L1 and so on. If the sizes of the two linked lists are m and n, then interleaving can be done in O(m+n)

```
#n1: head of the first linked list
#n2: head of the second linked list
#Return value: head of the result interleaved linked list
@staticmethod
def interleave(n1, n2):
    if (not n1):
        return n2 #If linked list1 is empty, return n2

    if (not n2):
        return n1 #If linked list2 is empty, return n1

    #Process the two linked lists
    result = n1
    while (n1 and n2):
        temp1 = n1.next
        temp2 = n2.next

        #Place node of second linked list next to the node of
        #the first linked list
        if (n1.next):
                n2.next = n1.next

        n1.next = n2

        n1 = temp1
        n2 = temp2

    return result
```

1.1 Linked Lists

is still M nodes ahead of n3. But M is a multiple of the loop length. So if n3 is at node B, M nodes ahead of B corresponds to node B itself. So n1 is also at B. So n1 and n3 meet at node B exactly where the loop starts.

```
#head: first node of the linked list
#Return value: first node in loop if loop exists, None otherwise
@staticmethod
def find_loop(head):
    n1 = n2 = head
    found_loop = False

    #n1 moves fast. So advance it by two steps
    #n2 is slow. So advance it by one step
    while (n1):
        n1 = n1.next
        if (n1):
            n1 = n1.next
            n2 = n2.next

        #If n1 and n2 meet then there is a loop in the linked list
        if (n1 == n2):
            found_loop = True
            break

    if (not found_loop):
        return None

    #Find the beginning of the loop
    n3 = head
    while (n1 != n3):
        n1 = n1.next
        n3 = n3.next

    return n1
```

10. Interleave two linked lists

Let's consider two linked lists, L1 having the members A->B->C->D and L2 having the members X->Y->Z. Interleaving the two linked lists will result in the single linked list A->X->B->Y->C->Z->D, wherein the first node of L2 is placed next to the first node of L1, second node of L2 is placed next to second node of L1 and so on. If the sizes of the two linked lists are m and n, then interleaving can be done in O(m+n)

```
#n1: head of the first linked list
#n2: head of the second linked list
#Return value: head of the result interleaved linked list
@staticmethod
def interleave(n1, n2):
    if (not n1):
        return n2 #If linked list1 is empty, return n2

    if (not n2):
        return n1 #If linked list2 is empty, return n1

    #Process the two linked lists
    result = n1
    while (n1 and n2):
        temp1 = n1.next
        temp2 = n2.next

        #Place node of second linked list next to the node of
        #the first linked list
        if (n1.next):
            n2.next = n1.next

        n1.next = n2

        n1 = temp1
        n2 = temp2

    return result
```

1.1 Linked Lists

11. Merge two sorted linked lists into a single sorted linked list

Let the nodes of the two linked lists be sorted in non-decreasing order. We can merge the linked lists in a single pass. We go on traversing the two linked lists and keep adding the smaller node in the two linked lists to the result. When we run out of nodes in one of the linked lists, we append the remaining portion of the other linked list to the result. If linked list1 has m nodes and linked list2 has n nodes, then the time complexity is O(m+n)

```python
#n1: head of the first linked list
#n2: head of the second linked list
#Return value: head of the merged linked list
@staticmethod
def merge( n1, n2):
    if (not n1):
        return n2 #If linked list1 is empty, return n2

    if (not n2):
        return n1 #If linked list2 is empty, return n1

    #make the result refer to the node with the smaller value
    if (n1.data <= n2.data):
        result = n1
        prev_merge_node = n1
        n1 = n1.next
    else:
        result = n2
        prev_merge_node = n2
        n2 = n2.next

    #Process the two linked lists
    while (n1 and n2):
        if (n1.data <= n2.data):
             prev_merge_node.next = n1
             n1 = n1.next
             prev_merge_node = prev_merge_node.next
        else:
             prev_merge_node.next = n2
             n2 = n2.next
             prev_merge_node = prev_merge_node.next


    #If there are still nodes present in the linked lists, then
    #append them to the result
    if (n1):
        prev_merge_node.next = n1
    else:
        prev_merge_node.next = n2

    return result
```

12. Each node in a linked list has two references. One of the references points to the next element in the linked list, while the other reference points to a random element in the linked list. Create another copy of this linked list in O(n) time using constant extra space

---

Let the next field in the linked list be connected as: A->B->C (indicated by solid lines in diagram below). Let the random field be connected as: A->C, C->B and B->A (indicated by the dashed lines in diagram below). Let the newly created nodes of the cloned linked list be represented as A', B' and C'

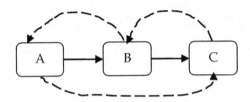

To solve the problem in O(n) using constant extra space, we do the following:

1. For each node in the original linked list, make a copy of the node and store it next to the original node. So the linked list A->B->C, now becomes A->A'->B->B'->C->C'

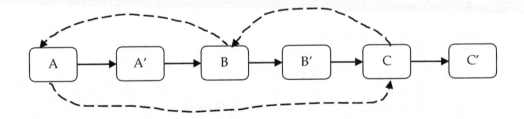

2. Next traverse the linked list again and for each of the <u>original</u> nodes do the following: n.next.random = n.random.next.

For instance, if n=A, then A.next.random = A.random.next
So A'.random = C.next [since A.next is A' and A.random = C]
So A'.random = C' [since C.next is C']

So we end up connecting the correct random field for the new nodes

1.1 Linked Lists

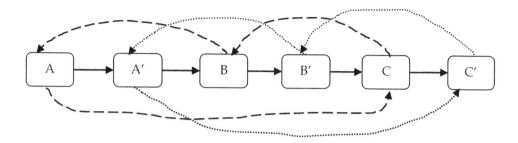

3. Remove the new nodes A′ B′ and C′ from the original linked list and form a new linked list with them. We end up with two identical linked lists.

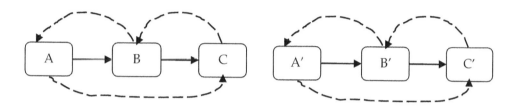

The code for the second solution is given below

```
#original_head: head of the original linked list
#Return value: head of the newly cloned linked list
@staticmethod
def clone(original_head):
    new_head = None

    #For each node in original linked list, create a new node. The new node
    #initially will be placed next to the original node
    n1 = original_head
    while (n1):
        next_node = n1.next

        n2 = LinkedListNode()
        if (not n2):
            return None

        n2.data = n1.data

        if (not new_head):
            new_head = n2
        n1.next = n2
        n2.next = next_node
        n1 = next_node

    #Set the random value correctly for the new nodes
    n1 = original_head
```

```
while (n1):
    n1.next.random = n1.random.next
    n1 = n1.next.next

#Disconnect the new nodes from the original linked list and
#form a new linked list for them
n1 = original_head
while (n1):
    n2 = n1.next
    n1.next = n1.next.next
    if (n2.next):
        n2.next = n2.next.next

    n1 = n1.next

return new_head
```

1.1 Linked Lists

13. Check if a linked list is a palindrome in O(n) time

To check if a linked list is a palindrome in O(n), we use the following approach

1. Find the length of the linked list and the middle node of the linked list.

2. Reverse the second half of the linked list. Then compare the first half of the linked list with the reversed second half. If the linked list is a palindrome then the nodes in the first half and the reversed second half should have the same data

3. Reverse the second half of linked list again so that we get back the original linked list

```
#head: first element of linked list.
#Returns: True if list is a palindrome, False otherwise
@staticmethod
def is_palindrome(head):
    if (not head):
        return False

    #Advance p by two nodes and q by one node in each loop.
    #So when p reaches the end of list, q will refer to middle of
    #the linked list
    p = q = head
    length = 0
    while (p):
        length += 1
        p = p.next
        if (p):
            length += 1
            p = p.next

        if (p):
            q = q.next

    #Reverse the second half of the linked list
    temp = r = LinkedListNode.reverse(q.next)
    p = head

    #Compare first half with reverse of second half
    is_palindrome = True
    for i in range(length // 2):
        if (p.data != r.data):
            is_palindrome = False
            break

        p = p.next
        r = r.next
```

```
#Reverse the second half of linked list to get back original
#linked list
LinkedListNode.reverse(temp)

return is_palindrome
```

1.1 Linked Lists

14. Each node of a linked list stores one digit of a number. The head of the linked list has the most significant digit. Find the sum of two such linked lists (result is also a linked list)

The head of the input linked list stores the most significant (MS) digit. However, we perform addition from the least significant (LS) digit to the most significant digit. So we have to reverse the input linked lists to perform an efficient addition in O(m+n) where m and n are the sizes of the two input linked lists. The procedure is:

1. Reverse the two input linked lists

2. Add the digits of the two input linked lists. A new node is created to store the result of the addition of two nodes and the new node is appended to the result linked list. The carry obtained by adding two nodes is carried forward to the next nodes.

3. Once the addition is done, we may have still have a non-zero carry. In this case, create a new node to store the carry and append it to the result linked list

4. Reverse the two input linked lists to get back the original input linked lists

Note that we are constructing the result linked list with nodes pointing from most significant to least significant direction. So there is no need to reverse the result linked list. The diagram below illustrates the addition of 23 with 89

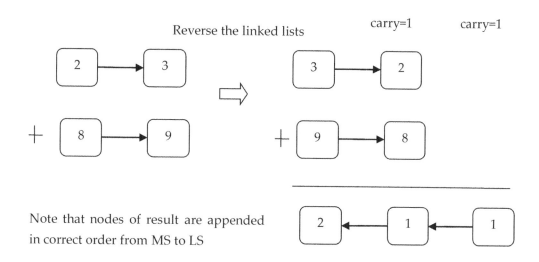

```python
#n1: head of the first linked list
#n2: head of the second linked list
#Return value: head of new linked list having the result of addition
@staticmethod
def add(n1, n2):
    #Reverse the two input linked lists
    h1 = p1 = LinkedListNode.reverse(n1)
    h2 = p2 = LinkedListNode.reverse(n2)

    #Add the nodes of the two linked lists
    current_sum = 0
    carry = 0
    result_node = None
    while (p1 and p2) :
        new_node = LinkedListNode()
        new_node.next = result_node
        result_node = new_node

        current_sum = p1.data + p2.data + carry
        new_node.data = current_sum % 10
        carry = current_sum // 10

        p1 = p1.next
        p2 = p2.next

    #If one of the two input linked lists still has nodes to be processed
    #then make p1 refer to the leftover input linked list
    if (p2):
        p1 = p2

    #Process the remaining input linked list
    while (p1) :
        new_node = LinkedListNode()
        new_node.next = result_node
        result_node = new_node

        current_sum = p1.data + carry
        new_node.data = current_sum % 10
        carry = current_sum // 10
        p1 = p1.next

    #If carry is non-zero, then store the carry in the result linked list
    if (carry != 0) :
        new_node = LinkedListNode()
        new_node.next = result_node
        result_node = new_node
        new_node.data = carry

    #Reverse back the two input linked lists
    LinkedListNode.reverse(h1)
    LinkedListNode.reverse(h2)

    #The result node already refers to MS node. So no need to reverse
    #result linked list
    return result_node
```

1.1 Linked Lists

15. Each node of a linked list stores one digit of a number. The head of the linked list has the most significant digit. Find the product of two such linked lists (result is also a linked list)

The head of the input linked list stores the most significant digit. However, we perform multiplication from the least significant digit to the most significant digit. So we have to reverse the input linked lists to perform an efficient multiplication. The time complexity is O(mn) where m and n are the sizes of the two input linked lists. The procedure is

1. To simplify processing, we first pre-create nodes of the result linked list and zero fill them. If sizes of input linked lists are m and n, then result linked list will have m+n nodes.

2. Reverse the two input linked lists

3. Consider the diagram below. Take the digit in second linked list (node 9) and multiply it with the first linked list (3->2). Add the result to the nodes in the result linked list (from node a onwards). Then move to the next node in the second linked list (node 8) and the next node in result (node b). Repeat this step for all the nodes in the second linked list.

4. Reverse the two input lists and the result list.

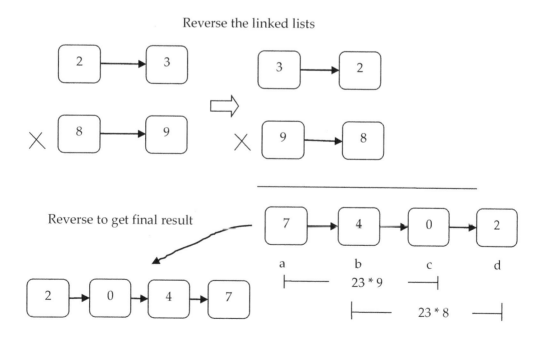

31

```python
#n1, n2: head of the first and second linked lists
#count1, count2: num elements in first and second linked lists
#Return value: head of new linked list having result of multiplication
@staticmethod
def multiply(n1, n2, count1, count2):
    #Reverse the two input linked lists
    h1 = LinkedListNode.reverse(n1)
    h2 = LinkedListNode.reverse(n2)

    #Pre-create the result linked list
    i = 0
    result_head = None
    while (i < count1 + count2 ) :
        cur_res_node = LinkedListNode(0)
        cur_res_node.next = result_head
        result_head = cur_res_node
        i += 1

    #Perform the multiplication
    result_start_node = result_head
    p1 = h1
    while (p1) :
        cur_res_node = result_start_node
        p2 = h2
        carry = 0
        while (p2) :
                product = p1.data * p2.data
                current_sum = product + cur_res_node.data + carry
                cur_res_node.data = current_sum % 10
                carry = current_sum // 10

                p2 = p2.next
                cur_res_node = cur_res_node.next

        cur_res_node.data = carry

        p1 = p1.next
        result_start_node = result_start_node.next

    #Reverse back the two input linked lists
    LinkedListNode.reverse(h1)
    LinkedListNode.reverse(h2)

    #Reverse the result linked list
    result_head = LinkedListNode.reverse(result_head)

    return result_head
```

1.2 Stacks and Queues

1. Implement a queue using stacks

To implement a queue using stacks, we have to perform the enqueue and dequeue operations of the queue using the push and pop operations supported by the stacks.

Let us say that we internally use stack S1 to implement a queue. When elements are added to the queue, they are pushed onto the internal stack S1. However when we have to remove an element from the queue, if we pop the element from S1, we will be returning the most recently added element instead of the element first added to the queue. We solve this problem by using an additional internal stack S2 that stores the elements to be removed from the queue in correct order. So S2 should store the elements in reverse order of S1. By popping each element from S1 and immediately pushing it into S2, S2 will store the elements in reverse order of S1. To remove an element from the queue, we will have to just pop the element from S2.

For instance, let us say that elements A, B and C are added to the queue. Then S1 will contain A, B and C while S2 will be empty as shown in the diagram below.

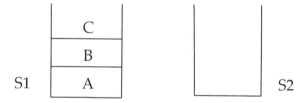

Now if an element has to be removed from the queue, since S2 is empty, each element of S1 is popped and immediately pushed into S2 as shown in the diagram below.

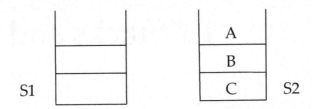

The top of stack S2 (which is element A) is then popped to remove the element from the queue.

It is important to note that, elements should be popped from S1 and pushed into S2 only when S2 is completely empty. For instance, after A is removed, let the element D be added to the queue. D is first added to S1. Suppose D is popped from S1 and pushed to S2 even before S2 is empty, then the state of the stacks is shown below

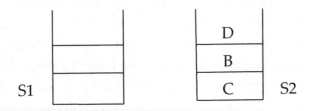

Clearly this results in an incorrect behavior since the next element that will be removed from the queue is D as D is at the top of S2 whereas the correct element to be removed from the queue is the element B. The code for a queue class using stacks is given below

```
#Queue in python 2.7 has been renamed to queue. So handling this so that code
#is portable on all versions of python
try:
    import queue
except ImportError:
    import Queue as queue


class QueueUsingStacks(object):
    def __init__(self):
        #Create the internal stacks
        self.s1 = queue.LifoQueue()
        self.s2 = queue.LifoQueue()

    def add(self, new_element):
        #Add elements only to stack s1
        self.s1.put(new_element)
```

1.2 Stacks and Queues

```
def remove(self):
    if(self.s2.empty()) :
            #We remove elements only from stack s2. So
            #if s2 is empty, then pop all the elements from s1 and
            #push them into s2.
            while(not self.s1.empty()) :
                    e = self.s1.get()
                    self.s2.put(e)

    #If s2 is not empty, then remove the element from top of s2.
    #This element corresponds to the head of the queue
    e = None
    if(not self.s2.empty()):
            e = self.s2.get()

    return e

def empty(self):
    #Queue is empty only if both stacks are empty
    if (self.s1.empty() and self.s2.empty()):
            return True
    return False
```

Note that each element that is added to the queue and removed from the queue later, will be first pushed into S1, then popped from S1, then pushed to S2 and finally popped from S2 thereby undergoing a total of 2 push and 2 pop operations.

The Big Book of Coding Interviews

2. Implement a stack using queues.

To implement a stack using queues, we have to perform the push and pop operations of the stack using the enqueue and dequeue operations supported by the queues.

A stack can be implemented using two internal queues Q1 and Q2. There are two ways to achieve this: one where the push operation is more efficient than the pop operation and the other where the pop operation is more efficient than the push operation.

<u>Case 1</u>: Push is more efficient than pop

When an element is pushed to the stack, the element is enqueued in Q1

When an element is popped from the stack, dequeue the first N-1 elements from Q1 (N is the number of elements currently present in Q1) and enqueue them in Q2, one element at a time. Dequeue the last element from Q1 and return it as the element popped from the stack. Now rename Q1 as Q2 and Q2 as Q1.

For instance, let us say that the elements A, B and C are added to the stack. Then A, B, C will be enqueued into Q1 as shown in the diagram below

Now if an element must be popped from the stack, dequeue A and B from Q1, then enqueue A and B in Q2. Finally dequeue the last element in Q1 which is C and return it as the popped element. Once this is done, the state of Q1 and Q2 are shown below

1.2 Stacks and Queues

In the last step of the pop operation, Q1 is renamed as Q2 and Q2 is renamed as Q1 as shown below

The code for implementing a stack class using queues where push is efficient is given below.

```
#Queue in python 2.7 has been renamed to queue. So handling this so that code
#is portable on all versions of python
try:
    import queue
except ImportError:
    import Queue as queue


class StackUsingQueues(object):
    def __init__(self):
        #Create the internal queues
        self.q1 = queue.Queue()
        self.q2 = queue.Queue()

    def empty(self):
        #Stack is empty if q1 is empty
        if (self.q1.empty()):
            return True
        return False

    def push(self, new_element):
        #Add elements only to queue q1
        self.q1.put(new_element)

    def pop(self):
        if (self.q1.empty()):
            return None

        #Remove all elements from q1 and add it to q2 except the last item
        while (self.q1.qsize() > 1):
            e = self.q1.get()
            self.q2.put(e)

        #Remove the last element in q1. It will contain the top of stack
        e = self.q1.get()
```

```
#Swap q1 and q2
self.q1, self.q2 = self.q2, self.q1

return e #Return the top of the stack
```

Case 2: Pop is more efficient than push

When an element is pushed to the stack, the element is enqueued in Q1. All the elements of Q2 are dequeued and enqueued in Q1. Rename Q1 as Q2 and Q2 as Q1. So Q2 will always contain elements in the reverse order of insertion.

When an element is popped from the stack, a dequeue operation is performed on Q2 to obtain the element at the top of the stack.

1.2 Stacks and Queues

3. Implement N stacks in a list

If there are just two stacks, the bottoms of the stacks can be at the opposite ends of the list and the stacks will grow in opposite direction towards the middle of the list. This way, the free space of the list is common to both the stacks and any stack can make use of the free space in between. So there will be no wastage of space.

bottom	top		top	bottom
S1	Free Space		S2	

If 3 or more stacks should be stored in a list, the possible size that each stack can grow to can be initially guessed. Based on the initial guess, the bottom of each stack is decided in the list. To fully utilize the free space in the list, the bottom of one or more stacks and their elements can be shifted at run time.

For instance, let us say that we have to implement 3 stacks in a list. The guess estimate for the sizes of stack S1 is 2, S2 is 3, and S3 is 4. Then the diagram below shows the initial layout of the list.

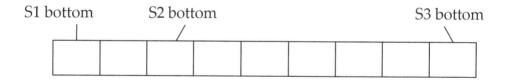

At run time let us say that the state of the stacks is as shown and we want to add C to S1

	S1 bottom	S1 top	S2 bottom		S2 top		S3 top	S3 bottom
	A	B	X	Y	Z		Q	P

Stack S1 is full. However there is still space available between S2 and S3. Stack S1 can make use of this space for storing C, if the bottom of stack S2 and elements in S2 are shifted as shown below.

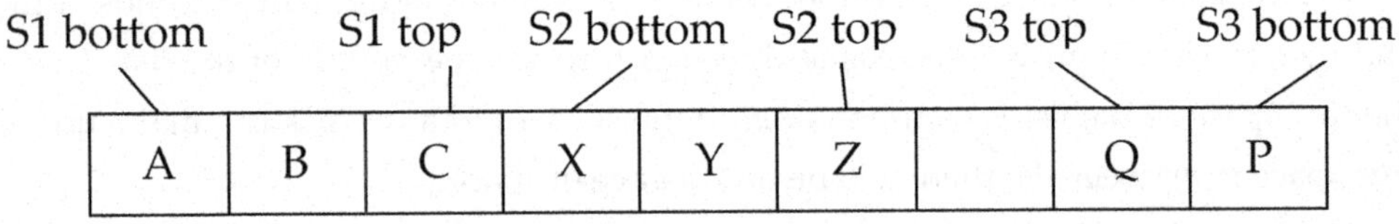

S1 bottom		S1 top	S2 bottom	S2 top		S3 top	S3 bottom
A	B	C	X	Y	Z	Q	P

1.2 Stacks and Queues

4. Implement a circular queue using lists. Take care of resize of the queue in-case the queue becomes full

---

In a circular queue implemented using lists, we keep track of the head (index of first element) and tail (index of last element) of the queue. The time complexity of enqueue and dequeue operations is O(1). When we resize the list of size N, we can't directly copy the first N locations of the old list into the first N locations in the new list. Instead we have to copy the elements from head to tail in the old list into the locations 0 to N-1 in the new list. The implementation for a circular queue using lists is given below

```python
class CircularQueue(object):
    def __init__(self) :
        self.head = -1 #index of first element in queue. -1 if queue is empty
        self.tail = -1 #index of last element in queue. -1 if queue is empty
        self.count = 0 #Number of elements currently present in the queue

        self.max_size = 0 #Max number of elements that can be stored in queue
        self.buf = [] #buffer for storing elements


    def add(self, new_element):
        if (self.count == self.max_size) :
            #If the queue is full, then resize the queue
            if (self.max_size == 0):
                new_size = 1
            else:
                new_size = self.max_size * 2

            new_buf = [new_element] * new_size
            old_pos = self.head
            new_pos = 0

            #Copy from the old queue buf to the new buf
            while (new_pos < self.count) :
                new_buf[new_pos] = self.buf[old_pos]
                new_pos += 1
                old_pos = (old_pos + 1) % self.max_size


            self.buf = new_buf
            self.head = 0
            self.tail = self.count - 1
            self.max_size = new_size

        #Advance the tail and insert the element at the tail
        self.tail = (self.tail + 1) % self.max_size
        self.buf[self.tail] = new_element
```

```python
        if (self.count == 0):
            self.head = self.tail

        self.count += 1

        #Return the result code indicating success
        return 0


    def remove(self):
        #Can't remove an item from an empty queue
        if (self.count <= 0):
            return None

        removed_element = self.buf[self.head]

        if (self.head == self.tail) :
            #There was only 1 item in the queue and that item has been
            #removed. So reinitialize self.head and self.tail to -1
            self.head = -1
            self.tail = -1
        else :
            #Advance the head to the next location
            self.head = (self.head + 1) % self.max_size

        self.count -= 1

        return removed_element
```

1.2 Stacks and Queues

5. Implement get minimum functionality in a stack which returns the smallest value stored in the stack in constant time.

We can find the smallest value stored in a stack in constant time by maintaining an additional stack called the min_stack. The top of the min_stack always has the smallest value stored so far in the main_stack.

When a push operation is performed on the main_stack, the item is first added to the main_stack. Then if the min_stack is empty or if the item being added is smaller than or equal to the item at the top of the min_stack, then the item is also pushed on to the min_stack.

When a pop operation is done on the main_stack, the top element is first removed from the main_stack and the value of this element is compared with the value of the top element of the min_stack. If both values match, then topmost element of min_stack is also popped.

To get the minimum value in the main_stack at any point of time, we just have to peek at the top of the min_stack.

```
#There is no peek functionality in python stack. So we are doing a get
#followed by an immediate put to mimic the peek
def peek(stack):
    result = stack.get()
    stack.put(result)
    return result


#main_stack: main stack
#min_stack: the additional stack for getting the minimum element
#data_to_add: data to be added to the stack
def add_element(main_stack, min_stack, data_to_add) :
    #Push the node being inserted onto the main stack
    main_stack.put(data_to_add)

    #If the min stack is empty or the data being inserted is <=
    #to the top of the min_stack, then add the data to the min_stack
    if (min_stack.empty()) :
        min_stack.put(data_to_add)
    else :
        peek_result = peek(min_stack)
        if (data_to_add <= peek_result):
            min_stack.put(data_to_add)
```

```
#main_stack: main stack
#min_stack: the additional stack for getting the minimum element
#Return value: data at the top of the main stack
def remove_element(main_stack, min_stack) :
    if (main_stack.empty()):
        raise NameError('Stack is empty')

    #Remove the topmost element from the main stack
    popped_element = main_stack.get()

    #Peek at the minimum value, which is stored at the top of the min_stack
    min_val = peek(min_stack)

    #If value popped from the main stack matches the value at the top
    # of min_stack, then remove the topmost element from the min_stack
    if (popped_element == min_val) :
        min_stack.get()

    return popped_element
```

1.2 Stacks and Queues

6. Sort the elements in a stack using the push, pop, peek and is_empty operations

Let the original stack be S1. We will use an additional stack S2 for sorting the elements of S1. The final sorted result will be stored in S2. Let the elements 3, 1, 2 be stored in S1.

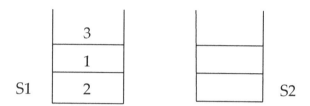

Initially S2 is empty. So 3 is popped from S1 and pushed into S2. Then 1 is popped from S1 and compared with the top element of S2 which is 3. Since 1 is <= 3, by pushing 1 on to S2, we can continue to maintain the sorted order of elements in S2. So 1 is also pushed into S2. Next 2 is popped from S1 as shown below.

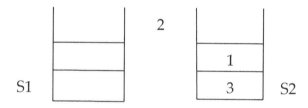

Then 2 is compared with the top element of S2 which is 1. Since 2 > 1, if we push 2 onto the stack, we can't maintain sorted order. So we pop elements from S2 and push them into S1 until we find an element >= 2 in S2 or until S2 becomes completely empty. So 1 is popped from S2 and pushed into S1. Next since 2 < 3, we have found the position where 2 can be inserted into S2 and we push 2 into S2 as shown below

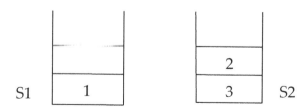

Then 1 is popped from S1 and compared with top of S2. Since 1 < 2, 1 is pushed into S2

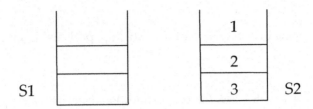

Now S2 contains the sorted elements. The code is given below

```
#Input elements are stored in original_stack. At the end of the operation,
#original_stack will be empty and sorted stack will have elements in sorted
#order
def stack_sort(original_stack, sorted_stack):
    while (not original_stack.empty()) :
        e1 = original_stack.get()
        e2 = None
        if(not sorted_stack.empty()):
            e2 = peek(sorted_stack)

        #If sorted stack is empty OR e1 is <= top element of
        #sorted stack, then push e1 onto the sorted stack
        if (e2 is None or e1 <= e2) :
            sorted_stack.put(e1)
            continue


        #While e1 > top element of sorted stack, remove the top
        #element of sorted stack and push it onto the original stack.
        while (not sorted_stack.empty()) :
            e2 = peek(sorted_stack)
            if (e1 > e2) :
                e2 = sorted_stack.get()
                original_stack.put(e2)
            else :
                break


        sorted_stack.put(e1) #Push e1 onto the sorted stack
```

7.

Given a string consisting of opening and closing braces '{', '}', opening and closing brackets '[', ']' and opening and closing parenthesis '(' and ')', check if the opening and closing characters are properly nested

To check if the opening and closing characters are properly nested we make use of a stack. Traverse the characters in the string and do the following:

1. If we get an opening character in the string, then push it on to the stack

2. If we get a closing character in the string, then the corresponding opening character must be present on top of the stack. So if we get ')' in the string, '(' should be present on top of the stack. Otherwise, the nesting is not proper. After checking the top of stack, pop the stack.

After processing all characters in the string, the stack should be empty. If the stack still has elements in it, then the nesting is not proper

```
#Verify if the braces, brackets and parenthesis are properly nested
#str1: input string containing braces, brackets and parenthesis
#Return value: True if the nesting is proper, False otherwise
def validate_nesting(str1) :
    s = queue.LifoQueue() #create a stack

    for c in str1 :
        if (c == '{' or c == '[' or c == '(') :
            #If we get an opening brace, bracket or parenthesis
            #in string, then push it on to the stack
            s.put(c)
        elif (c == '}' or c == ']' or c == ')'):
            #If we get a closing brace, bracket or parenthesis
            #in string, then the character on top of stack should be
            #the corresponding opening character
            if (s.empty()):
                return False

            top_char = peek(s)
            if (c == '{' and top_char != '}'):
                return False
            elif (c == ']' and top_char != '['):
                return False
            elif (c == ')' and top_char != '('):
                return False

            #Since we have matched the opening and closing character,
            #remove the opening character from the stack
            s.get()
```

```
        else :
                #We found a character other than a brace, bracket
                #or parenthesis
                return False


#At the end of processing, the stack should be empty
if (not s.empty()):
    return False

return True
```

1.3 Trees

1. Convert a binary tree into its mirror image

An example of a binary tree and its mirror image is shown below.

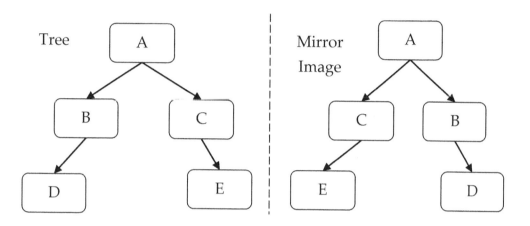

So to convert the binary tree to its mirror image, the left child and the right child of each node in the tree should be swapped.

```
@staticmethod
#cur_node: current node of the tree whose mirror image should be computed
def compute_mirror_image(cur_node):
    if (cur_node) :
        #Swap the left child and right child of the current node
        cur_node.left, cur_node.right = cur_node.right, cur_node.left

        #Recursively compute the mirror image
        TreeNode.compute_mirror_image(cur_node.left)
        TreeNode.compute_mirror_image(cur_node.right)
```

The Big Book of Coding Interviews

2. Find if a binary tree is symmetric

A binary tree is symmetric, if the left sub-tree of each node is a mirror image of the right sub-tree. An example of a symmetric binary tree is given below

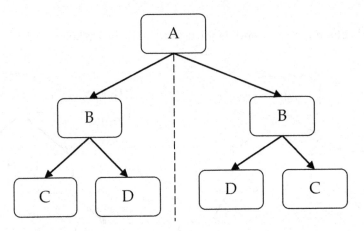

```
@staticmethod
def compare_nodes(n1, n2):
    if (not n1 and not n2):  #If both the nodes are None
        return True  # return symmetric

    #If one node is None and the other is not None
    if ( (n1 and not n2) or (not n1 and n2)):
        return False #return not symmetric

    if (n1.data != n2.data): #If data of two nodes don't match
        return False # return not symmetric

    if (not TreeNode.compare_nodes(n1.left, n2.right)):
        return False

    if (not TreeNode.compare_nodes(n1.right, n2.left)):
        return False

    return True #Return symmetric


@staticmethod
#Returns True if the tree is symmetric, False otherwise
def is_symmetric(root):
    if (not root):
        return True

    return TreeNode.compare_nodes(root.left, root.right)
```

3. Find if a binary tree is balanced

A binary tree is balanced if at every node in the tree, the absolute difference between the height of the left-subtree and the height of the right sub-tree doesn't exceed 1. To solve the problem we recursively traverse the tree and calculate the height of the nodes in a bottom up manner. If at any node, the difference between the height of the left and right sub-trees exceeds 1, we report that the tree is unbalanced.

```
#cur_node: cur node of the binary tree being checked
#Return values: 1. True if the tree is balanced, False otherwise
#               2. height of the cur_node is also returned
@staticmethod
def is_balanced(cur_node) :
    if (not cur_node) :
        height = 0
        return True, height

    is_left_balanced, left_height = TreeNode.is_balanced(cur_node.left)
    is_right_balanced, right_height = TreeNode.is_balanced(cur_node.right)

    #To get the height of the current node, we find the maximum of the
    #left subtree height and the right subtree height and add 1 to it
    height = max(left_height, right_height) + 1

    if (not is_left_balanced or not is_right_balanced):
        return False, height

    #If the difference between height of left subtree and height of
    #right subtree is more than 1, then the tree is unbalanced
    if (abs(left_height - right_height) > 1):
        return False, height

    return True, height
```

4. Find if a binary tree is a binary search tree

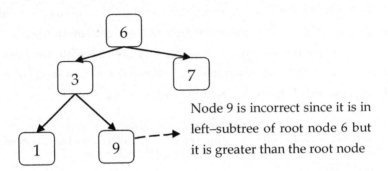

Node 9 is incorrect since it is in left-subtree of root node 6 but it is greater than the root node

The initial approach that comes to mind is to check if the left child node is smaller than the parent node and the right child node is greater than the parent node for all the nodes in the tree. However this solution will not work as shown in the binary tree above. Every node satisfies the condition that the left child is smaller than the parent and the right child is greater than the parent. But the tree is still not a binary search tree since node 9 is incorrect. To correctly find out if a tree is a binary search tree, we should traverse the tree in-order and check if the nodes are present in ascending order.

```
#cur_node: current node
#prev_node_list: prev_node_list[0] has in-order predecessor of cur_node
#Return values: True if the tree is a binary search tree, False otherwise
@staticmethod
def is_bst(cur_node, prev_node_list):
    if (not cur_node):
        return True

    #Check if the left sub-tree is a BST
    if (not TreeNode.is_bst(cur_node.left, prev_node_list)):
        return False

    #If data in cur_node is <= previous node then it is not a BST
    prev_node = prev_node_list[0]
    if (prev_node and cur_node.data <= prev_node.data):
        return False

    #Update previous node to current node
    prev_node_list[0] = cur_node

    #Check if the right sub-tree is a BST
    return TreeNode.is_bst(cur_node.right, prev_node_list)
```

1.3 Trees

5. Print the nodes of a binary tree in level order

To print the nodes of the binary tree in level order, we start with the root node and then print the child nodes in each level from left to right. Consider the binary tree below

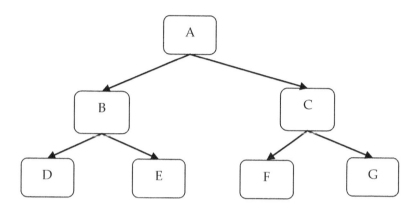

The level order printing will result in the following output: ABCDEFG. To achieve this we make use of a queue and use the following strategy:

1. Add the root node to the queue
2. Remove the head element of the queue and print it. Then add the children of the removed element back to the queue. Repeat step-2 until the queue becomes empty.

1. Add root of tree to queue

2. Remove A, print it and add its children B and C to the queue

3. Remove B, print it and add its children D and E to the queue

4. Remove C, print it and add its children F and G to the queue

```python
#root: root node of the tree
#q: python Queue object used for printing the tree
@staticmethod
def print_level_order(root, q):
    if (not root):
        return

    #Add the root node to the empty queue
    q.put(root)
    num_nodes_in_cur_level = 1
    num_nodes_in_next_level = 0

    #Process the nodes in the queue in Breadth First manner
    while (not q.empty()) :
        #Remove the node at the head of the queue
        n = q.get()

        TreeNode.print_data(n.data) #print the data in the node

        #Add the left child to the queue
        if (n.left) :
            q.put(n.left)
            num_nodes_in_next_level += 1

        #Add the right child to the queue
        if (n.right) :
            q.put(n.right)
            num_nodes_in_next_level += 1

        num_nodes_in_cur_level -= 1

        #go to next line, if all nodes in current level are processed
        if (num_nodes_in_cur_level == 0) :
            print('')
            num_nodes_in_cur_level = num_nodes_in_next_level
            num_nodes_in_next_level = 0
```

1.3 Trees

6. Print the nodes of a binary tree in spiral (zigzag) order

Consider the following binary tree

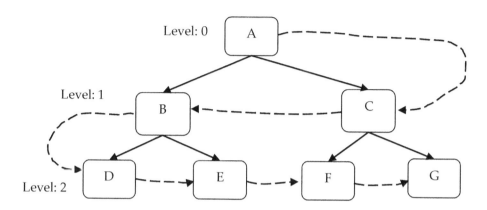

To print in spiral (zigzag) order, we have to print the nodes from right to left in one level and left to right in the next level. So the output for this tree is ACBDEFG. To achieve this, we make use of two stacks: Stack-0 and Stack-1. Stack-0 is used when printing nodes at an even level and Stack-1 is used when printing nodes at an odd level. The algorithm that we use to print spirally is as follows:

1. Initially push the root into Stack-0 and start processing Stack-0

2. For an even level, pop an element from Stack-0 and print it. Then add its left child followed by its right child into Stack-1. Repeat step-2 until Stack-0 becomes empty

3. For an odd level, pop an element from Stack-1 and print it. Then add its right child followed by its left child into Stack-0. Repeat step-3 until Stack-1 becomes empty

The algorithm comes to a halt when both stacks become completely empty

The steps of the algorithm are shown below. First push root node into Stack-0.

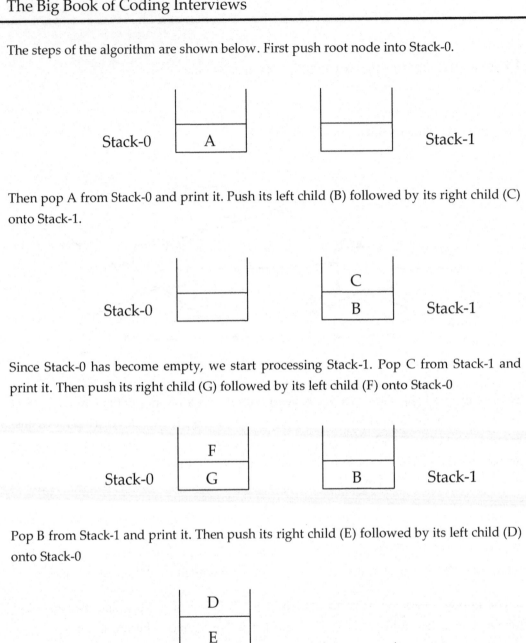

Then pop A from Stack-0 and print it. Push its left child (B) followed by its right child (C) onto Stack-1.

Since Stack-0 has become empty, we start processing Stack-1. Pop C from Stack-1 and print it. Then push its right child (G) followed by its left child (F) onto Stack-0

Pop B from Stack-1 and print it. Then push its right child (E) followed by its left child (D) onto Stack-0

Since Stack-1 is empty, start processing Stack-0. Since the nodes in Stack-0 have no children, we end up popping and printing them and finally both stacks become empty.

1.3 Trees

```
#Helper function for printing in zig zag order:
#print_stack: stack used for printing the nodes:
#store_stack: stack that stores the children of nodes in print_stack
#left_to_right: if set to 1, left child is stored first followed by right child
@staticmethod
def process_stacks(print_stack, store_stack, left_to_right):
    while (not print_stack.empty()) :
        cur_node = print_stack.get()
        TreeNode.print_data(cur_node.data)

        if (left_to_right) :
                if (cur_node.left):
                        store_stack.put(cur_node.left)
                if (cur_node.right):
                        store_stack.put(cur_node.right)
        else :
                if (cur_node.right):
                        store_stack.put(cur_node.right)
                if (cur_node.left):
                        store_stack.put(cur_node.left)


#root: root of the binary tree to be printed spirally
#s0, s1: stacks used for storing nodes of the binary tree
@staticmethod
def print_zig_zag(root, s0, s1):
    if (not root):
        return

    #Push root into stack s0 and start processing
    s0.put(root)

    while (not s0.empty()) :
       #s0 is used for printing. The children of nodes in s0 are
       #stored in s1 in left to right direction
       TreeNode.process_stacks(s0, s1, True)
       print('')

       #s1 is used for printing. The children of nodes in s1 are
       #stored in s0 in right to left direction
       TreeNode.process_stacks(s1, s0, False)
       print('')
```

The Big Book of Coding Interviews

7. Find the least common ancestor for two nodes in a tree given only parent references

Each node in the tree has a parent reference. To find the least common ancestor of two nodes N1 and N2 in the tree we use the following procedure:

1. Find the depths of the two nodes N1 and N2 by traversing up the tree using the parent references until we reach the root node

2. Let us say that N1 is deeper than N2. Pick the deeper node N1 and traverse up the parents until we reach a node whose depth is equal to the depth of the shallower node N2.

3. If the nodes in the two paths are the same then the common node is the least common ancestor. Otherwise go up the tree by one level on both paths and repeat this step until we reach a common node

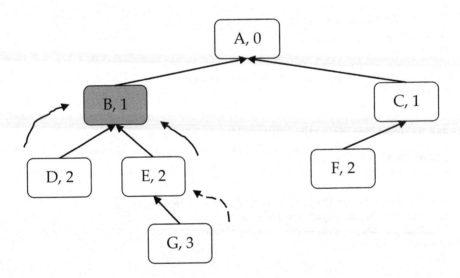

Consider the following tree, where the depth of the nodes are indicated for each node. Node A has depth of 0, node B and C have a depth of 1 and so on. Suppose we have to find the least common ancestor of node D and node G. D has a depth of 2 while G has a depth of 3. Since G is the deeper node, we find the ancestor of G which is at the same depth as the shallower node D. In this case E has the same depth as D. Then we advance from D and E by one node up along both paths until we reach a common node. So we reach node B along both paths. So B is the least common ancestor of nodes D and G.

1.3 Trees

```
#n: node in the binary tree
#Return value: depth of the node
@staticmethod
def find_depth(n) :
    depth = 0

    while (n.parent) :
        n = n.parent
        depth += 1

    return depth

#Find the Least Common Ancestor of a BINARY TREE
#n1 and n2 are two nodes in the tree
#Return value: least common ancestor node of n1 and n2
@staticmethod
def lca(n1, n2):
    depth1 = TreeNode.find_depth(n1)
    depth2 = TreeNode.find_depth(n2)

    # If n1 is deeper than n2, then move n1 up the tree
    #till the depth of n1 and n2 match
    while (depth1 > depth2) :
        n1 = n1.parent
        depth1 -= 1

    # If n2 is deeper than n1, then move n2 up the tree
    #till the depth of n1 and n2 match
    while (depth2 > depth1) :
        n2 = n2.parent
        depth2 -= 1

    #Move n1 and n2 up the tree until a common node is found
    while (n1 != n2 ) :
        n1 = n1.parent
        n2 = n2.parent

    return n1
```

The Big Book of Coding Interviews

8. Convert a sorted list into a binary search tree with least depth.

Let the elements of the input list [1, 2, 3, 4, 5] be sorted in ascending order. If we store the first element of the list in the root of the binary search tree, then place the next element to the right of the root and so on, we will end up with the tree shown below.

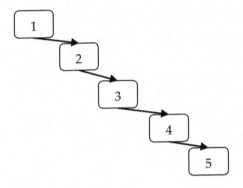

Although this is still a valid binary search tree, the tree is too deep. The tree is now more like a linked list and we can't get the speed up while searching it. So to build a binary search tree with the least depth, we use the following approach

1. Place the middle item in the list into the root of the tree

2. Recursively construct the left sub-tree using elements between (start, middle − 1) and the right sub-tree using the elements between (middle + 1, end)

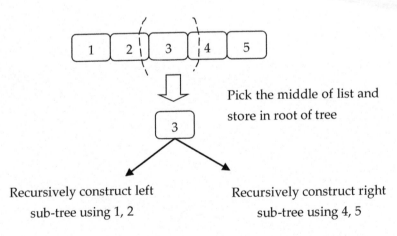

1.3 Trees

```python
#parent: parent of the BST node currently being constructed
#values: sorted list to be converted into BST
#low, high: lower and upper indexes of the list region being operated on
#Return value: BST node created that corresponds to values[(low+high)//2]
@staticmethod
def construct_bst(parent, values, low, high):
    middle = (low + high) // 2

    if (low > high):
        return None

    new_node = TreeNode()
    if (not new_node):
        return None

    #Construct the new node using the middle value
    new_node.data = values[middle]
    new_node.parent = parent

    #Construct the left sub-tree using values[low] to values[middle-1]
    new_node.left = TreeNode.construct_bst(new_node, values, low, middle - 1)

    #Construct the right sub-tree using values[middle+1] to values[high]
    new_node.right = TreeNode.construct_bst(new_node, values, middle + 1, high)

    return new_node
```

The Big Book of Coding Interviews

9. Convert a sorted doubly linked list in place into a binary search tree with least depth

Each node has 2 members: left and right. In the doubly linked list, left stores the previous node and right stores the next node. In the BST, left stores the left child and right stores the right child. We reuse the doubly linked list nodes to create the BST. The procedure is:

- Find the middle node in the doubly linked list
- Recursively construct left sub-tree using the nodes that are before the middle node and connect the left sub-tree to the middle node
- Recursively construct right sub-tree using the nodes that are after the middle node and connect the right sub-tree to the middle node

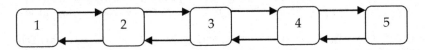

1. Given doubly linked list to be converted to BST

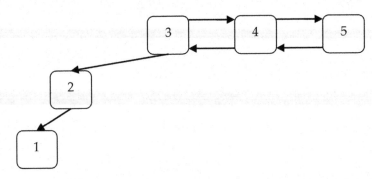

2. Recursively compute left sub-tree and connect to middle node

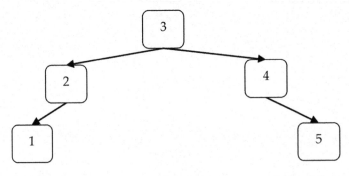

3. Recursively compute right sub-tree and connect to middle node

1.3 Trees

The code to convert a doubly linked list to a binary search tree is given below.

```
#node_list:  helper list of size 1 that contains a node.
#       this list is used for traversing the doubly linked list
#start: index of node in linked list at beginning of region being operated on
#end: index of node in linked list at end of region being operated on
@staticmethod
def construct_bst (node_list, start, end):
    if (start > end):
        return None

    middle = (start + end) // 2

    #Recursively construct the left subtree  using the nodes before the
    #middle node and get the root of the left sub-tree
    left_child = TreeNode.construct_bst(node_list, start, middle - 1)

    #node_list[0] will now be refering to the middle node
    middle_node = node_list[0]

    #Connect the left sub-tree to the middle node
    middle_node.left = left_child

    #Advance to the next node after the middle node
    node_list[0] = middle_node.right

    #Recursively construct the right subtree using the nodes after the
    #middle node and connect the root of right subtree to middle node
    middle_node.right = TreeNode.construct_bst(node_list, middle + 1, end)

    return middle_node
```

10. Convert a binary search tree in place into a sorted doubly linked list

Each node has 2 members: left and right. In the doubly linked list, left stores the previous node and right stores the next node. In the BST, left stores the left child and right stores the right child. We reuse the BST nodes to create the doubly linked list. The procedure is:

1. Recursively convert left sub-tree into a doubly linked list and connect it to the root

2. Recursively convert right sub-tree into a doubly linked list and connect it to the root

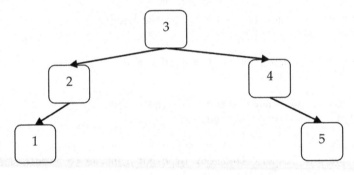

1. Given BST to be converted to doubly linked list

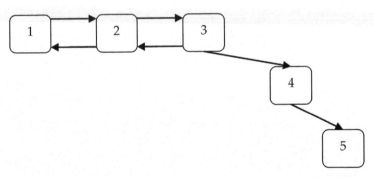

2. Recursively convert left sub-tree to doubly linked list

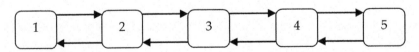

3. Recursively convert right sub-tree to doubly linked list

1.3 Trees

The code to convert a binary search tree to a doubly linked list is given below.

```
#cur_node: current BST node being processed
#prev_node_list: prev_node_list[0] has node that is previous to cur_node in
#         linked list
#head_list: head of the result linked list will be passed in head_list[0]
#Returns: 0 on success
@staticmethod
def bst_to_linked_list(cur_node, prev_node_list, head_list) :
    if (not cur_node):
        return 0

    #In-Order Traversal of the BST

    #Convert the left sub-tree of node to linked list
    TreeNode.bst_to_linked_list(cur_node.left, prev_node_list, head_list)

    #Link the previous node with the current node
    prev_node = prev_node_list[0]
    cur_node.left = prev_node

    if (prev_node) :
        prev_node.right = cur_node
    else :
        #Since previous node is None, this is the first node
        #of the linked list. So make head refer to it
        head_list[0] = cur_node


    #Make the current node the previous node
    prev_node_list[0] = cur_node

    #Convert the right sub-tree of node to linked list
    TreeNode.bst_to_linked_list(cur_node.right, prev_node_list, head_list)

    return 0 #return success
```

11. Given a node in a binary search tree, find its previous and next nodes

We can traverse to the previous and next node of a given node in a binary search tree provided that the nodes maintain references to the parent.

To find the previous element in a binary search tree, we will encounter two cases.

Case-1: the current node has a left child. Suppose we have to find the node previous to node 5 in the diagram below. Node 5 has a valid left child. In this case, the previous node is the rightmost node in the left sub-tree of the current node. So to find the element previous to 5, we find the rightmost element in the left sub-tree of 5 which in this case is 4.

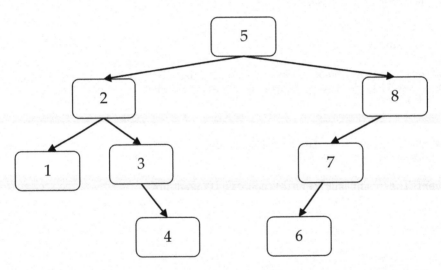

Case 2: the current node doesn't have a left child. For instance, in the diagram above, node 6 has no left child. In this case, we have to keep on traversing up the tree until we find the ancestor node whose right sub-tree has the current node. The ancestor node whose right sub-tree has the current node is the previous element of the current node. So to find the element previous to 6, we traverse up the tree since 6 has no left child. 6 is in the left sub-tree of 7. So we continue up to reach node 8. Again 6 is in the left sub-tree of 8. We continue up again to reach node 5. 6 is in the right sub-tree of 5. So the element previous to 6 is 5.

```
#x: any node in the binary search tree
#Return value: the node previous to node x
@staticmethod
def get_previous(x) :
    #Handle Case-1, left child exists
    if (x.left) :
        y = x.left
        while (y.right) :
            y = y.right

        return y

    #Handle Case-2, left child doesn't exist
    y = x.parent
    while (y and y.left == x) :
        x = y
        y = y.parent

    return y
```

To find the next element in a binary search tree, we will again encounter two cases.

Case-1: the current node has a valid right child. Suppose we have to find the node next to node 5. Node 5 has a valid right child. In this case, the next node is the left most node in the right sub-tree of the current node. So to find the element next to 5, we find the leftmost element in the right sub-tree of 5 which in this case is 6.

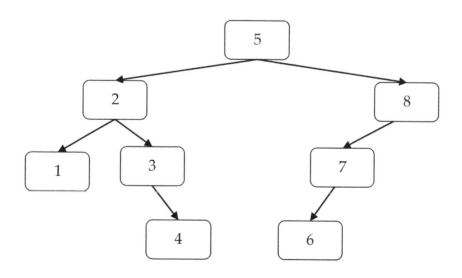

Case-2: the current node doesn't have a right child. For instance, in the diagram above, node 4 has no right child. In this case, we have to keep on traversing up the tree until we find the ancestor node whose left sub-tree has the current node. The ancestor node whose left sub-tree has the current node is the next element of the current node. So to find the element next to 4, we traverse up the tree since 4 has no right child. 4 is in the right sub-tree of 3. So we continue up to reach node 2. Again 4 is in the right sub-tree of 2. We continue up again to reach node 5. 4 is in left sub-tree of 5. So the element next to 4 is 5.

```
#x: any node in the binary search tree
#Return value: the node after node x
@staticmethod
def get_next(x) :
    #Handle Case-1: right child exists
    if (x.right) :
        y = x.right
        while (y.left) :
            y = y.left

        return y

    #Handle Case-2: right child doesn't exist
    y = x.parent
    while (y and y.right == x) :
        x = y
        y = y.parent

    return y
```

12. Find the kth largest element in a binary search tree

The largest element in a binary search tree is the rightmost element in the tree. To find the kth largest element, we first find the largest element and then traverse the k-1 elements previous to the largest element. For instance, to find the 3rd largest element, we find the largest element and then traverse 2 nodes before the largest element. We make use of the get_previous function described in page 67.

```
#root: the root node of the binary search tree
#k: indicates the kth largest value. k >= 1
#Return value: kth largest node in the binary search tree
@staticmethod
def find_kth_largest(root, k) :
    if (not root or k < 1):
        return None

    #Find the node with the maximum value
    n = root
    while (n.right):
        n = n.right

    #Find the k-1 previous nodes
    for i in range(1, k) :
        n = TreeNode.get_previous(n)
        if (not n) :
            return None

    return n
```

13. Find if the sum of any two nodes in a binary search tree equals K

Suppose instead of a binary search tree, we were given a sorted list A = [0, 1, 3, 4, 6, 7, 8, 9] and asked to find if any two numbers sum up to 11. Then we can do the following:

- Initialize left = 0 and right = number of elements in A - 1
- Compute sum = A[left] + A[right]. If the sum is equal to 11 then we have found the pair
- If the sum is less than 11, then we have to increase the sum. So left = left + 1
- If the sum is greater than 11, then we should decrease the sum. So right = right - 1

This process is repeated until we find the pair whose sum is k or left becomes >= right. The running time of this algorithm is O(n).

The same algorithm can be extended to binary search trees since a binary search tree is also a data structure meant for representing sorted data. We make use of the get_previous function and get_next functions described on pages 67 and 68.

```
#root: root of the binary search tree
#k: sum of two nodes should equal k
#Return value: list with the 2 tree nodes which sum up to k if they
#       exist, None otherwise
@staticmethod
def find_pair_sum_to_k(root, k) :
    if (not root):
        return None

    #Store the leftmost node in n1
    n1 = root
    while (n1.left):
        n1 = n1.left

    #Store the right most node in n2
    n2 = root
    while (n2.right):
        n2 = n2.right

    #Process the tree by picking one node from left and one node from right
    while (n1 != n2) :
        current_sum = n1.data + n2.data

        #check if the left node and right node sum to k
        if (current_sum == k) :
            return [n1, n2]
```

```
        if (current_sum < k) :
                #Pick the next higher value node from the left
                n1 = TreeNode.get_next(n1)
        else :
                #Pick the next smaller value from the right
                n2 = TreeNode.get_previous(n2)

    return None
```

The Big Book of Coding Interviews

14. In each node of a binary search tree, store the sum of all nodes that are greater than it

---

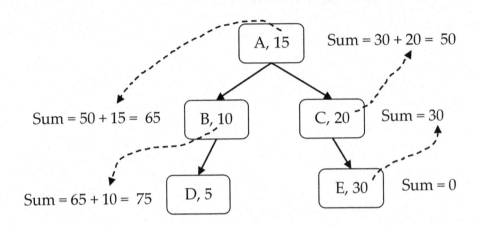

In the above diagram, the values of the nodes in a binary search tree are shown. Node E is the rightmost node and there are no nodes greater than it. So the sum for node E is 0. Node E is greater than node C. So the sum stored in C is 30. Nodes C and E are greater than A. So the sum stored in A = 20 + 30 = 50.

To compute the sum of all the nodes greater than a node, we initialize sum to zero, traverse the tree in post-order and use the following approach at each node starting with the root

1. First process the right sub-tree of the current node and add the values of the nodes in the right subtree

2. In the current node, store the sum of the values in the right sub-tree

3. Add the value of the current node to the sum

4. Pass the sum to the left subtree of the current node and recursively process the left subtree.

```
#cur_node: current node of the binary search tree
#bst_sum_list: has single element that stores the sum of nodes greater
#       than current node
@staticmethod
def compute_sum_of_greater_nodes(cur_node, bst_sum_list):
    if (not cur_node):
        return

    #Since greater elements are in the right sub-tree, first process the
    #right sub-tree
    TreeNode.compute_sum_of_greater_nodes(cur_node.right, bst_sum_list)

    #Assign the sum of the greater nodes
    cur_node.sum = bst_sum_list[0]

    #Add the current node's data to the sum
    bst_sum_list[0] += cur_node.data

    #Process the left sub-tree
    TreeNode.compute_sum_of_greater_nodes(cur_node.left, bst_sum_list)
```

15. Compute the vertical sum of a binary tree

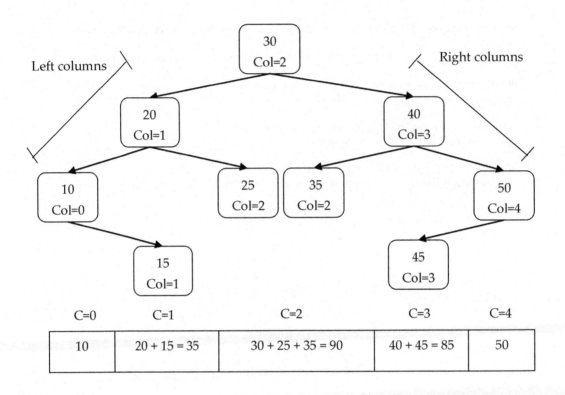

The number of left columns in the tree can be found by repeatedly traversing left in the left sub-tree of the root. In this example, the number of left columns = 2 (corresponding to nodes 20 and 10). Similarly the number of right columns can be found by repeatedly traversing right in the right sub-tree of the root. In this example, the number of right columns = 2 (corresponding to the nodes 40 and 50). The total columns of the tree including root = 1 + left columns + right columns = 1+ 2+ 2 = 5

Each node in the tree above is also assigned a column number as follows:

- the Col. number of the root is initialized to the number of left columns = 2
- if node is left child of its parent, its Col. number = Col. number of parent − 1
- if node is right child of its parent, its Col. number = Col. number of parent + 1

1.3 Trees

The procedure to find the vertical sum is:

1. Create the sum list whose size is equal to the total number of columns in the tree. Initialize the sum list to 0 for all columns.

2. Assign the column numbers to each node in the tree as we traverse the tree. Use the column number assigned to a node as the index into the sum list and add the value of the node to the sum list. After traversing all nodes in the tree, the sum list will have the vertical sum for each column.

```
#Helper function to find the vertical sum
#cur_node: current node being processed in the binary tree
#col: column of the current node
#sum_list: list containing the sum of nodes in each column
@staticmethod
def process_sum(cur_node, col, sum_list):

    if (not cur_node):
        return

    sum_list[col] += cur_node.data

    #column number of left child is col - 1
    TreeNode.process_sum(cur_node.left, col - 1, sum_list)

    #column number of right child is col+1
    TreeNode.process_sum(cur_node.right, col + 1, sum_list)


#Main function to find the vertical sum
#root: root of the binary tree
#Return values: list which contains the vertical sum
@staticmethod
def compute_vertical_sum(root):
    if (not root):
        return None

    #Compute the number of left columns
    cur_node = root.left
    num_left_cols= 0
    while (cur_node) :
        num_left_cols += 1
        cur_node = cur_node.left

    #Compute the number of right columns
    cur_node = root.right
    num_right_cols = 0
    while (cur_node) :
        num_right_cols += 1
        cur_node = cur_node.right
```

```
total_num_cols = num_left_cols + num_right_cols + 1

#Dynamically create the list for storing the column sum based on total
#columns
sum_list = [0] * total_num_cols

root_col = num_left_cols

#Compute the vertical sum starting with the root
TreeNode.process_sum(root, root_col, sum_list)

return sum_list
```

1.3 Trees

16. Remove all nodes in a binary tree that don't lie in a K-heavy path

K-heavy path is a path in which the sum of the values of the nodes in the path is at least K. Suppose K = 10, then in the binary tree below, the path ABDH has a net value of 3+ 2+ 2+ 1 = 8 and so is not a K-heavy path. On the other hand, path ACG has a net value of 3+ 2+ 7 = 12 and is a K-heavy path.

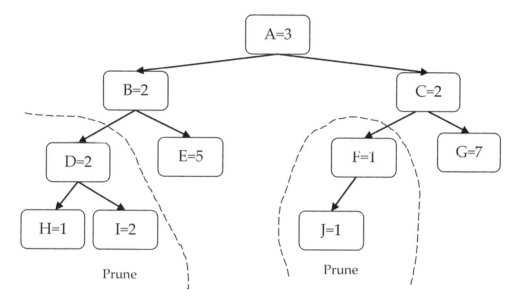

In this problem, we have to prune out the nodes that don't lie in any K-heavy path.

Consider node D. The paths running through D from the root are ABDH with a net value of 8 and ABDI with a net value of 9. Since none of the paths through D are at least 10, the node D should be completely pruned.

Consider node B. The path ABE through the node B has a net value of 10. Since there is at least one path through node B with net value >= K, node B should not be pruned.

To remove nodes that are not in a K-heavy path, traverse the tree and perform the following at each node

- Compute the value (X) of the path from the root to the current node
- Compute the longest path from the current node to any of its leaf nodes in its left and right sub-trees (Y)
- If X+Y < K, then prune the node

Consider node D. Then value of path from root to D = 3 + 2 + 2 = 7. The longest path from D to leaf = 2. So X+Y = 7 + 2 which is less than 10. So D should be pruned.

```python
#cur_node: current node of the binary tree
#above_sum: sum of the nodes from root to the parent of current node
#k: the threshold path value for retaining the nodes
#Return value: length of the longest path from root to leaf in which current
#       node is present
@staticmethod
def k_heavy_path(cur_node, above_sum, k):
    if (not cur_node):
        return above_sum

    above_sum += cur_node.data

    #Find longest path in left sub-tree that contains current node
    max_left_path = TreeNode.k_heavy_path(cur_node.left, above_sum, k)

    #If longest left sub-tree path is below threshold, prune left sub-tree
    if (max_left_path < k):
        cur_node.left = None

    #Find longest path in right sub-tree that contains current node
    max_right_path = TreeNode.k_heavy_path(cur_node.right, above_sum, k)

    #If longest right sub-tree path is below threshold, prune right sub-tree
    if (max_right_path < k):
        cur_node.right = None

    #longest_path is the maximum of max_left_path and max_right_path
    longest_path = max(max_left_path, max_right_path)

    return longest_path
```

1.3 Trees

17. Find the diameter of a binary tree

The diameter of a binary tree is the number of nodes in the longest path between any two leaves in the tree. It is not necessary that the diameter of the binary tree should pass through the root of the tree. For instance, the diameter in the binary tree below is IGDBEHJ and it doesn't pass through the root node A

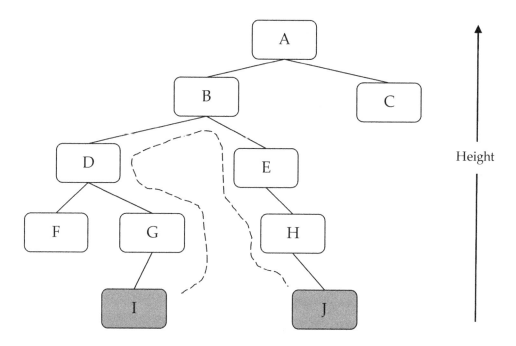

To calculate the diameter we need to know the left and right height of a node. The left height of a node is the maximum number of nodes in a path from the node to any leaf in left sub-tree of the node. So the left height of D is 1 (path F)

Similarly the right height of a node is the maximum number of nodes in a path from the node to any leaf in right sub-tree of the node. So right height of D is 2 (path GI)

Height of a node is 1 + max(left height, right height). So the height of D is 1 + max (1, 2) = 1 + 2 = 3.

We can compute the left and right height of the nodes in the tree in a bottom up manner. So if we know the heights of the children, we can calculate the height of the parent.

Once we know the left height and the right height of a node X, we can find the longest path between any two leaves passing through this node X using the formula longest path through node = 1 + left height + right height.

So longest path through D = (1 + left height of D + right height of D) = 1+ 1+ 2 = 4. The longest path through B = (1 + left height of B + right height of B) = 1+ 3+ 3 = 7.

The diameter of the tree is the maximum longest path among all nodes in the tree.

```
#cur_node: current node of the tree
#diameter: diameter of the tree computed till now is passed here
#Return values: height of cur_node and diameter of the tree
@staticmethod
def find_diameter(cur_node, diameter):
    if (not cur_node) :
        height = 0
        return height, diameter

    #Find the height of the left sub-tree
    left_height, diameter = TreeNode.find_diameter(cur_node.left, diameter)

    #Find the height of the right sub-tree
    right_height, diameter = TreeNode.find_diameter(cur_node.right, diameter)

    #Calculate height of cur_node
    height = 1 + max(left_height, right_height)

    #Calculate longest path between any two leafs passing through cur_node
    longest_path = left_height + right_height + 1

    #If the length of longest path through cur_node is greater than
    #the current diameter then assign it to the diameter
    if (longest_path > diameter):
        diameter = longest_path

    return height, diameter
```

1.3 Trees

18. Form a binary tree given its in-order and pre-order traversals

We can reconstruct a binary tree in the following cases

- in-order and pre-order traversals are known
- in-order and post-order traversals are known
- in-order and level-order traversals are known

Note that if in-order traversal is not known, then even if we have pre-order, post-order and level-order traversal, we still can't reconstruct the tree. In the current problem, we know the in-order and pre-order traversals. So we can reconstruct the binary tree. Let the in-order traversal = [B,D,A,E,C,F] and pre-order traversal = [A,B,D,C,E,F]. The traversals are stored in lists. The procedure to reconstruct the binary tree is as follows:

1. Choose the first element (A) in the pre-order list as the pivot. Since the root of the binary tree is stored as the first element of the pre-order list, pivot A is the root of the tree. So we create the root node with data equal to A

2. Next find the location of the pivot A in the in-order list.

3. The elements [B, D] that are to the left of A in the in-order list will be in the left sub-tree. Advance to the next element in the pre-order list (B) and form the left sub-tree recursively on the left in-order sub-list [B, D]. When the left subtree processing is complete, we would have advanced to element C in pre-order list

4. The elements [E, C, F] that are to the right of A in the in-order list will be in the right sub-tree. Advance to the next element in the pre-order list (E) and form the right sub-tree recursively on the right in-order sub-list [E, C, F].

Pre-order = **A**, B, D, C, E, F

In-order = B, D, **A**, E, C, F

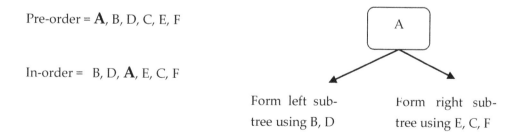

```python
#pre_order: list containing the data of nodes of the binary tree in pre-order
#in_order: list containing the data of nodes of the binary tree in in-order
#in_start: starting index of current region in the in_order list
#in_end: ending index of current region in the in_order list
#pre_pos: it is an object. pre_pos.value has the index in the pre-order list
#Return value: newly created binary tree node
@staticmethod
def construct_tree(pre_order, in_order, in_start, in_end, pre_pos) :
    #Termination condition for recursion
    if (in_start > in_end):
        return None

    # Assign the pivot from pre-order list
    pivot = pre_order[pre_pos.value]

    #Find pivot in in-order list
    for in_location in range(in_start,  in_end + 1) :
        if (in_order[in_location] == pivot) :
            break

    #Create the new node and assign the pivot data
    new_node = TreeNode()
    new_node.data = pivot

    #Advance to the next member in the pre-order list
    pre_pos.value += 1

    #First recursively construct the left sub-tree
    new_node.left = TreeNode.construct_tree(pre_order, in_order,
                            in_start, in_location - 1, pre_pos)

    #Recursively construct the right sub-tree
    new_node.right = TreeNode.construct_tree(pre_order, in_order,
                            in_location + 1, in_end, pre_pos)

    return new_node
```

1.3 Trees

18. Form a binary tree given its in-order and pre-order traversals

We can reconstruct a binary tree in the following cases

- in-order and pre-order traversals are known
- in-order and post-order traversals are known
- in-order and level-order traversals are known

Note that if in-order traversal is not known, then even if we have pre-order, post-order and level-order traversal, we still can't reconstruct the tree. In the current problem, we know the in-order and pre-order traversals. So we can reconstruct the binary tree. Let the in-order traversal = [B,D,A,E,C,F] and pre-order traversal = [A,B,D,C,E,F]. The traversals are stored in lists. The procedure to reconstruct the binary tree is as follows:

1. Choose the first element (A) in the pre-order list as the pivot. Since the root of the binary tree is stored as the first element of the pre-order list, pivot A is the root of the tree. So we create the root node with data equal to A

2. Next find the location of the pivot A in the in-order list.

3. The elements [B, D] that are to the left of A in the in-order list will be in the left sub-tree. Advance to the next element in the pre-order list (B) and form the left sub-tree recursively on the left in-order sub-list [B, D]. When the left subtree processing is complete, we would have advanced to element C in pre-order list

4. The elements [E, C, F] that are to the right of A in the in-order list will be in the right sub-tree. Advance to the next element in the pre-order list (E) and form the right sub-tree recursively on the right in-order sub-list [E, C, F].

Pre-order = **A**, B, D, C, E, F

In-order = B, D, **A**, E, C, F

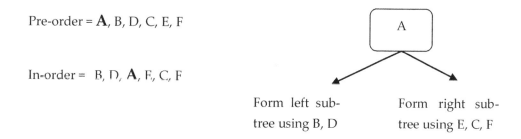

Form left sub-tree using B, D

Form right sub-tree using E, C, F

```
#pre_order: list containing the data of nodes of the binary tree in pre-order
#in_order: list containing the data of nodes of the binary tree in in-order
#in_start: starting index of current region in the in_order list
#in_end: ending index of current region in the in_order list
#pre_pos: it is an object. pre_pos.value has the index in the pre-order list
#Return value: newly created binary tree node
@staticmethod
def construct_tree(pre_order, in_order, in_start, in_end, pre_pos) :
    #Termination condition for recursion
    if (in_start > in_end):
        return None

    # Assign the pivot from pre-order list
    pivot = pre_order[pre_pos.value]

    #Find pivot in in-order list
    for in_location in range(in_start,  in_end + 1) :
        if (in_order[in_location] == pivot) :
            break

    #Create the new node and assign the pivot data
    new_node = TreeNode()
    new_node.data = pivot

    #Advance to the next member in the pre-order list
    pre_pos.value += 1

    #First recursively construct the left sub-tree
    new_node.left = TreeNode.construct_tree(pre_order, in_order,
                        in_start, in_location - 1, pre_pos)

    #Recursively construct the right sub-tree
    new_node.right = TreeNode.construct_tree(pre_order, in_order,
                        in_location + 1, in_end, pre_pos)

    return new_node
```

1.3 Trees

19. Serialize and Deserialize a binary tree

Serialization converts a data structure into a format that can be stored in persistent memory (such as a file) or that can be sent across a network. The process of reconstructing the format back to get the original data structure is called deserialization.

In our case, we will convert the binary tree into a format so that it can be stored in a file. As we traverse the nodes of the binary tree, the data in each node is written to a file. If a node has no child, then a special value (say #) is written to the file in place of the child.

Since in-order traversals are ambiguous, pre-order tree traversal is used.

Consider the tree below

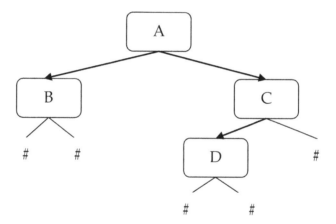

The output written to the file using pre-order traversal and the special value # for empty nodes is A B # # C D # # #.

To deserialize the tree, the file is read and the tree is constructed in pre-order.

```python
#cur_node: current node of the binary tree
#fo: file object to store the binary tree
#Return value: 0 on sucess
@staticmethod
def serialize_tree(cur_node, fo) :
    #If cur_node is None, then store the special value and return
    if (not cur_node) :
        fo.write(str(SPECIAL_VALUE) + '\n')
        return 0


    #Traverse the nodes in pre-order
    #First write the data of the node into the file
    fo.write(str(cur_node.data) + '\n')

    #Traverse the left subtree
    TreeNode.serialize_tree(cur_node.left, fo)

    #Traverse the right subtree
    TreeNode.serialize_tree(cur_node.right, fo)

    return 0


#fo: file object to read the binary tree data
#Return value: the reconstructed node of the binary tree
@staticmethod
def deserialize_tree(fo):
    #Read the data from the line in the file
    value = int(fo.readline())

    #If the special value is read, then return None
    if (value == SPECIAL_VALUE):
        return None

    #Traverse in pre-order
    #Store the value read from the file in the new_node
    new_node = TreeNode()
    new_node.data = value

    new_node.left = TreeNode.deserialize_tree(fo) #Construct left subtree

    new_node.right = TreeNode.deserialize_tree(fo) #Construct right sub-tree

    return new_node
```

1.3 Trees

20. Print the border nodes of a binary tree

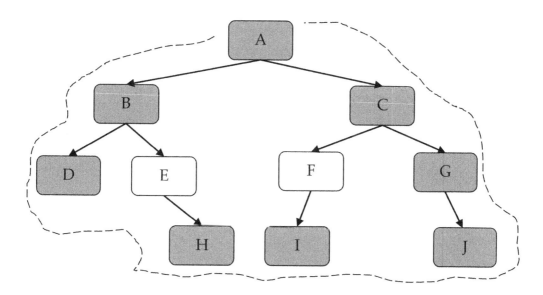

The border nodes in a binary tree consist of

- the left border nodes: the root node and all nodes that we can reach by starting from the root and repeatedly traversing left constitute the left border nodes. In the diagram above, A, B and D are left border nodes
- the right border nodes: the root node and all nodes that we can reach by starting from the root and repeatedly traversing right constitute the right border nodes. In the diagram above, A, C, G and J are right border nodes.
- the leaf nodes: in the diagram above, D, H, I and J are leaf nodes

Note that node D is a left border node and also a leaf node. Similarly node J is a right border node and also a leaf node. These nodes should be printed only once. So the convention we follow is that when printing left/right border nodes, we don't print the leaf nodes to avoid printing the same node twice. To print the border nodes to form a continuous boundary, we print in the following order

- the non-leaf left border nodes starting from the top of the tree (A, B)
- the leaf nodes (D, H, I, J)
- the non-leaf right border nodes in bottom up manner (G, C, A)

```python
#Print the left border
@staticmethod
def print_left_border(cur_node) :
    #Keep traversing left and print the non-leaf nodes
    while (cur_node) :
        #If node has a left or right child, then it is a non-leaf node
        if (cur_node.left or cur_node.right):
                TreeNode.print_data( cur_node.data)

        cur_node = cur_node.left


#Print the leaf nodes of the tree
@staticmethod
def print_leaf_nodes(cur_node) :
    if (not cur_node):
        return

    if (not cur_node.left and not cur_node.right):
        TreeNode.print_data(cur_node.data)

    TreeNode.print_leaf_nodes(cur_node.left)
    TreeNode.print_leaf_nodes(cur_node.right)


# Print the right border nodes of the tree
@staticmethod
def print_right_border(cur_node) :
    if (not cur_node):
        return

    #First reach the deepest right node and then start printing bottom-up
    TreeNode.print_right_border(cur_node.right)

    #If the node has a left or right child, then it is a non-leaf node.
    #So print it
    if (cur_node.left or cur_node.right):
        TreeNode.print_data(cur_node.data)



#Main function that prints the border nodes of a binary tree
@staticmethod
def print_border_nodes(root):
    if (not root):
        return

    TreeNode.print_left_border(root)
    TreeNode.print_leaf_nodes(root)
    TreeNode.print_right_border(root)
```

1.3 Trees

21. Print the right view of a binary tree

The right view of a binary tree consists of the last nodes at each level of the tree. For instance, for the tree below, the right view is ACF.

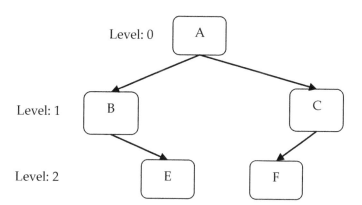

To print the right view, we will first traverse the right child of a node and then the left child of the node. By doing this we will now have to print the first node that we encounter in each level as we traverse the tree instead of printing the last node in each level. We will also keep a track of the level of the current node and the maximum level reached in the tree. If the level of the current node exceeds the max level reached in the tree so far, then we have reached a new level and we will print the current node.

```
#cur_node: current node in the tree being processed
#cur_level: the depth of the current node. Root node of tree has a level of 0
#max_level_list: max_level_list[0] has the maximum level seen in the tree so
#    far. We pass -1 for the root node
@staticmethod
def print_right_view(cur_node, cur_level, max_level_list) :
    if (not cur_node):
        return

    #If the current node is the first node we have observed in current level,
    #then print it
    if (max_level_list[0] < cur_level) :
        TreeNode.print_data(cur_node.data)
        max_level_list[0] = cur_level

    #First expand the right child and then the left child
    TreeNode.print_right_view(cur_node.right, cur_level + 1, max_level_list)
    TreeNode.print_right_view(cur_node.left, cur_level + 1, max_level_list)
```

22. Given two binary trees t1 and t2, find out if t2 is the sub-tree of t1

To check if tree t2 is a sub-tree of t1, we pick each node (let's call it the chosen node) from t1 and check if all nodes of t2 are present under the chosen node in the same manner. To achieve this we make use of two recursive functions. The first recursive function (is_sub_tree) first traverses the tree t1 to pick the chosen node of t1 from where to start the comparison and then invokes the second recursive function (compare_nodes) which compares the sub-tree under the chosen node of t1 with the nodes of t2.

There is one boundary condition we need to take care of. If t2 is empty, then we treat t2 as a sub-tree of t1.

If t1 has m nodes and t2 has n nodes, then the worst case time complexity is O(m*n). However if the root of t2 occurs only k times in t1, then the time complexity reduces to O(m + (n*k)).

```python
#Helper function that compares the nodes
#n1: node belonging to the main tree
#n2: node belonging to sub-tree being searched
#Return value: True if sub-tree of n1 matches sub-tree of n2. False otherwise
@staticmethod
def compare_nodes(n1, n2) :
    if (not n1 and not n2):
        return True

    if (not n1 or not n2):
        return False

    if (n1.data != n2.data):
        return False

    return (TreeNode.compare_nodes(n1.left, n2.left)
        and TreeNode.compare_nodes(n1.right, n2.right))
```

1.3 Trees

```python
#Main function that checks if tree under root2 is a subtree of tree under root1
#root1: main tree node
#root2: root of the sub-tree being searched
#Return value: True if tree under root2 is present in tree under root1
@staticmethod
def is_sub_tree(root1, root2) :
    #empty tree is treated as a sub-tree of the main tree
    if(not root2):
        return True

    if (not root1):
        return False

    if (TreeNode.compare_nodes(root1, root2)):
        return True

    #Check if tree of root2 is present in left sub-tree of root1
    #or right sub-tree of root1
    return (TreeNode.is_sub_tree(root1.left, root2)
        or TreeNode.is_sub_tree(root1.right, root2))
```

23. Two nodes of a binary search tree have been accidentally swapped. How will you correct the tree?

Let us not worry about the binary search tree and just consider the sorted data [10, 20, 30, 40, 50]. Suppose two members in this data get accidentally swapped. Then there are two possibilities

1. Non-adjacent members are swapped. 20 and 40 are not adjacent to each other. If they get swapped, then we get [10, 40, 30, 20, 50]. In this case, when we traverse the data and compare the previous element with the current element, we will get two inconsistencies. The first inconsistency is when we compare current element 30 with previous element 40. The second inconsistency is when we compare current element 20 with previous element 30. To get back the original sorted data, we have to swap the previous element of the first inconsistency (40) with the current element of the second inconsistency (20).

2. Adjacent members are swapped. 20 and 30 are adjacent to each other. If they get swapped, then we get [10, 30, 20, 40, 50]. In this case, when we traverse the data and compare the previous element with the current element, we will get only one inconsistency. The inconsistency happens when we compare the current element 20 with the previous element 30. To get back the original sorted data, we have to swap the previous element (30) and current element (20).

If we are given a binary search tree, then we have to traverse the tree in-order and keep comparing the previous node with the current node to find the inconsistencies. When we find the first inconsistency, we will store the previous node as error node 1 and current node as error node 2. When the second inconsistency happens, we will store the current node of the second inconsistency as error node 2. Finally we swap the data of error node 1 and error node 2 to correct the binary search tree.

```python
#Helper function for finding the error nodes in a Binary Search Tree
#cur_node: current tree node
#prev_node_list: contains node that is the in-order predecessor of cur_node
#error1: list in which the first error node is returned
#error2: list in which the second error node is returned
@staticmethod
def find_error_nodes(cur_node, prev_node_list, error1, error2):
    if (not cur_node):
        return

    #Check for error node in the left sub-tree
    TreeNode.find_error_nodes(cur_node.left, prev_node_list, error1, error2)

    #cur_node should be greater than previous node. So if data in cur_node
    #is less than or equal to previous node then we have found an error
    prev_node = prev_node_list[0]
    if (prev_node and cur_node.data <= prev_node.data) :
        if (not error1[0] ) :
            error1[0] = prev_node
            error2[0] = cur_node
        else :
            error2[0] = cur_node
            return

    #Update previous node to current node
    prev_node_list[0] = cur_node

    #Check for error node in the right sub-tree
    TreeNode.find_error_nodes(cur_node.right, prev_node_list, error1, error2)


#Main function for correcting the Binary Search Tree
#root: root node of the Binary Search Tree in which two nodes have been swapped
@staticmethod
def correct_bst(root):
    error1 = [None]
    error2 = [None]
    prev_node_list = [None]

    #Find the two error nodes
    TreeNode.find_error_nodes(root, prev_node_list, error1, error2)

    #If we found two error nodes, then swap their data
    if (error1[0]  and error2[0] ) :
        error1[0].data, error2[0].data = error2[0].data, error1[0].data
```

24. Traverse a binary tree in-order without using recursion

For traversing the tree without recursion, we make use of a stack. We start with the current node initialized to the root node and push it on to the stack. Then we push on to the stack all the nodes that we encounter by repeatedly traversing left from the current node. Once we can no longer travel left, we pop the node from the top of the stack, make it the current node, process it and then traverse to the right of the current node.

```python
#root: root node of the binary tree
#s: stack for storing the nodes for in-order traversal
@staticmethod
def non_recursive_in_order(root, s) :
    cur_node = root
    while (cur_node or not s.empty()) :
        if (cur_node) :
                #push the current node onto stack
                s.put(cur_node)

                #Traverse to the left sub-tree
                cur_node = cur_node.left

        else :
                #pop the node from stack and process it
                cur_node = s.get()

                #process or print the node in-order
                TreeNode.process(cur_node)

                #Traverse to the right sub-tree
                cur_node = cur_node.right
```

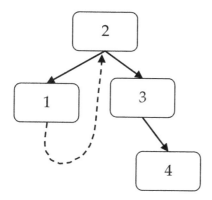

1.3 Trees

25. Traverse a binary tree in-order without using recursion and without using a stack

To traverse a binary tree without using recursion and without using a stack, we make use of threaded binary trees. In threaded binary trees, if a node does not have a right child, then instead of storing None for the right child, a link (also referred to as a thread) is stored pointing to the in-order successor of the node. For instance, consider the binary tree below.

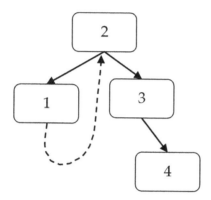

There is a thread shown as a dotted line from node 1 to node 2 (node 2 is the in-order successor of node 1). The main idea is that when we hit a dead end while traversing the tree, the threads help us figure out the next node. So for instance, we reach the node 1 from the root node 2. Without using a stack and without recursion, we reach a dead end at node 1. However if we maintain a thread from node 1 to node 2, we can continue the traversal. So to avoid using stacks and recursion, we construct the threads as we traverse the tree and once we no longer need the threads, we remove the threads during the tree traversal itself. This method of tree traversal is called Morris traversal. In Morris traversal, we start from the root node and perform the following:

1. If the current node has no left child, then process this node and go to the right child of the current node

2. If the current node has a left child, then find the predecessor of the current node in its left sub-tree and do the following:

The Big Book of Coding Interviews

    - If the predecessor has no right child, then we have not yet traversed this portion of the tree. Construct a thread linking the right child of predecessor and the current node so that when we reach the predecessor, we can then follow the thread to reach back the current node. Then proceed to the left child of current node

    - If the predecessor has a right child, then it is a thread that we had actually formed earlier to help us traverse the tree. Now that we have finished traversing this portion of the tree, we can remove the thread. So make the right child of the predecessor None. Process the current node. Then proceed to the right child of the current node.

Let us take an example and work out the details.

1. We start with the root (Node-2) as the current node. Node-2 has a left child. So we find the predecessor of Node-2 in its left sub-tree. The left predecessor of Node-2 is Node-1. Node-1 has no right child. So we construct a thread from Node-1 to the current node (Node 2). The left child of Node-2 which is Node-1, then becomes the current node

2. The current node (Node-1) has no left child. So we immediately process it. The right child of Node-1 which in this case is Node-2 (because of the thread we constructed) then becomes the current node.

3. The current node (Node-2) has a left child. So we again find the predecessor of Node-2 in its left sub-tree. The left predecessor of Node-2 is Node-1. But now, Node-1 has a right child. So make the right child of Node-1 equal to None. Process the current node (Node-2) and then move to its right child (Node-3).

4. The current node (Node-3) has no left child. So immediately process it and move to its right child (Node-4)

5. The current node (Node-4) has no left child. So immediately process it and move to its right child (None)

6. Since current node is None, we have finished the processing.

```
#root: root node of the tree
@staticmethod
def morris_in_order(root):
    cur_node = root
    while (cur_node) :
        #If cur_node has no left sub_tree, then print/process the
        #cur_node then move over to cur_node.right and continue
        if (not cur_node.left) :
            TreeNode.print_morris(cur_node)
            cur_node = cur_node.right
            continue


        #The cur_node has a left sub-tree. First store the left
        #predecessor of current node in left_pre. The left predecessor
        #can be found by traversing to the left of current node and
        #then repeatedly going to the right till we hit a leaf node
        left_pre = cur_node.left
        while (left_pre.right and left_pre.right != cur_node) :
            left_pre = left_pre.right


        if (not left_pre.right) :
            #If left predecessor is None, it means we have
            #not yet traversed the left sub-tree of current node.
            #So create a thread from left_pre.right to the current
            #node to remember that on reaching left_pre the next
            #in-order node is cur_node. Then proceed to cur_node.left
            left_pre.right = cur_node
            cur_node = cur_node.left
        else :
            #If left predecessor is not None, then it
            #means that we have finished traversing the left
            #sub-tree of current node. So remove the thread from
            #left_pre.right to current node. The current node is
            #the in-order node to be processed. So process it and
            #then move to right sub-tree of cur_node
            left_pre.right = None
            TreeNode.print_morris(cur_node)
            cur_node = cur_node.right
```

26. Merge two binary search trees

To merge two binary search trees, we do the following:

1. Convert each binary search tree into a doubly linked list (binary search tree to doubly linked list conversion has already been solved on page 65).

2. The two doubly linked lists will be sorted. Now merge the two sorted linked lists into one result doubly linked list (merging two sorted linked lists has already been solved on page 23)

3. Convert the result doubly linked list back into a binary search tree (doubly linked list to binary search tree conversion has already been solved on page 63).

1.4 Lists

1. Replace each element in a list with the next greatest

Consider the list A = [0, 2, 8, 1, 3, 5, 4].

The greatest number after 0 in A is maximum of [2, 8, 1, 3, 5, 4] = 8. So 0 is replaced by 8.

The greatest number after 8 in A is maximum of [1, 3, 5, 4] = 5. So 8 is replaced with 5.

4 is the last number in A. There are no more elements to its right. So 4 is replaced by an invalid number or the smallest possible number.

So the resulting list is = [8, 8, 5, 5, 5, 4, INVALID_NUMBER].

The brute force approach will try to compute the next greatest of an element by scanning all the elements to its right. This will have a time complexity of $O(n^2)$.

However we can achieve the same in $O(n)$ by traversing from the end of the list to the beginning and maintaining the maximum element seen so far. The code is given below

```
#a: non-empty list in which each element should be replaced with next greatest
def replace_with_next_greatest(a) :
    n = len(a)

    next_greatest = a[n-1]
    a[n-1] = INVALID_NUMBER

    #Process the list from the back
    for i in range(n-2, -1, -1) :
        temp = a[i]

        a[i] = next_greatest

        if (temp > next_greatest):
            next_greatest = temp
```

2. Given a list, efficiently remove all occurrences of an element from the list in place without creating a new list and without using the Python remove function

---

Suppose the given list is A = [1, 4, 2, 1, 5, 2] and we have to remove all occurrences of 1 from it, then the result list is [4, 2, 5, 2]. The element to be removed from the list can be present in multiple locations. We can efficiently remove all occurrences of the element in O(1) space and O(n) time in a single pass through the list by doing the following:

1. Maintain a variable called fill_pos to keep track of where we should store the next element of the list that should not be deleted. Initialize fill_pos to 0.

2. Traverse through the list. If the current element in the list should be deleted then skip it. If current element in the list should not be deleted, then store the current element at fill_pos in the list and increment fill_pos.

```
#a: input list from which all occurrences of an element should be removed
#x: element to be removed
def remove_element(a, x) :
    fill_pos = 0
    for  cur_value in a:
        if (cur_value != x) :
            a[fill_pos] = cur_value
            fill_pos += 1

    #delete all the elements from fill_pos onwards
    if (fill_pos < len(a)) :
        del a[fill_pos:]
```

1.4 Lists

3. Given a list, efficiently remove all the duplicates from the list in place without creating a new list and without using the Python remove function

---

Suppose the given list is A = [1, 4, 2, 1, 5, 2] and we have to remove all duplicates from it, then the result list is [1, 4, 2, 5]. All duplicates in a list A can be removed using the following approaches

1. Brute force approach. Pick every element in A and remove all the duplicates of that element. Removing all duplicates of one element can be done in O(n). Since we have to do this for n elements, the time complexity will be $O(n^2)$ and no extra space is needed

2. Dictionary approach. Traverse the elements in A and add the elements to a dictionary. If we encounter an element which is already in the dictionary, then we exclude it from the result. The time complexity is O(n) but we will need extra space for the dictionary.

3. Sorting. Sort the list A. After sorting, the duplicates will be arranged next to each other. Then iterate through the sorted list and retain an element in A only if it is different from the previous element. We will be using this approach in the code below. The time complexity is O(nlog(n)) and we don't need additional space.

```python
#a: non-empty input list from which duplicates should be removed.
#   this list will be modified in-place
def remove_duplicates(a) :
    #Sort the list
    a.sort()

    fill_pos = 1
    for  i in range(1, len(a)):
        if (a[i] != a[i - 1]) :
              a[fill_pos] = a[i]
              fill_pos += 1

    #remove the remaining items in the list from fill_pos onwards
    if (fill_pos < len(a)):
        del a[fill_pos:]
```

The Big Book of Coding Interviews

4. Move all the zeroes in a list to the right end of the list without creating a new list

We can move all the zeroes to one end of the list (in this case, the right end) in O(n) using the following technique:

1. Scan for the first zero from the left side of the list.

2. Scan for the first non-zero from the right side of the list.

3. Swap the zero and non-zero provided that the zero appears to the left of the non-zero.

```
#a: input list in which the zeroes should be moved to one end
def move_zeroes(a) :
    left = 0
    right = len(a) - 1

    while (left < right) :
        #Locate the first zero from the left
        while (left < len(a) and a[left] != 0):
            left += 1

        #Locate first non-zero from the right
        while (right >= 0 and a[right] == 0):
            right -= 1

        if (left < right) :
            #Swap a[left] and a[right]
            a[left], a[right] = a[right], a[left]
```

1.4 Lists

5. Rotate a list by k times in place without creating a new list

Consider the list [10, 20, 30, 40, 50]. Suppose we rotate the list once, we have to move the elements 10, 20, 30, 40 right by 1 position and move the last element 50 to the beginning to get [50, 10, 20, 30, 40]. So if we have a list of size n, then for 1 rotate operation we will need n moves. If we rotate the list k times then there will be k*n moves. There is a faster method for rotating a list. Let the list be A = [10, 20, 30, 40, 50] and the number of rotations k = 2. The procedure is:

1. Reverse the entire list. So we get [50, 40, 30, 20, 10]

2. Reverse the list in the region 0 to k -1. If k = 2, we reverse the region A[0] to A[1]. So we get the list [40, 50, 30, 20, 10]

3. Finally reverse the list in the region k to n-1 where n is the length of the list. If k=2, we reverse the region A[2] to A[4]. So we get the required result [40, 50, 10, 20, 30].

With this technique, we always need 2*n moves irrespective of the value of k.

```
#Main function to rotate a 1 dimensional list
#a: list which should be rotated.
#num_rotations: how many times to rotate the list. Should be >= 0
def rotate_list(a, num_rotations) :
    length = len(a)
    if (length == 0):
        return

    #Suppose a list has a length of 5, every time we rotate by
    #5 locations, we end up with the same list. So obtain num_rotations
    #value from 0 to length - 1
    num_rotations = num_rotations % length

    if (num_rotations == 0):
        return

    #Reverse the entire list
    a.reverse()

    #Reverse the list in the region (0, num_rotations - 1)
    reverse_list(a, 0, num_rotations - 1)

    #Reverse the list in the region (num_rotations, length - 1)
    reverse_list(a, num_rotations, length - 1)
```

```python
#Helper function which reverses a list in region (low, high)
#a: list which needs to be reversed
#low: lower index of region to be reversed
#high: higher index of region to be reversed
def reverse_list(a, low, high) :
    while (low < high) :
        a[low], a[high] = a[high], a[low]
        low += 1
        high -= 1
```

1.4 Lists

6. A list is used to store the values of the digits of a large number. So if the number is 789, then a[0] = 7, a[1] = 8, a[2] = 9. Perform subtraction of two such lists and store the result in a list

We do the following:

1. Find the larger of the two numbers. The list which has more elements will have the larger number. If both lists have the same number of elements, then compare the digits from the most significant digit to the least significant digit to find the larger number.

2. Subtract the smaller number from the larger number. Initialize borrow to 0 and start finding the difference of the digits of the two numbers from least significant digit to most significant digit. The difference between the digits of the two numbers at a particular position = digit of larger number – digit of smaller number – borrow. If the difference is negative, then add 10 to the difference and set borrow to 1.

3. If the user has requested (smaller number – larger number), then the result will be negative.

```
#num1 and num2: lists which store the digits of the two numbers.
#   The two lists store numeric value of the digits and not ascii values
#Returns: 1. result list which contains num1 - num2
#         2. boolean value which indicates if result is negative
def large_subtract(num1, num2) :
    is_negative = False

    #Store larger number in num1
    #So if num1 is smaller than num2, then swap num1 and num2
    if (is_smaller(num1, num2) ) :
        #Swap num1 and num2
        num1, num2 = num2, num1

        #If num1 was smaller than num2, then result will be negative
        is_negative = True


    #initialize result list
    result = [0] * len(num1)

    #Perform the subtraction for all the digits in num2
    pos1 = len(num1) - 1
    pos2 = len(num2) - 1
    borrow = 0
    while (pos2 >= 0) :
        difference = num1[pos1] - num2[pos2] - borrow
        if (difference < 0) :
            difference += 10
```

```
                    borrow = 1
            else :
                    borrow = 0

        result[pos1] = difference
        pos1 -= 1
        pos2 -= 1


    #Process any digits leftover in num1
    while (pos1 >= 0) :
        difference = num1[pos1] - borrow
        if (difference < 0) :
                difference += 10
                borrow = 1
        else :
                borrow = 0

        result[pos1] = difference
        pos1 -= 1


    return result, is_negative



#Helper function which returns True if num1 is smaller than num2
def is_smaller(num1, num2) :
    if (len(num1) > len(num2)):
        return False

    if (len(num1) < len(num2)):
        return True

    for  digit1, digit2 in zip(num1, num2):
        if (digit1 > digit2):
                return False

        if (digit1 < digit2):
                return True


    return False
```

7. Given a list, find the power set of the elements in the list

The power set will contain all subsets of the list including the empty set. Consider the list = [A, B, C]. The power set consists of {}, {A}, {B}, {C}, {A,B}, {A,C}, {B,C}, {A, B, C}.

We can generate the power set either non-recursively or recursively. The non-recursive method is as follows: Initialize an integer to 0. Then go on incrementing the integer until we reach $2^n - 1$, where n is the number of elements in the list. Each integer generated represents one subset. If the ith bit in the integer is set to 1, then the ith element in the list is included in the subset, otherwise the ith element is excluded from the subset. So when the integer is 0, it represents the empty subset. The code for the non-recursive method is given below

```
#Helper function for printing a subset
#input_list: list containing the input elements
#selection: if bit i is 1 in selection, then element i is present in subset
def printSubset(input_list, selection):
    print('{', end='')

    for i, cur_value in enumerate(input_list):
        if (selection & (1 << i)):
            print('{} '.format(cur_value) , end='')

    print('}')


#Main function for generating the subsets
#input_list: list containing the input elements
def generateSubsets(input_list):
    num_subsets = 1 << len(input_list)

    for i in range(num_subsets):
        printSubset(input_list, i)
```

The Big Book of Coding Interviews

8. Given a list of N elements, produce all the subsets of size R that can be formed from the elements.

To find the subset of size R, we will use recursion. Cycle through all elements in the list recursively. First exclude the current item from the subset and recursively fill the remaining items into the subset until the subset contains R items. Then include the current item in the subset and recursively fill the remaining items into the subset until the subset contains R items.

```
#a: input list containing the elements
#is_selected: if is_selected[i] = True, then the ith element
#   of the input_list is present in the current subset
#pos: current position in the input
#subset_size: total number elements that should be present in the final subset
#cur_num_selections: currently how many elements have been selected
def generate_combinations(a, is_selected, pos, subset_size, cur_num_selections):
    if (cur_num_selections == subset_size) :
        print_combination(a, is_selected, subset_size)
        return #Terminate the recursion


    if (pos >= len(a)) :
        return #Terminate the recursion

    #Exclude the item from the subset
    is_selected[pos] = False

    generate_combinations(a, is_selected, pos+1, subset_size,
                    cur_num_selections)

    #Include the item in the subset
    is_selected[pos] = True

    generate_combinations(a, is_selected, pos+1, subset_size,
                    cur_num_selections + 1)
```

1.4 Lists

9. Efficiently find the intersection and union of two lists without converting the lists into sets or dictionaries

---

We are not allowed to convert the lists into sets. So we can find the intersection of two lists, A (size = m) and B (size = n) using the following techniques

1. Brute force approach: For every element in A, check if the element is present in B and if yes add it to the result. The time complexity will be O(mn) and no extra space is needed.

2. Sorting: Sort the lists A and B. This can be done in O(mlogm) and O(nlogn). Then iterate through the sorted lists and pick the elements that are common to both lists. This can be done in O(m+n). We don't need additional space. We will be using this approach in the code below.

To find the union of two lists without using sets, we can again apply the same techniques

1. Brute force approach: Pick each element of A and if it is not already present in the result then add it to the result. Then pick each element of B and if it is not already in the result, then add it to the result. The time complexity is O(mn) and we don't need additional space.

2. Sorting: Sort the two lists and then pick up the unique elements from the two lists and add them to the result. Sorting can be done in O(mlogm) and O(nlogn). Adding the unique elements to the result can be done in O(m+n). We will be using this approach in the code below. Note that we don't need additional space but since we sort the input lists, they will get modified. Suppose we don't want the input lists to get modified, then we can do the following: Add all the elements of A and B into the result list. Then sort the result list. This can be done in O((m+n)log(m+n)). Then remove the duplicates from it. If there are any duplicates in the result, they will be next to each other. So removal of the duplicates can be done in O(m+n).

The Big Book of Coding Interviews

In the code below, we use the sorting approach to find the intersection of lists

```
#a, b: two input lists whose intersection has to be found
#Returns: list containing the result of intersection of a and b
def find_intersection(a, b) :
    result = []

    #Sort the two lists
    a.sort()
    b.sort()

    i = j = result_pos = 0
    while (i < len(a) and j < len(b)) :
        #Check if the elements in a and b match
        if (a[i] == b[j]) :
            #Add only unique elements to the result
            if (i == 0 or a[i] != a[i - 1]) :
                result.append(a[i])

            i += 1
            j += 1

        elif (a[i] < b[j]):
            i += 1
        else :
            j += 1

    return result
```

1.4 Lists

In the code below, we use the sorting approach to find the union of two lists

```
#a, b: two input lists whose union has to be found
#Returns: list containing the result of union of a and b
def find_union(a, b) :
    if (len(a) + len(b) == 0):
        return []

    result = []

    #sort a and b
    a.sort()
    b.sort()

    #Process as long as there are elements in both a and b.
    #Pick the smaller element among a[i] and b[j] and if it
    #doesn't match with last element in result, add it to result
    i = j = 0
    while (i < len(a) and j < len(b)) :
        if (a[i] <= b[j]) :
            if (len(result) == 0 or a[i] != result[-1]):
                result.append(a[i])

            if (a[i] == b[j]):
                j += 1 #advance b

            i += 1

        else :
            if (len(result) == 0 or b[j] != result[-1]):
                result.append(b[j])
            j += 1

    #Process the remainder elements in a
    while (i < len(a)) :
        if (len(result) == 0 or a[i] != result[-1]):
            result.append(a[i])
        i += 1

    #Process the remainder elements in b
    while (j < len(b)):
        if (len(result) == 0 or b[j] != result[-1]):
            result.append(b[j])
        j += 1

    return result
```

The Big Book of Coding Interviews

10. An unsorted list of size N, contains elements whose values are between 0 to K − 1 where K <= N. Find the most frequently occurring element in O(n) time and O(1) space. For instance if N = 5 and K = 4, given the list [1, 3, 0, 2, 0], then 0 is the most frequently occurring element

---

The main idea is to use the element value in the list as an index into the list. It is safe to do so since the value of an element in the list is less than the size of the list (K <= N). To solve the problem, we iterate through the elements in the list a and do the following:

1. Compute index = a[i] % K

2. Add K to a[index].

Once we have processed all the elements in the list, we find the maximum element in the list. The index of the maximum element will give the most repeated element.

Note that to calculate the index in step 1 above, we perform a[i] % K. This is because by the time we come to location i, we might have already added K to the value at this location one or more times. So we take a[i] % K to get the original value at location i.

Also note that the elements in the list have been modified. To get back the original elements, we simply perform a[i] = a[i] % K for each element in the list

Let a = [1, 3, 0, 2, 0]. N = 5 and K = 4. The table below illustrates how we calculate the most repeated element

i	a[i]	index = a[i] % K	Add K to a[index]
0	1	1 % 4 = 1	a = [1, **3+4**, 0, 2, 0], So a = [1, 7, 0, 2, 0]
1	7	7 % 4 = 3	a = [1, 7, 0, **2+4**, 0], So a = [1, 7, 0, 6, 0]
2	0	0 % 4 = 0	a = [**1+4**, 7, 0, 6, 0], So a = [5, 7, 0, 6, 0]
3	6	6 % 4 = 2	a = [5, 7, **0+4**, 6, 0], So a = [5, 7, 4, 6, 0]
4	0	0 % 4 = 0	a = [**5+4**, 7, 2, 6, 0], So a = [9, 7, 2, 6, 0]

So the maximum value in list a is 9 which is present at index 0. So 0 is the most repeated element in the list.

1.4 Lists

```
#a: list consisting of numbers. A number can have a value between 0 to k-1
#k: k should be <= num elements in list
def find_most_repeated(a, k) :
    #For each number found in the list, go to the index corresponding to
    #the number and add k to the value at the index.
    for i, cur_value in enumerate(a):
        #By the time we come to location i, we might have already added k
        #to the value at this location one or more times.
        #So take a[i] % k to get the original value
        index = cur_value % k
        a[index] += k

    most_repeated = -1
    max_value = MIN_INT
    for i, cur_value in enumerate(a):
        if (cur_value > max_value) :
            #Note that index i will give the most repeated number
            most_repeated = i
            max_value = cur_value

        #Get back the original value in the list
        a[i] = cur_value % k


    return most_repeated
```

11. Find the lowest absolute difference between any two elements in a list

Using the brute force approach, we can compute the absolute difference between every pair of elements in the list and find the lowest absolute difference in $O(n^2)$. However there is a faster technique as described below

1. Sort the list in non-decreasing order. This can be done in O(nlogn)

2. Find the difference between adjacent pairs of elements, i.e. (a[1] – a[0]), (a[2] – a[1]), etc. This can be done in O(n).

The lowest difference between the adjacent pairs of elements gives the lowest absolute difference between any two elements in the list. The overall time complexity is O(nlogn).

```
#a:input list
#Returns: the least absolute difference between any two elements in the list
def find_least_difference(a) :
    assert (len(a) > 1)

    #Sort the list in non-decreasing order
    a.sort()

    least_difference = a[1] - a[0]
    for  i in range(1, len(a) - 1):
        if (a[i+1] - a[i] < least_difference):
            least_difference = a[i+1] - a[i]

    return least_difference
```

1.4 Lists

12. Given a list of integers, find a 3-element subset that sums to S

A minor variation of this problem is to find if any 3 elements in a list sum up to zero.

Using a brute force approach, it is possible to solve the problem with a time complexity of $O(n^3)$ by generating all the 3-element subsets. There is a more efficient solution that uses sorting as described below:

1. Sort the input list A in non-decreasing order. This can be done in O(nlogn).

2. Pick each element x in the list A. Let the index of the element x in list A be i. Let the total number of elements in the list be n. Then start picking one element A[low] from i+1 in the forward direction, where low >= i + 1 and another element A[high] from n-1 in the backward direction, where high <= n - 1. Let total = x + A[low] + A[high]. If total is equal to S, then we have found the sum. If total is less than S, then we increment low. If total is greater than S, then we decrement high. For one element this can be done in O(n). For n elements this can be done in $O(n^2)$

The total time complexity is $O(n^2)$ and we don't need additional space. We will however end up sorting the input list.

```
#a: input list
#S: the addition of any 3 elements in list should be equal to S
#Returns: Number of 3 elements subsets where sum of 3 elements is equal to S
def find_3_element_sum(a, S) :
    #Sort the list in non-decreasing order
    a.sort()

    count = 0
    for  i in range(len(a) - 2):
        #Choose a[i]. Start picking the other two elements from
        #opposite ends. So start choosing from i+1 on one side and
        #length - 1 on the other side
        low = i + 1
        high = len(a) - 1
        while (low < high) :
                total = a[i] + a[low] + a[high]
                if (total == S) :
                    count += 1
                    print('{} + {} + {} = {} '.format(a[i], a[low],
                                                    a[high], total) )

                    low += 1
                    high -= 1
```

```
            elif (total > S):
                    high -= 1 #We need to pick a smaller element
            else :
                    low += 1 #We need to pick a larger element

    return count
```

13. Find the maximum product of any 3 numbers in a list

We can find the highest 3 numbers in the list and multiply them to get the maximum product of 3 numbers in the list. However if the list contains negative numbers, then we may not get the correct result. For instance, consider the list [-10, -9, 1, 2, 3]. The product of the highest 3 numbers is 1 * 2 * 3 = 6. But the maximum product that we can get is -10 * -9 * 3 = 270. So the maximum product of 3 numbers in a list is either the product of the 3 highest numbers OR the product of the 2 lowest numbers and the highest number.

So we need to find the 2 lowest numbers and the 3 highest numbers in the list. We can do this in a single scan of the list. We will maintain the list called max_values for storing the 3 highest numbers. max_values[0] will store the highest value, max_values[1] will store the second highest number and max_values[2] will store the third highest number. Similarly, we will maintain the list called min_values for storing the 2 lowest numbers. min_values[0] will store the lowest value and min_values[1] will store the second lowest value. The code is given below

```
#a:input list
#Returns: the maximum product of 3 elements in the list
def find_max_product(a) :
    max_value = [MIN_INT] * 3
    min_value = [MAX_INT] * 2
    assert (len(a) >= 3)

    for  cur_val in a:
       #Check if cur_val is among the 3 largest values
       if (cur_val > max_value[0]) :
             max_value[2] = max_value[1]
             max_value[1] = max_value[0]
             max_value[0] = cur_val
       elif (cur_val > max_value[1]):
             max_value[2] = max_value[1]
             max_value[1] = cur_val
       elif (cur_val > max_value[2]):
             max_value[2] = cur_val

       #Check if cur_val is among the 2 smallest values
       if (cur_val < min_value[0]) :
             min_value[1] = min_value[0]
             min_value[0] = cur_val
       elif (cur_val < min_value[1]):
             min_value[1] = cur_val

    return max(max_value[0] * max_value[1] * max_value[2],
               min_value[0] * min_value[1] * max_value[0])
```

The Big Book of Coding Interviews

14. For every element in a list, efficiently find the product of all other elements except that element. Division is not allowed. For instance, given A = [2, 6, 4, 5], the product of all elements except 2 is 6*4*5 = 120. So if we do this for every element, we get [120, 40, 60, 48]

For one element, we can find the product of all elements except itself in O(n). If we do this for all elements, we can find the result in $O(n^2)$. However there is an efficient solution that can do the job in O(n). The idea is as follows:

1. In the first pass through the list A, we process it from left to right and keep multiplying the adjacent elements from the left. In result[i], we store the product of elements from A[0] to A[i-1]

2. In the second pass through the list A, we process it from right to left and go on accumulating the product of adjacent elements from the right. So at location i, we will have the product of elements from A[n-1] to A[i+1]. We multiply this product with result[i] which already has A[0] *...*A[i-1]. So result[i] will now have A[0] * ... A[i-1] * A[i+1] * .... * A[n-1]

```
#a: input list
#Returns: result[i] will contain product of all elements of list a except a[i]
def compute_product(a) :
    n = len(a)
    result = []

    #Compute the product of elements of list a in forward direction.
    #Store product of a[0] to a[i-1] in result[i]
    product = 1
    for  cur_value in a:
        result.append(product)
        product = cur_value * product


    #Next compute the product of elements of list a in reverse direction
    #So we now compute product of a[n-1] to a[i+1] and multiply it with
    #value in result[i]. In this way result[i] will contain product of
    #a[0]...a[i-1]*a[i+1]....a[n-1]
    product = 1
    for  i in range(n - 1, -1,-1):
        result[i] = result[i] * product
        product = a[i] * product

    return result
```

1.4 Lists

15. Efficiently find the equilibrium point in a list. The equilibrium point is the location where the sum of elements to the left of the location equals the sum of the elements to the right of the location. For instance, given A = [-50, 100, 80, 30, -60, 10, 70], the equilibrium point is 2, since sum of elements to left of index 2 = -50 + 100 = 50 and sum of elements to the right of index 2 = 30 – 60 + 10 + 70 = 50

We can apply the brute force approach and check if each point is an equilibrium point. We can find if one point is an equilibrium point in O(n) and since we have to do this for n points, the complexity of brute force approach is $O(n^2)$. There is a more efficient way that gives the equilibrium point in O(n) that is described below:

1. First compute the sum of all elements in the list A. This value will be stored in right_sum. Next initialize left_sum to 0.

2. Process the elements of the list from left to right. When we pick A[i], we subtract A[i] from right_sum so that right_sum has sum of all elements to the right of index i. Then we compare left sum and right sum. If they match, we have found the equilibrium point. If not, we increment left_sum with A[i] and go to the next element.

```
#a: input list whose equilibrium point has to be found.
#Return value: index of the equilibrium point if it exists, -1 otherwise
def find_equilibrium_point(a) :
    #Compute the sum of all elements and store in right_sum
    right_sum = 0
    for  cur_value in a:
        right_sum += cur_value

    #Go on computing sum of all elements from the left to right and
    #compare with right sum
    left_sum = 0
    for  i, cur_value in enumerate(a):
        #Subtract cur_value from right_sum to find out sum of
        #the elements to the right of i
        right_sum -= cur_value

        if (left_sum == right_sum) :
                return i #We have found the equilibrium point

        left_sum += cur_value

    return -1
```

16.

In a list consisting of 0's and 1's, find the longest sub-list which has equal number of 0's and 1's

---

Consider the list [1, 1, 0, 1, 0, 1, 1, 1, 1, 0]. The longest sub-list with equal 0's and 1's is [1, 0, 1, 0] from index 1 to index 4 of the main list.

To find the longest sub-list, we first compute the running sum of 0's and 1's. The running sum is initialized to 0 and every time we get a 1, we increment the running sum by 1 and if we get a 0, we decrement the running sum by 1. So if there are N elements in the list and all of them are 0's we get a running sum of –N. If all the N elements are 1's, then we get a running sum of N. So the running sum for a list can vary from –N to N. We normalize the running sum from the range (–N, N) to the range (0, 2*N) by adding N to the running sum.

We maintain the first_ix_for_sum list that gives the first index in the list at which we observed a particular normalized sum. Initially first_ix_for_sum list is initialized with MIN_INT.

first_ix_for_sum[N] corresponds to normalized running sum of N. Normalized running sum of N corresponds to running sum of 0. We can consider that we have already observed a running sum of 0 at index of -1 ie, before starting to process the list. So first_ix_for_sum[N] is initialized to -1.

The list [1, 1, 0, 1, 0, 1, 1, 1, 1, 0] has N = 10 elements in it. Consider the first 5 elements of the list.

Index	Element	Running Sum	Normalized Sum = Running sum + N	Is first occurrence of normalized sum	Action
0	1	1	11	Yes	first_ix_for_sum[11] = 0
1	1	2	12	Yes	first_ix_for_sum[12] = 1
2	0	1	11	No	
3	1	2	12	No	
4	0	1	11	No	

1.4 Lists

Each time that we obtain a normalized running sum that we have already observed, it means that we have traversed an equal number of 0's and 1's between the index corresponding to the first occurrence of the normalized running sum and the current index. For instance, we observe the normalized running sum of 11 for the first time at index 0 . Subsequently we observed normalized running sum of 11 again at index 2. So there are equal number of 0's and 1's in between index 1 to index 2. We again observe normalized running sum of 11 at index 4. So again there are equal number of 0's and 1's from index 1 to index 4.

So every time we hit a normalized sum that we have already encountered before, the difference between the current index and the index when we first observed the normalized sum will give us the length of the region with equal 0's and 1's. The longest such region will give us the result.

```
#a:input list
#Returns: 1. the length of the longest sub-list with equal 0's and 1's
#         2. start index of longest sub-list
#         3. end index of longest sub-list
def find_sub_list(a) :
    num_elements = len(a)

    #first_ix_for_sum will store the first seen index for a particular
    #normalized running sum. Initialize the sum table. MIN_INT should be < -1
    #normalized running sum = num_elements + running_sum
    first_ix_for_sum = [MIN_INT] * (2 * num_elements + 1)

    #Before we start processing, we say that at index -1, running sum is 0
    #The normalized running sum =  num_elements + running_sum = num_elements
    #+ 0 = num_elements. So first_ix_for_sum[num_elements] is set to -1
    first_ix_for_sum[num_elements] = -1
    max_length = 0
    running_sum = 0
    start_index = end_index = -1
    for  i, cur_element in enumerate(a):
        #If we get a 1, increment the running sum. If we get a 0
        #then decrement the running sum
        if (cur_element == 1):
             running_sum += 1
        else:
             running_sum -= 1

        #If there are 10 elements, then running sum can vary from -10
        #to +10. Normalize the running sum into an index from 0 to 20
        normalized_sum = num_elements + running_sum
        if (first_ix_for_sum[normalized_sum] == MIN_INT) :
             #We are observing the normalized running sum
             #for the first time. Store the index in first_ix_for_sum
             first_ix_for_sum[normalized_sum] = i
        else :
```

```
            #We have already observed the normalized running sum
            #before. Suppose we have a normalized running sum of 3
            #at index 10 and we again observe normalized running sum
            #of 3 at index 18, then there are equal 0's and 1's
            #from index 11 to index 18
            first_index = first_ix_for_sum[normalized_sum]
            if (i - first_index > max_length) :
                    max_length = i - first_index
                    start_index = first_index + 1
                    end_index = i

    return max_length, start_index, end_index
```

1.4 Lists

17. Rotate a two dimensional square matrix by 90 degrees

To rotate a square matrix in the clockwise direction by 90° we have to take the first row in the original matrix and make it the last column in the rotated matrix. The second row becomes the second last column and so on. This can be done easily by using an additional matrix. But we want to rotate the matrix in-place without using up a lot of additional memory.

To solve this problem, we do the following:

- choose one quadrant of the square matrix
- take each element in the chosen quadrant and circularly rotate the corresponding elements in all the quadrants

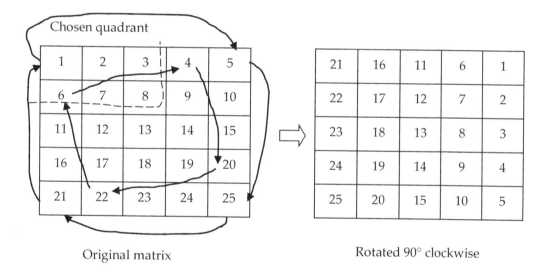

Original matrix   Rotated 90° clockwise

So in the diagram above, 1, 5, 25, 21 are circularly swapped (1 moves to 5, 5 moves to 25, 25 moves to 21 and 21 moves to 1). The other circular movements are

- 6->4->20->22
- 2->10->24->16
- 7->9->19->17
- 3->15->23->11
- 8->14->18->12

The Big Book of Coding Interviews

The code for rotating 90° clockwise is given below

```
#m: 2-D square matrix to be rotated by 90 degrees in clockwise direction
def rotate_square_matrix90(m) :
    n = len(m) #Get the number of rows in the square matrix

    #max_i and max_j have the boundaries of the first quadrant
    max_i = (n // 2) - 1
    max_j = ((n+1) // 2) - 1

    for i in range(max_i + 1):
        for j in range(max_j + 1):

                    #Perform a four way swap
                    temp = m[i][j]

                    m[i][j] = m[n - j - 1][i]

                    m[n - j - 1][i] = m[n - i - 1][n - j - 1]

                    m[n - i - 1][n - j - 1] = m[j][n - i - 1]

                    m[j][n - i - 1] = temp
```

There is another technique that uses matrix transpose for rotating a matrix in-place. The transpose of a matrix interchanges the rows and columns (so first row becomes first column, second row becomes second column and so on).

To rotate a matrix by 90° clockwise using matrix transpose, do the following:

- take the transpose of the matrix
- then interchange the columns: interchange first column and last column, interchange the second column and second last column and so on

To rotate a matrix by 90° anti-clockwise using matrix transpose, do the following:

- take the transpose of the matrix
- then interchange the rows: interchange first row and last row, then interchange the second row and second last row and so on

To rotate a matrix by 180°, do the following:

- interchange the rows: interchange first row and last row, then interchange the second row and second last row and so on
- interchange the columns: interchange first column and last column, interchange the second column and second last column and so on

Note that for 180°, the direction of rotation does not matter (we will get the same result if we rotate a matrix by 180° clockwise or 180° anti-clockwise). So to get a matrix rotated by 180° we can also first interchange all the columns and then interchange all the rows.

18. Print the elements of a two dimensional matrix in spiral order

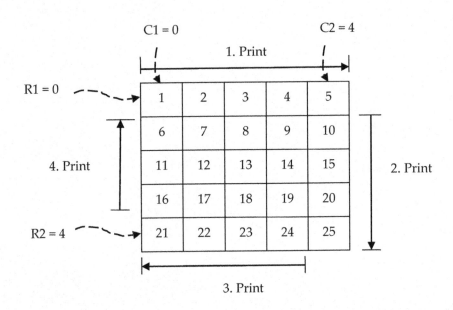

Consider the matrix above. To print in spiral order we have to print 1, 2, 3, 4, 5, 10, 15, 20, 25, 24, 23, 22, 21, 16, 11, 6, 7, 8, 9, 14, 19, 18, 17, 12 and 13.

The start row R1 is initialized to 0, end row R2 is initialized to number of rows − 1 = 5 - 1 = 4, start column C1 is initialized to 0 and end column C2 is initialized to number of columns − 1 = 5 − 1 = 4. The algorithm to print the matrix spirally is:

- print the cells in R1 (0) from columns C1 (0) to C2 (4). So we print 1, 2, 3, 4, 5.
- increment R1 (R1 becomes 1).
- print the cells in C2 (4) from rows R1 (1) to R2 (4). So we print 10, 15, 20, 25
- decrement C2 (C2 becomes 3)
- print the cells in R2 (4) from columns C2 (3) to C1 (0). So we print 24, 23, 22, 21.
- decrement R2 (R2 becomes 3)
- print the cells in C1 (0) from rows R2 (3) to R1 (1). So we print 16, 11, 6
- increment C1 (C1 becomes 2)

The above steps are repeated as long as R1 <= R2 and C1 <= C2.

```
#m: 2-D matrix that should be printed spirally
def print_spiral(m) :
    num_rows = len(m)
    num_cols = len(m[0])
    r1 = 0
    r2 = num_rows - 1
    c1 = 0
    c2 = num_cols - 1

    while (r1 <= r2 and c1 <= c2) :
        #Print row r1
        cur_row = r1
        for  cur_col in range(c1, c2+1):
                print('{} '.format(m[cur_row][cur_col]) , end='')

        r1 += 1 #Advance r1 to next row

        #Print column c2
        cur_col = c2
        for  cur_row in range(r1, r2+1):
                print('{} '.format(m[cur_row][cur_col]) , end='')

        c2 -= 1 #Advance c2 to previous column

        if (r1 != r2) :
                #Print row r2
                cur_row = r2
                for  cur_col in range(c2, c1-1,-1):
                        print('{} '.format(m[cur_row][cur_col]) , end='')

                r2 -= 1 #Advance r2 to previous row

        if (c1 != c2) :
                #Print column c1
                cur_col = c1
                for  cur_row in range(r2, r1-1,-1):
                        print('{} '.format(m[cur_row][cur_col]) , end='')

                c1 += 1 #Advance c1 to next column
```

The Big Book of Coding Interviews

19. A two dimensional matrix M consists of 0's and 1's. If M[i][j] is 1, then make all the elements in row i and all elements in column j equal to 1 using minimal additional space.

We can solve this problem by having two additional lists: row_list and colum_list. The row_list[i] will be set to 1 if there is at least one cell in row i of matrix M that is set to 1. The column_list[j] will be set to 1 if there is at least one cell in column j of matrix M set to 1. Once the lists are computed, we go ahead and modify the matrix as follows:

- If row_list[i] = 1, then make all the cells in row i of matrix M to 1
- If column_list[j] = 1, then make all cells in column j of matrix M to 1

There is a better solution that requires just two variables instead of two lists. By having these two variables, it is possible to use the first row of the matrix M to serve as row_list and first column of matrix M to serve as column_list. The steps of this solution are:

1.) Maintain the variables is_1_in_first_row (which is set to True if there is at least one cell in the first row set to 1) and is_1_in_first_col (which is set to True if there is at least one cell in the first column set to 1). In the input matrix below, is_1_in_first_col is set to True since there is a 1 in first column and is_1_in_first_row is set to False since all the cells are 0 in the first row.

0	0	0	0	0
1	0	0	0	0
0	0	1	0	0
0	0	0	0	0

is_1_in_first_row = False

is_1_in_first_col = True

2.) Now scan the region M[1][1] to M[num_rows-1][num_cols-1] and check the cells. If M[i][j] is set to 1, then make M[i][0] = 1 and M[0][j] = 1

1.4 Lists

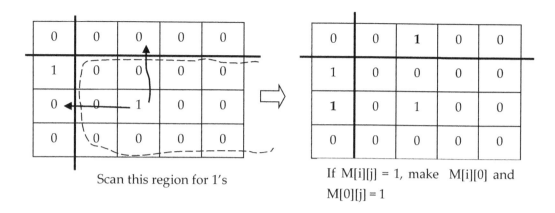

Scan this region for 1's

If M[i][j] = 1, make M[i][0] and M[0][j] = 1

3. Go through the first column of M and if M[i][0] is 1, then set all cells in row i to 1. Also go through the first row of M and if M[0][j] is 1, then set all cells in column j to 1.

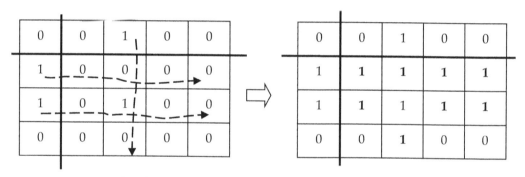

Set the cells to 1 based on first row and first column of M

4. If is_1_in_first_col is True, then set all cells in first column to 1. If is_1_in_first_row is True, then set all cells in the first row to 1.

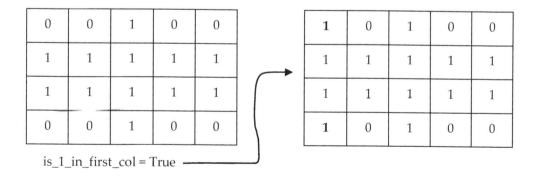

is_1_in_first_col = True

```python
#m: 2-D matrix to be processed having at least 1 row and 1 column
def process_matrix(m) :
    is_1_in_first_row = 0
    is_1_in_first_col = 0

    num_rows = len(m)
    num_cols = len(m[0])

    #Check if any cell in the first row is set to 1
    for  i in range(num_rows):
        if (m[i][0] == 1) :
            is_1_in_first_row = True
            break

    #Check if any cell in first column is set to 1
    for  j in range(num_cols):
        if (m[0][j] == 1) :
            is_1_in_first_col = True
            break

    #Scan the matrix. If m[i][0] is equal to 1 then, set m[i][0] to 1
    #and set m[0][j] to 1
    for  i in range(1, num_rows):
        for  j in range(1, num_cols):
            if (m[i][j] == 1) :
                m[i][0] = 1
                m[0][j] = 1

    #Mark the cells as 1 as indicated by m[i][0] and m[0][j]
    for  i in range(1, num_rows):
        for  j in range(1, num_cols):
            if (m[i][0] == 1 or m[0][j] == 1):
                m[i][j] = 1

    #If there was a 1 initially in first column, set 1 in all the
    #cells of first column
    if (is_1_in_first_col):
        for  i in range(num_rows):
            m[i][0] = 1

    #If there was a 1 initially in first row, set 1 in all the
    #cells of the first row
    if (is_1_in_first_row):
        for  j in range(num_cols):
            m[0][j] = 1
```

1.4 Lists

20. A two dimensional matrix M represents a maze. If M[i][j] is -1, then the cell is blocked. Find how many paths are present between M[0][0] and M[num_rows - 1] [num_cols-1]

Consider the grid in the diagram below. We are treating M[num_rows-1][num_cols-1] as the source and M[0][0] as the destination. We have three possible movements from a cell:

- we can move above to the previous row
- we can move to the left to the previous column.
- we can move diagonally to the cell in the previous row and previous column

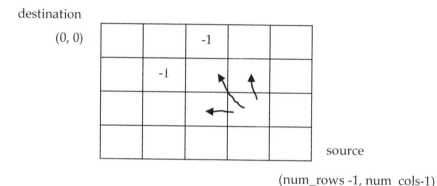

We can solve this problem using recursion. At each cell, we apply the following steps

- if we reach a cell that is marked with -1, then we stop traversing on that path and backtrack to the previous cell we had traversed
- if we reach a normal cell, then we explore all possible paths through the cell. So we first jump to the cell above and try to recursively traverse further to reach the destination. We then jump to the cell to the left and try to recursively traverse further to reach the destination. We then jump to the diagonally above cell and recursively try to reach the destination.

```
#m: matrix that has to be navigated
#cur_row: row of the current cell
#cur_col: column of the current cell
#Return value: the total number of paths possible is returned
def navigate_maze(m, cur_row, cur_col) :
    if (cur_row < 0 or cur_col < 0):
        return 0

    if (m[cur_row][cur_col] == -1):
        return 0 #We can't traverse this cell, so simply return

    if (cur_row == 0 and cur_col == 0) :
        #We have reached the destination
        return 1

    #Try continuing the path by going to the cell in previous row
    num_paths = navigate_maze(m, cur_row - 1, cur_col)

    #Try continuing the path by going to the cell in previous column
    num_paths += navigate_maze(m, cur_row, cur_col - 1)

    #Try continuing the path by going to the diagonally above cell
    num_paths += navigate_maze(m, cur_row - 1, cur_col - 1)

    return num_paths
```

1.5 Strings

1. Find if two string words are anagrams of each other

Two strings are anagrams of each other if re-arrangement of characters in one string results in the other string. This implies that two string words are anagrams if for each character, the number of times the character occurs in the first string is equal to the number of times it occurs in the second string. The code for finding if two words are anagrams is given below

```
#str1, str2: the two strings which we want to compare
#Return value: True if the two strings are anagrams, False otherwise
def are_anagrams(str1, str2) :
    count1 = [0] * NUM_CHARACTERS  #NUM_CHARACTERS is 256
    count2 = [0] * NUM_CHARACTERS

    #Compute the character counts for str1 and str2
    for  c in str1:
        count1[ord(c)] += 1

    for  c in str2:
        count2[ord(c)] += 1

    #Compare the counts
    is_anagram = True
    if (count1 != count2):
        is_anagram = False

    return is_anagram
```

2. Count the number of words in a string

We will define a word as a collection of one or more characters from a-z and A-Z. The words in a string can be separated by multiple spaces, tabs, punctuation marks etc. To count the number of words, as we traverse the string we will keep track of the previous character and the current character. If the previous character is not an alphabet from a-z and A-Z and the current character is an alphabet from a-z and A-Z, then we have encountered a new word and we increase the word count by 1.

```python
#str1: string in which the number of words have to be counted
#Return value: number of words in the string
def count_words(str1) :
    if (not str1):
        return 0

    num_words = 0
    is_prev_char_alphabet = False
    for c in str1 :
        is_cur_char_alphabet = c.isalpha()

        #If previous character is not an alphabet and current character is
        #an alphabet then we have found a new word
        if (not is_prev_char_alphabet and is_cur_char_alphabet) :
            num_words += 1

        is_prev_char_alphabet = is_cur_char_alphabet

    return num_words
```

1.5 Strings

3. Convert a string to an integer without using the int() built-in function.

The function for converting a string to an integer is given below

```
#str1: string to be converted to integer
#result: integer value of string
def str_to_int(str1):
    result = 0
    count = 0
    is_negative = False

    for c in str1:
        if (c == '-' and count == 0):
            is_negative = True

        if ('0' <= c and c <- '9'):
            result = (result * 10) + (ord(c) - ord('0'))

        count += 1

    if (is_negative):
        result = -1 * result

    return result
```

The Big Book of Coding Interviews

4. Given a number from 0 to 999,999,999, print the number in words. So 200,145,700 should be printed as two hundred million one hundred forty five thousand seven hundred

We will break the input number into millions, thousands and the remaining 3 least significant digits. So in this case 200,145,700 gets broken down to 200, 145 and 700. Then we make use of a helper function that prints 3 consecutive digits.

```
#Helper function to print number from 1 to 999
#number: number from 1 to 999
def print_3_digits(number) :
    #basic_lookup[0] is empty. We want basic_lookup[1] to map to 'One'
    #and so on.
    basic_lookup = ['', 'One', 'Two', 'Three', 'Four', 'Five', 'Six',
             'Seven', 'Eight', 'Nine', 'Ten', 'Eleven', 'Twelve',
             'Thirteen', 'Fourteen', 'Fifteen', 'Sixteen',
             'Seventeen', 'Eighteen', 'Nineteen']

    #tens_lookup[0] and tens_lookup[1] are empty.
    #We want tens_lookup[2] to map to 'Twenty' and so on.
    tens_lookup = ['', '','Twenty', 'Thirty', 'Fourty', 'Fifty', 'Sixty',
             'Seventy', 'Eighty', 'Ninety']

    #Suppose number is 987, then hundreds_digit is 9
    hundreds_digit = number // 100
    if (hundreds_digit > 0) :
        print(basic_lookup[hundreds_digit] + ' Hundred ', end='')


    #Suppose number is 987, then remainder will be 87
    remainder = number % 100
    if (remainder > 0) :
        if (remainder <= 19) :
            print(basic_lookup[remainder] + ' ', end='')
        else :
            tens_digit = remainder // 10
            unit_digit = remainder % 10
            print(tens_lookup[tens_digit] + ' ', end='')
            print(basic_lookup[unit_digit] + ' ', end='')
```

1.5 Strings

```python
#Main function to print the number in words
#number: any number from 0 to 999999999
def print_num_in_words(number) :
    #If number is 0, handle it here and return
    if (number == 0) :
        print('Zero ')
        return

    #Suppose number is 123456789, then millions = 123, remainder = 456789
    millions = number // 1000000
    remainder = number - (millions * 1000000)

    #Suppose remainder = 456789, then thousands = 456, remainder = 789
    thousands = remainder // 1000
    remainder = remainder - (thousands * 1000)

    if (millions > 0) :
        print_3_digits(millions)
        print('Million ', end='')

    if (thousands > 0) :
        print_3_digits(thousands)
        print('Thousand ', end='')

    if (remainder > 0) :
        print_3_digits(remainder)

    print('')
```

5. Convert a string having Roman numerals into an integer.

The integer equivalent for the Roman numerals is given below:

Roman numeral	Integer value
I	1
V	5
X	10
L	50
C	100
D	500
M	1000

To find the integer equivalent of a string containing Roman numerals, we process the string from the rear. This simplifies the computation. If the current Roman numeral is greater than the next numeral, we add the current numeral to the result. For instance consider XI. When processing X, since X is greater than I, we add 10 to the result. If the current Roman numeral is less than the next numeral, then we subtract the current numeral from the result. For instance consider IX. When processing I, since I is less than X, we subtract 1 from the result.

```
#str1: valid input string with Roman alphabets
#Return value: integer equivalent of the Roman string
def roman_to_int(str1) :
    table = {'I': 1, 'V': 5, 'X': 10, 'L': 50, 'C': 100, 'D': 500, 'M': 1000}

    i = len(str1) - 1 #Process the string from the rear
    if (i < 0):
        return 0

    result = table[str1[i]]
    i -= 1
    while (i >= 0) :
        cur_digit_val = table[str1[i]]
        next_digit_val = table[str1[i+1]]
        if (cur_digit_val < next_digit_val):
                result -= cur_digit_val
        else:
                result += cur_digit_val
        i -= 1

    return result
```

1.5 Strings

6. Compress a string using run length encoding. So the string "aaabcccbbbb" becomes "a3b1c3b4"

We start at the beginning of the input string and traverse it. Each time we encounter a character, we parse out all identical characters that are adjacent to it and find out the count of identical characters. The character and the count are then written out to the result.

```
#Performs run length encoding on a string
#str1: input string (example: 'aaabb')
#Returns: output string (example: 'a3b2')
def run_length_encode(str1) :
    if (not str1):
        return str1

    pos1 = 0
    result = []
    while (pos1 < len(str1)) :
        c = str1[pos1]

        #Count the number of consecutive occurrences of character c
        count = 0
        while (pos1 < len(str1) and c == str1[pos1]) :
                count += 1
                pos1 += 1

        #Store character c and the count in the result
        result.append(str(c))
        result.append(str(count))

    #convert list to string
    return ''.join(result)
```

A variation of this question is, given the run length encoded string "a3b2" decode it back to the original string "aaabb"

7. Remove all duplicate characters in a string

If we are given the string "hehllho", after removing the duplicate characters we get "helo". We can remove all the duplicate characters in a string s1 in O(n) as indicated below:

1. Maintain a list called was_char_observed which indicates if a character has been observed in s1 until now.

2. Traverse s1 and if the was_char_observed list indicates that the current character has not been observed so far, then append the current character to the result list. Finally convert the result list to a string and return the string.

```
#str1: input string from which duplicate characters should be removed
#Returns: output string which doesn't contain any duplicates
def remove_duplicates(str1) :
    if (not str1):
        return str1

    result = []
    was_char_observed = [False] * NUM_CHARACTERS #NUM_CHARACTERS is 256

    for  c in str1:
        #Only if the current character was not observed so far, add the
        #current character to fill position and advance the fill position
        if (not was_char_observed[ord(c)]) :
             result.append(c)

        was_char_observed[ord(c)] = True

    #convert list to string
    return ''.join(result)
```

A variation of this question is to remove all the characters of string s2 from string s1. In this case, we fill was_char_observed using the characters in s2 and use the same approach above.

1.5 Strings

8. Replace all spaces in a string with "%20"

When a URL is sent to a web server, the space characters (' ') in it are first converted to "%20" and then sent. Each space occupies 1 character whereas "%20" occupies 3 characters. So the result will be longer than the original string. To solve the problem with least number of moves, we process the string from the rear as described below:

1. Count the number of spaces in the original string.

2. Initialize fill position (fill_pos) to original string length + (2 * number of spaces) - 1

3. Go on copying the characters from the rear of the original string to the fill position and keep decrementing the fill position. If we encounter a space in the original string, then we insert the characters "%20" at the fill position.

```
#str1: input string
#Return value: string where spaces in input string are replaces with %20
def replace_space(str1) :
    #Count the number of spaces
    num_spaces = 0
    for c in str1:
        if (c == ' '):
            num_spaces += 1

    new_length = len(str1) + (2 * num_spaces)

    #Since result will be longer, create a bigger list
    result = [' '] * new_length

    #Keep copying characters from rear of original string to fill_pos
    fill_pos = new_length - 1
    for c in reversed(str1) :
        if (c == ' ') :
            result[fill_pos] = '0'
            result[fill_pos - 1] = '2'
            result[fill_pos - 2] = '%'
            fill_pos -= 3
        else :
            result[fill_pos] = c
            fill_pos -= 1

    #convert the list to a string
    return ''.join(result)
```

The Big Book of Coding Interviews

9. Given two strings, find if one string can be formed by rotating the characters in the other

Let the strings be str1 and str2. We need to check if str2 can be formed by rotating str1. If the two strings are not of the same length, then we can immediately conclude that str2 is not a rotation of str1. If the two strings are of equal length, then we can generate every rotation of str1 and compare with str2. If the size of str1 is n, then there are n possible rotations and each comparison takes O(n). So the total time complexity is $O(n^2)$.

We can find out if str2 is a rotation of str1 in O(n), if we are allowed to use additional space. The algorithm is as follows:

1. If the two strings have different lengths then return indicating str2 is not a rotation of str1.

2. Form a new string str3 and copy str1 into str3. Then again concatenate str1 into str3.

3. Search for str2 in str3. If str2 is found in str3, then str2 is a rotation of str1.

For instance, let str1="PQR" and str2 = "QRP". Then str3 will be str1 repeated twice which in this case is "PQRPQR". The rotations of str1 are "PQR", "RPQ" and "QRP". str3 will have all the rotations of str1 in it as shown below.

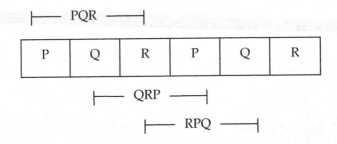

So all the rotations of str1 are present in str3. So when we check if str2 is present in str3, we will find it if str2 is a rotation of str1.

```python
#str1 and str2 are the two strings which need to be checked
#Return value: True if the strings are rotations of each other, False otherwise
def is_string_rotation(str1, str2) :
    #If lengths of two strings are not equal, then they can't be rotations
    if (len(str1) != len(str2)):
        return False

    str3 = str1 + str1

    #find returns -1 if it can't find str2 in str3
    result = str3.find(str2)

    is_rotation = True
    if (result == -1):
        is_rotation = False

    return is_rotation
```

The Big Book of Coding Interviews

10. Reverse the words in a string in-place. So the string "Hello how are you" should become "you are how Hello"

We can reverse the words in a string in O(n) without using additional space, by doing the following:

1. Reverse the entire string. So if the input string is "Hello how are you", after reversal it becomes "uoy era woh olleH".

2. Then reverse all the words in the string. So "uoy era woh olleH" now becomes "you are how Hello"

```
#Main function to reverse the words in a string
#str1: the string in which the words have to be reversed
#Returns: string in which the words have been reversed
def reverse_words(str1) :
    #convert input string to a list
    result = list(str1)

    #if length is < 2 then convert the result list to string and return
    if (len(str1) < 2):
        return ''.join(result)

    #Reverse the entire list
    result = result[::-1]

    #Reverse the individual words
    pos = 0
    while (pos < len(result)) :
        if (result[pos].isalpha()) :
            low = pos
            while (pos < len(result) and result[pos].isalpha()) :
                pos += 1

            high = pos - 1
            reverse_list(result, low, high)
        else :
            pos += 1

    #convert list to string
    return ''.join(result)
```

1.5 Strings

```
#Helper function which reverses a list between indexes low and high
#list1: list which needs to be reversed
#low: lower index of region to be reversed
#high: higher index of region to be reversed
def reverse_list(list1, low, high) :
    while (low < high) :
        list1[low], list1[high] = list1[high], list1[low]
        low += 1
        high -= 1
```

The Big Book of Coding Interviews

11. Find the first non-repeating character in a string. For instance, in string "ABBCAEEF", the first non-repeating character is C.

To find the first non-repeating character in the string, we use the following approach which has a time complexity of O(n):

1. First scan the string and count the number of occurrences for each character

2. Next scan the string again from left to right and the first character that we encounter with a count of 1 is the first non-repeating character.

```
#str1: string to be searched
#Return value: first unique character if it exists, '\0' otherwise
def find_first_unique_char(str1) :
    count = [0] * NUM_CHARS  #NUM_CHARS is 256

    #count the number of occurrences of each character
    for  c in str1:
        count[ord(c)] += 1


    #traverse str1 and find first character which occurs only once
    first_unique_char = '\0'
    for  c in str1:
        if (count[ord(c)] == 1) :
            first_unique_char = c
            break

    return first_unique_char
```

1.5 Strings

12. Find the first non-repeating character in a stream of characters

When we are given a stream of characters, we can inspect only one character at a time. To find the first non-repeating character in a stream, we need to maintain information about the characters that we have observed previously in the stream. For each character we maintain:

- the first position of the character observed in the stream. If we have not yet observed the character in the stream, we store -1 as the first position
- whether the character has been repeated in the stream, i.e. the character has already appeared two or more times in the stream

We also maintain the current first unique (non-repeating) character in the stream. If there are no unique characters in the stream, we store a special character, say '#', as the first unique. When we process the current character in the stream, we do the following:

1. If the first position of the current character is -1, then we update the first position of the character to the current position. If the first unique doesn't exist, then the current character becomes the first unique.

2. If the first position of the current character is not -1, then we have already observed the character. So we mark the character as a repeated character. If the current character is the first unique, then we need to find the new first unique. Scan the first positions and character repeated information of all characters to find the new first unique. If there are m characters in the alphabet, then each scan can be done in $O(m)$ and we will have to do at most m such scans. So the complexity of scanning is $O(m^2)$

If the length of the stream is n, then the total complexity of the algorithm is $O(n + m^2)$. If n is very large compared to m^2 then the complexity reduces to $O(n)$.

```
class StreamParam(object):

    def __init__(self):
        #If we have seen the character 2 or more times in the stream,
        #then is_repeated[character] = True
        self.is_repeated = [False] * NUM_CHARS

        #For every character, we maintain the position of its first
        #occurrence. If the character has not yet occured in stream,
        #we store -1
        self.first_pos = [-1] * NUM_CHARS
```

```python
        #the first unique character in the stream
        self.first_unique = '#'

        #the current position in the stream
        self.cur_pos    = 0


#p: contains the parameters for processing the stream
#cur_char: indicates the current character in the stream
#Returns: first unique character in the stream if it exists, '#' otherwise
def first_unique_in_stream(p, cur_char) :
    if (p.first_pos[ord(cur_char)] == -1) :
        #We are seeing the character for the first time in the stream.
        #So update its first position
        p.first_pos[ord(cur_char)] = p.cur_pos

        #If there are no unique characters in the stream, then make
        #this the first unique character
        if (p.first_unique == '#') :
            p.first_unique = cur_char


        p.cur_pos += 1
        return p.first_unique


    #We have already seen this character before
    p.is_repeated[ord(cur_char)] = 1

    #If the current character is the first unique character in the stream,
    #then we need to replace it with next unique character
    if (p.first_unique == cur_char) :

        #Find the first character that occurs only once in stream
        smallest_pos = MAX_POS
        p.first_unique = '#'
        for  i in range(NUM_CHARS):
                if (p.is_repeated[i] == 0 and p.first_pos[i] != -1
                    and p.first_pos[i] < smallest_pos) :
                        smallest_pos = p.first_pos[i]
                        p.first_unique = chr(i)


    p.cur_pos += 1
    return p.first_unique
```

13. Find the length of the longest palindrome in a string

To find the length of the longest palindrome we use the following procedure:

1. Pick each character in the string and treat it as the middle of a possible palindrome.

2. Then keep extending the substring, one character at a time, in the left and right directions from the chosen character until there is a mismatch in the characters on the left end and right end of the substring. This is the longest possible palindrome with the chosen character at the center.

3. The longest amongst all palindromes generated is the longest palindrome in the string

It is important to note that when we pick a character as the middle of a possible palindrome, the chosen character may be the middle of an odd length palindrome or an even length palindrome. For example, in the string ABCBACDEED, C is the middle of the odd length palindrome ABCBA and E is the middle of the even length palindrome DEED. We have to check for both possibilities at each character. So we do the following:

- to find the longest odd length palindrome with location p as center, simply extend in the left direction (from p-1 onwards) and the right direction (from p+1 onwards) by one character at a time until the left most and right most characters mismatch

- to find the longest even length palindrome with location p as center, first choose the next character p+1 as well. If the characters at p and p+1 match, then extend in the left direction (from p-1 onwards) and the right direction (from p+2 onwards) by one character at a time until the left most and right most characters mismatch

The time complexity of this approach is $O(n^2)$

```python
#str1: valid input character string
#Return value: length of longest palindrome
def find_longest_palindrome(str1) :
    max_pal_len = 0
    for  pos in range(len(str1)):
        #Check for odd length palindromes by comparing the characters
        #to the left of pos with the characters to the right of pos
        left = pos - 1
        right = pos + 1
        cur_pal_len = 1
        while (left >= 0 and right <= len(str1) - 1):
                if (str1[left] != str1[right]):
                        break
                cur_pal_len += 2
                left -= 1
                right += 1


        if (cur_pal_len > max_pal_len):
                max_pal_len = cur_pal_len


        #Check for even length palindromes. If str1[pos], matches
        #with str1[pos+1], then compare the characters to the left of
        #pos with the characters to the right of pos+1
        if (pos < len(str1) - 1 and str1[pos] == str1[pos + 1]):
                left = pos - 1
                right = pos + 2
                cur_pal_len = 2
                while (left >= 0 and right <= len(str1) - 1):
                        if (str1[left] != str1[right]):
                                break
                        cur_pal_len += 2
                        left -= 1
                        right += 1


                if (cur_pal_len > max_pal_len):
                        max_pal_len = cur_pal_len


    return max_pal_len
```

1.5 Strings

14. Find if any permutation of a string is a palindrome. For instance, the string "EVELL" has a permutation "LEVEL" which is a palindrome

---

The permutations of a string are all the possible rearrangements of the characters in the string. We can check if any permutation of a string is a palindrome in O(n) as follows:

1. For each character in the string, count the number of times it occurs in the string

2. If the number of characters that appear odd number of times is less than 2, then at least one permutation of the string will form a palindrome.

For instance in "EVELL", E occurs 2 times, L occurs 2 times and V occurs once. So the number of characters that occurs odd number of times is 1 (which is less than 2). So at least one permutation of "EVELL" will form a palindrome

```
#str1: input string
#Returns: True if there is at least one permutation of string str1 which is
#    a palindrome, False otherwise
def is_permutation_palindrome(str1) :
    count = [0] * NUM_CHARACTERS

    #Find out how many times a character appears in the string
    for c in str1:
        count[ord(c)] += 1

    num_odd_char = 0
    for  cur_count in count:
        if (cur_count % 2 == 1):
            num_odd_char += 1

        #If there are 2 or more characters that appear odd number
        #of times, then we can't form a palindrome with any permutation
        #of the string
        if (num_odd_char >= 2):
            return False

    return True
```

15. Print all the substrings in a string

Let S be the input string of length n and let S(x, y) denote the substring of S starting at position x and ending at position y. We first generate the substrings S(0,0), S(0, 1), S(0, 2), ... S(0, n-1). We then generate the substrings S(1,1), S(1,2), ... S(1, n-1) and so on.

```
#str1: string whose substrings should be printed
def print_all_sub_strings(str1) :
    #Generate all pairs (i,j) where i <= j
    for  i in range(len(str1)):
        for  j in range(i, len(str1)):

            #print the substring str1[i] to str1[j]
            print(str1[i:j+1])
```

Suppose we are asked to generate all the repeating substrings (also referred to as repeating sequences) in a string, we can maintain a dictionary. Every time a substring is generated, the count for the substring in the dictionary is incremented. At the end, all substrings in the dictionary whose count is 2 or more are the repeated substrings.

1.5 Strings

16. Generate all permutations of the characters in a string

The permutations of a string are all the possible rearrangements of the characters in the string. The permutations will have the same length as the original string. There are n! permutations for a string with length n. Consider the string ABC. The permutations are ABC, ACB, BCA, BAC, CAB, and CBA

To generate all the permutations of a string, we make use of recursion. Each call to the recursive function at level i will cycle through all the possible characters at position i. To prevent the same character from being added more than once to the permutation, we maintain a visited list where visited[i] = True if i[th] character in the input string has already been added to the current permutation.

```
#str1: valid input string whose permutations have to be formed
#buf: list for storing the current permutation
#pos: current position in the buf list
#visited: indicates if character in input string has already been visited
def generate_permutations(str1, buf, pos, visited):
    #Recursion termination condition
    if (pos == len(str1)) :
        print(buf)
        return

    for i in range(len(str1)):
        if (visited[i] == False) :
            buf[pos] = str1[i]
            visited[i] = True
            generate_permutations(str1, buf, pos+1, visited)
            visited[i] = False
```

17.

You are playing the scrabble game. Given a bunch of characters, generate all possible strings that you can form using the characters.

If we are given the characters A, B, C, then we will have to generate A, B, C, AB, BA, AC, CA, BC, CB, ABC, ACB, BAC, BCA, CAB, and CBA. To achieve this we make use of recursion. Each call to the recursive function at level i will cycle through all the possible characters at position i. To prevent the same character being added more than once to the permutation, we maintain a visited list where visited[i] = True if i^{th} character in the input has already been added to the current permutation. The solution to this problem is similar to the previous problem where we generated all the permutations of a string. The only difference is that, if there are n characters in the input, then we don't need to wait until all n characters have been generated in the output. During recursion, all strings that we construct having 1 to n characters are treated as output strings.

```
#str1: valid input string whose permutations have to be formed
#buf: list for storing the current permutation
#pos: current position in the buf list
#visited: indicates if character in input string has already been visited
def generate_permutations(str1, buf, pos, visited):
    #print out the current permutation formed till now
    print(buf[0:pos])

    #Recursion termination condition
    if (pos >= len(str1)) :
        return

    for i in range(len(str1)):
        if (visited[i] == False) :
            buf[pos] = str1[i]
            visited[i] = True
            generate_permutations(str1, buf, pos+1, visited)
            visited[i] = False
```

1.5 Strings

18. Print all possible interleavings of two strings. For instance if str1 = "abc" and str2 = "123", then "abc123", "a1b2c3", "ab123c", "12a3bc", etc. are all valid interleavings.

When we interleave two strings str1 and str2, the order of characters in each string should be preserved. For instance, if character 'a' appears before character 'b' in str1, then the same should hold good in the interleaved string. To generate all possible interleavings of str1 and str2, we make use of recursion. At each position of the interleaved string, we can choose between the current character in str1 and str2. So first choose the current character from str1 at the position and recursively process the next positions. Then choose the current character from str2 at the position and recursively process the next positions.

```
#str1, str2: two valid input strings that have to be interleaved
#buf: list that contains the result of interleaving the two strings
#pos1: current position in string str1
#pos2: current position in string str2
#buf_pos: current position in the buf list
def string_interleave(str1, str2, buf, pos1, pos2, buf_pos):
    #If we have finished processing both strings, print buf and
    #terminate the recursion
    if (pos1 == len(str1) and pos2 == len(str2)) :
       print_result(buf, buf_pos, '')
       return

    #If we have finished processing str2, concatenate remaining str1 to buf,
    #print buf and terminate the recursion
    if (pos2 == len(str2)) :
       print_result(buf, buf_pos, str1[pos1:])
       return

    #If we have finished processing str1, concatenate remaining str2 to buf,
    #print buf and terminate the recursion
    if (pos1 == len(str1)) :
       print_result(buf, buf_pos, str2[pos2:])
       return

    #Include the next character of str1 into buf
    buf[buf_pos] = str1[pos1]
    string_interleave(str1, str2, buf, pos1 + 1, pos2, buf_pos + 1)

    #Include the next character of str2 into buf
    buf[buf_pos] = str2[pos2]
    string_interleave(str1, str2, buf, pos1, pos2 + 1, buf_pos + 1)
```

```
#Helper function for printing the result
def print_result(buf, buf_pos, remainder) :
    result = ''.join(buf[0:buf_pos])
    result = result + remainder
    print(result)
```

1.5 Strings

18. Print all possible interleavings of two strings. For instance if str1 = "abc" and str2 = "123", then "abc123", "a1b2c3", "ab123c", "12a3bc", etc. are all valid interleavings.

When we interleave two strings str1 and str2, the order of characters in each string should be preserved. For instance, if character 'a' appears before character 'b' in str1, then the same should hold good in the interleaved string. To generate all possible interleavings of str1 and str2, we make use of recursion. At each position of the interleaved string, we can choose between the current character in str1 and str2. So first choose the current character from str1 at the position and recursively process the next positions. Then choose the current character from str2 at the position and recursively process the next positions.

```
#str1, str2: two valid input strings that have to be interleaved
#buf: list that contains the result of interleaving the two strings
#pos1: current position in string str1
#pos2: current position in string str2
#buf_pos: current position in the buf list
def string_interleave(str1, str2, buf, pos1, pos2, buf_pos):
    #If we have finished processing both strings, print buf and
    #terminate the recursion
    if (pos1 == len(str1) and pos2 == len(str2)) :
       print_result(buf, buf_pos, '')
       return

    #If we have finished processing str2, concatenate remaining str1 to buf,
    #print buf and terminate the recursion
    if (pos2 == len(str2)) :
       print_result(buf, buf_pos, str1[pos1:])
       return

    #If we have finished processing str1, concatenate remaining str2 to buf,
    #print buf and terminate the recursion
    if (pos1 == len(str1)) :
       print_result(buf, buf_pos, str2[pos2:])
       return

    #Include the next character of str1 into buf
    buf[buf_pos] = str1[pos1]
    string_interleave(str1, str2, buf, pos1 + 1, pos2, buf_pos + 1)

    #Include the next character of str2 into buf
    buf[buf_pos] = str2[pos2]
    string_interleave(str1, str2, buf, pos1, pos2 + 1, buf_pos + 1)
```

```python
#Helper function for printing the result
def print_result(buf, buf_pos, remainder) :
    result = ''.join(buf[0:buf_pos])
    result = result + remainder
    print(result)
```

1.5 Strings

19. On the telephone keypad, digit 2 represents characters "ABC", digit 3 represents the characters "DEF" and so on. Given a telephone number, find all the strings that can be generated from it. For instance, if the telephone number is 23, we can form the strings "AD", "AE", "AF", "BD", "BE", "BF", "CD", "CE" and "CF".

The digits 0 and 1 don't have any alphabetical character associated with them. So we assume digit 0 represents "0" and digit 1 represents "1". To generate all possible strings, we make use of recursion and for each digit in the telephone number, we cycle through all possible characters that we can assign to the digit.

```python
#Helper function for printing the words corresponding to the telephone number
#digits: list of digits from 0-9
#key_pad: contains the characters corresponding to each digit
#buf: contains the word formed corresponding to the telephone digits
#pos: current position in buf and digits
def keypad_string_gen(digits, keypad, buf, pos) :
    if (pos == len(digits)) :
        #We have processed all the digits. So print the
        #word and terminate the recursion
        print(buf)
        return

    cur_digit = digits[pos]
    key_string = keypad[cur_digit]

    #key_string is the string corresponding to the current digit
    #So if current digit is 2, key_string will be 'ABC'.
    #Cycle through all the characters in the key_string.
    for c in key_string :
        buf[pos] = c
        keypad_string_gen(digits, keypad, buf, pos+1)
```

```
#Main function for printing the words corresponding to the telephone number
#digits: list of digits from 0-9 in the telephone number
def telephone_digits_to_string(digits) :
    num_digits = len(digits)
    #Create a temporary buffer for storing the words corresponding to
    #the digits
    buf = ['A'] * num_digits

    #digit 2 corresponds to ABC, 3 corresponds to DEF and so on
    keypad = ['0', '1', 'ABC', 'DEF', 'GHI', 'JKL', 'MNO',
        'PQRS', 'TUV', 'WXYZ']

    keypad_string_gen(digits, keypad, buf, 0)
```

1.5 Strings

20. Generate all valid permutations of N opening braces '{', brackets '[', parenthesis '(' and N closing braces '}', brackets ']' and parenthesis ')'

To generate all valid permutations of braces, brackets and parenthesis, we use recursion. At the current position in the output string, we can either pick an opening character or a closing character using the conditions given below:

1. If the number of the opening characters in the output string is less than N, then we are free to choose any of the opening characters in the current position

2. While picking the closing character, we have to ensure that the opening and closing characters are properly nested. So we first check the most recent unmatched opening character and place the equivalent closing character at the current position. For instance, if we have generated the string "{[()". Then the most recent unmatched opening character is '['. So we can place ']' at the current position

```
#Helper function for finding the nearest unmatched opening character
#buf: list containing braces, brackets and parenthesis
#pos: we will search for unmatched character from pos - 1 to 0
#Return value: index of the first unmatched character when traversing from
#   pos - 1 to 0 if it exists, -1 otherwise
def find_unmatched(buf, pos) :
    back_pos = pos - 1
    n_braces = n_brackets = n_parenthesis = 0

    #When we get a closing character, decrement the count by 1,
    #when we get an opening character, increment the count by 1
    while (back_pos >= 0) :
        if (buf[back_pos] == '{') :
              n_braces += 1
        elif (buf[back_pos] == '['):
              n_brackets += 1
        elif (buf[back_pos] == '('):
              n_parenthesis += 1
        elif (buf[back_pos] == '}'):
              n_braces -= 1
        elif (buf[back_pos] == ']'):
              n_brackets -= 1
        elif (buf[back_pos] == ')'):
              n_parenthesis -= 1

        #If we encounter more opening characters than closing
        #characters as we traverse backwards, then we have found
        #the location of the mismatch
        if (n_braces > 0 or n_brackets > 0 or n_parenthesis > 0):
              return back_pos
```

```
        back_pos -= 1

    return -1

#Main function for printing the braces, brackets and parenthesis
#buf: list used to store braces, brackets and parenthesis
#pos: next free position in buf
#n_max: maximum number of opening characters (equal to max closing characters)
#n_open: number of opening characters currently in buf
#n_close: number of closing characters currently in buf
def print_nesting(buf, pos, n_max, n_open, n_close):
    #Condition for terminating the recursion
    if (n_close == n_max) :
        print_output(buf)
        return

    if (n_open < n_max) :
        #Add an opening brace and call print_nesting recursively
        buf[pos] = '{'
        print_nesting(buf, pos+1, n_max, n_open + 1, n_close)

        #Add an opening bracket and call print_nesting recursively
        buf[pos] = '['
        print_nesting(buf, pos+1, n_max, n_open + 1, n_close)

        #Add an opening parenthesis and call print_nesting recursively
        buf[pos] = '('
        print_nesting(buf, pos+1, n_max, n_open + 1, n_close)

    unmatched_pos = find_unmatched(buf, pos)
    if (n_open > n_close and unmatched_pos >= 0) :
        #to balance the characters, add closing character corresponding
        #to the unmatched character and call print_nesting recursively
        unmatched_char = buf[unmatched_pos]
        if (unmatched_char == '{') :
            buf[pos] = '}'
            print_nesting(buf, pos+1, n_max, n_open, n_close + 1)
        elif (unmatched_char == '['):
            buf[pos] = ']'
            print_nesting(buf, pos+1, n_max, n_open, n_close + 1)
        elif (unmatched_char == '('):
            buf[pos] = ')'
            print_nesting(buf, pos+1, n_max, n_open, n_close + 1)
```

1.6 Bitmaps

Python doesn't have an upper limit on the number of bits in an integer. However for practical purposes we will be restricting the number of bits in an integer to 32 bits unless otherwise indicated.

1. Given an integer, a.) set a particular bit position to 1, b.) reset a particular bit position to 0 and c.) toggle a particular bit position

---

Let n be the integer and pos be the position of the bit

To set a bit to 1, n = n | (1 << pos)

To reset a bit to 0, n = n & ~(1 << pos)

To toggle a bit, n = n ^ (1 << pos)

2. Efficiently count the number of bits set in an integer

One way to find the number of bits set in an integer is to check each bit. However there is a faster method to count the number of bits set using the function below

```
#Returns the number of bits set to 1 in n
def count_num_bits_set(n) :
    count = 0
    
    while (n != 0) :
        n &= n - 1
        count += 1
    
    return count
```

The following code works because each time we perform the operation n &= n - 1, the first bit that has a value of 1 from the right (from the least significant bit) is reset to 0.

For instance if n = 1100, then

n	= 1 1 0 0
n − 1	= 1 0 1 1
n & (n-1)	= 1 0 0 0

So 1100 is converted to 1000 wherein, the first bit that has a value of 1 from the right in 1100 is now reset to 0.

3. Find if an integer is a power of 2 using bit wise operators

The condition (x & (x-1) == 0) checks if an integer is a power of 2 or not. From the previous question, we know that x & (x-1) will reset the first bit that has a value of 1 from the right to 0. If x is a power of 2, then only one of the bits will be set to 1 and all the remaining bits will be set to 0 (for instance, 8 is a power of 2 and 8 in binary is 1000). So x & (x-1) will reset the only bit that has a value of 1 resulting in 0.

x & (x-1) == 0 however incorrectly indicates that 0 is also a power of 2, since (0 & (0 − 1)) = (0 & 0xffffffff) = 0. Since 0 is not a power of 2, we modify the condition as shown below

```
(x != 0) and ((x & (x-1)) == 0)
```

4. Reverse the bits in an integer

We can reverse the bits in an integer one bit at a time. However there is a faster technique. To reverse the bits in an integer efficiently, a lookup table is pre-computed to give the reverse values for every byte. This lookup table is then referred to for performing the reversal of the integer. The code for this is given below

1.6 Bitmaps

```
#input_value: the integer that has to be reversed
#reverse_table: lookup table that has the reversed values for every byte.
#   Example: reverse_table[0x1] = 0x80, since reverse of 00000001 is 1000000
#Return value:  integer that is the reverse of the input integer
def reverse_integer(input_value,  reverse_table) :
    result = 0
    num_bytes = 4
    for  i in range(num_bytes):
        #Get the least significant byte from the input
        cur_byte_value = input_value & 0xFF

        #Left shift the result by 8 and append the reverse of the
        #least significant byte of input
        result = (result << 8) | reverse_table[cur_byte_value]

        #Right shift out the least significant byte from the input
        input_value = input_value >> 8

    return result
```

5. Given two integers, find the number of bits that are different between the two integers

Consider the integers 2 (0010 in binary) and 9 (1001 in binary). Three bits are different and one bit is identical. To efficiently find the number of bits that are different, we do the following:

1. XOR the two integers.

2. In the result of the XOR, if the bit is 1, then the two integers are different at this bit position. So the number of 1's present in the result gives the number of different bits between the two integers. For counting the number of 1's in the result, we make use of the technique we described in page 159

```
#a, b: the two input integers
#Return value: Number of bits that have different values in a and b
def count_different_bits( a, b) :
    c = a ^ b
    count = 0

    #Since c = a xor b, the positions where a and b are different will
    #be set to 1 in c. So by counting the number of 1's in c, we will get the
    #number of bits that are different between a and b
    while (c != 0) :
        count += 1
        c = c & (c - 1)

    return count
```

6. Given an integer, swap the bit at position 1 with the bit at position 2

We first extract the bits at position 1 and position 2. We then have to swap the two bits only if the two bits are different. The code for swapping the bits is given below

```
#writes the bit_value (0/1) into position pos in x and returns the result
def write_bit(x, bit_value, pos):
    mask = 1 << pos
    if (bit_value == 1):
        x = x | mask
    else:
        x = x & ~mask

    return x

#x: integer in which the bits should be swapped
#pos1: position of first bit to be swapped
#pos2: position of the second bit to be swapped
def swap_bits(x, pos1, pos2):
    #get the bits at position pos1 and pos2
    bit1 = (x >> pos1) & 1
    bit2 = (x >> pos2) & 1

    #swap the bits
    if (bit1 != bit2) :
        x = write_bit(x, bit1, pos2)
        x = write_bit(x, bit2, pos1)

    return x
```

1.6 Bitmaps

7. Given an integer, compute the parity bit for the integer

There are two types of parity bit schemes

1. Even parity: if the total number of 1's is odd, then the parity bit will be 1 to make the total number of 1's (including the parity bit) even

2. Odd parity: if the total number of 1's is even, then the parity bit will be 1 to make the total number of 1's (including the parity bit) odd.

We will implement an even parity scheme here. We count the number of 1's in the integer using the scheme described in page 159.

```
#x: input integer
#Return value: parity bit, 1 if there are odd number of 1's, 0 otherwise
def compute_parity(x):
    #for each bit set to 1 in x, toggle the parity bit
    parity = 0
    while (x):
        parity = parity ^ 1
        x = x & (x - 1)

    return parity
```

8. Copy the bits between the specified start bit and end bit positions of one integer into another integer. For instance if source integer is 0xBBB and destination integer is 0xAEC and we copy the bits from 4 to 7 from source to destination, the result is 0xABC

Let the source integer be 0xBBB, destination integer be 0xAEC and we have to copy bits from position 4 to 7. The strategy we use is as follows:

1. Construct a mask (let's call it ones mask) in which all the bits are initially set to 1. If we need to copy n bits and the total number of bits in the integer is m, then right shift the ones mask by (m-n). So if we need to copy 4 bits between bit 4 and bit 7, and total number of bits in integer is 32, we perform ones_mask >> (32 – 4). So ones_mask will have a value 0xF.

2. Left shift the ones mask to the starting position from where we have to copy the bits. The ones mask will now have 1's from the start bit position to the end bit position. In this example, starting bit position is 4, so we perform (ones_mask << 4) = (0xF << 4) = 0xF0.

3. Construct a zeroes mask which is the complement of the ones mask. The zeroes mask will have 0's from the start bit to the end bit. So if ones mask is 0xF0, then zeroes mask will be 0xFFFFFF0F.

4. AND the destination integer with the zeroes mask to clear out the bits in the destination from start bit to end bit. So if destination is 0xAEC, then 0xAEC & 0xFFFFFF0F will give 0xA0C.

5. AND the source integer with the ones mask so that only the bits from start and end bit positions remain and the rest of the bits are cleared. If the source integer is 0xBBB, then 0xBBB & 0xF0 will give 0xB0

6. OR the source and destination. So 0xA0C | 0xB0 will give 0xABC

1.6 Bitmaps

```
#dest: destination integer into which the bits have to be copied
#src: source integer from which the bits have to be copied
#end_pos: Most Significant bit position upto where the bits should be copied
#start_pos: Least Significant bit position from where the bits should be copied
#    end_pos should be >= start_pos
#Return value: result integer after copying bits from source to destination
def copy_bits(dest, src, end_pos, start_pos) :
    num_bits_to_copy = end_pos - start_pos + 1
    num_bits_in_int = 32
    ones_mask = (1 << 32) - 1

    #Use the bit-wise right shift operator to remove the excess 1's
    #in the mask
    ones_mask = ones_mask >> (num_bits_in_int - num_bits_to_copy)

    #Left shift the 1's to the starting position. ones_mask will contain 1's
    #from start_pos to end_pos
    ones_mask = ones_mask << start_pos

    #zeroes_mask will contain 0's from start_pos to end_pos
    zeroes_mask = ~ones_mask

    #clear the bits in destination from start_pos to end_pos
    dest = dest & zeroes_mask

    #retain the bits in source from start_pos to end_pos and
    #clear the remaining bits
    src = src & ones_mask

    #copy the source bits into the destination
    dest = dest | src

    return dest
```

The Big Book of Coding Interviews

9. Implement circular shift left and circular shift right on an integer

Let n be the number of bits to shift. Let m be the total number of bits present in the integer. If we circular shift an integer m times, then we get back the original integer. So the actual number of shifts we need to perform is n % m.

The functions for circular shift left (also called left shift rotate) and circular shift right (right shift rotate) are given below

```
#value: input value which has to be circularly shifted left
#n: number of positions to shift
#Return value: result after circularly left shifting input value
def circular_left_shift(value, n) :
    num_bits_in_int = 32
    n = n % num_bits_in_int
    mask = (1 << num_bits_in_int) - 1
    result = (value << n) | (value >> (num_bits_in_int - n))
    result = result & mask
    return result


#value: input value which has to be circularly shifted right
#n: number of positions to shift
#Return value: result after circularly right shifting input
def circular_right_shift(value, n) :
    num_bits_in_int = 32
    n = n % num_bits_in_int
    mask = (1 << num_bits_in_int) - 1
    result = (value >> n) | (value << (num_bits_in_int - n))
    result = result & mask
    return result
```

1.6 Bitmaps

10. Find the maximum of 2 integers without using if-else or any other comparison operator

---

We can find the maximum of 2 integers without making use of if else or any comparison operator using the function below

```
#Returns the maximum of x and y without using if-else and comparison
# Maximum value of x and y should not exceed 31 bits
def find_max(x, y) :
    difference = x - y
    sign_bit = (difference >> 31) & 0x1

    #Sign bit can be 0 or 1
    #If sign bit is 0, max = x - (0 * difference) = x
    #If sign bit is 1, max = x - (1 * (x-y)) = x - x + y = y
    max_value = x  - (sign_bit * difference)
    return max_value
```

First we compute the difference between x and y. Next we find the sign bit of the difference. We are assuming that the maximum value of x and y does not exceed 31 bits. In the 2's complement notation, the most significant bit indicates the sign of the number. If the sign bit is 0, then the number is positive and if the bit is 1, then the number is negative.

If x >= y, then the difference x − y is positive and so the sign bit of the difference is 0. If x < y, then the difference x − y is negative and sign bit of the difference is 1.

Then we compute max = x - (sign_bit * difference).

If x >= y, then sign_bit = 0 and max = x - (0 * difference) = x. So we return x as the maximum value

If x < y, then sign_bit = 1 and max = x - (1 * difference) = x - difference = x - (x - y) = y. So we return y as the maximum value

11. Implement addition without using the addition (+) operator

When we add two bits X and Y, the result consists of the sum bit and the carry bit as shown in the table below

X	Y	Sum	Carry
0	0	0	0
0	1	1	0
1	0	1	0
1	1	0	1

So we find that Sum = X XOR Y, Carry = X AND Y. When adding two integers, we go on computing the Sum and Carry for all bits in the integers as shown below

```
#Returns the sum bit and carry bit on adding the bits a,b
def compute_sum(a, b):
    return a ^ b, a & b

#x, y: two integers, can be negative. x may be bigger, equal or smaller than y
#   Maximum value of x and y should not exceed 31 bits
#Return value: x + y using bit wise operators
def add(x, y) :
    result = 0
    carry_bit = 0
    #x and y can be represented within 32 bits in 2's complement format
    for cur_pos in range(32) :
        #extract the last bit of x and y
        x_last_bit = x & 1
        y_last_bit = y & 1

        #compute the sum of last bit of x and y
        sum_bit, carry_1 = compute_sum(x_last_bit, y_last_bit)

        #now add the carry_bit to the sum_bit
        sum_bit, carry_2 = compute_sum(sum_bit, carry_bit)

        #compute the carry bit for the next bit position
        carry_bit = carry_1 | carry_2

        #store the sum bit at cur_pos in the result
        result = result | (sum_bit << cur_pos)

        #shift out the last bit of x and y
        x = x >> 1
        y = y >> 1
```

1.6 Bitmaps

```
#Python doesn't have an upper limit on the number of bits in an integer.
#So if the result of addition is negative, we have to do the sign
#extension. Since we are dealing with only 32 bit integers, bit 31 will
#serve as the sign bit. If the sign bit is 1, then it means the result
#is negative.
if (result & (1 << 31)):
    #Propagate the negative sign bit. (~0) will give a continuous
    #set of 1's. Then stitch in the 32 bit result into the continuous
    #set of 1's
    result = ((~0) << 32) | result

return result
```

12. Implement subtraction without using the subtraction (-) operator

To perform x − y, we find the 2's complement of y and add it to x. For performing addition, we reuse the add function described in the previous problem.

```
#x, y: two integers, can be negative. x may be bigger, equal or smaller than y
#   Maximum value of x and y should not exceed 31 bits
#Return value: x - y using bit wise operators
def subtract(x, y):
    #Find the 2's complement of y
    y = (~y) + 1

    #Add the 2's complement of y to x. This will give us x - y
    result = add(x, y)

    return result
```

13. Implement multiplication without using the multiplication operator (*)

Let us say that we have to evaluate X * Y. We do the following:

1. Initialize the result to 0.

2. Examine the least significant bit of Y. If the least significant bit is 1, then add X to the result

3. Shift out the least significant bit of Y and double the value of X.

4. Repeat steps 2 and 3 until Y becomes 0.

```
#x, y: two integers >= 0
#Return value: x multiplied with y
def multiply(x, y) :
    result = 0
    while (y != 0) :
        #if the least significant bit of y is 1, then add x to result
        if ( (y & 1) == 1) :
            result += x

        y = y >> 1 #shift out the least significant bit of y
        x = x << 1 #double the value of x

    return result
```

The Big Book of Coding Interviews

14. Implement division without using the division (/) or mod (%) operators. The answer should return the quotient and remainder

---

The code to evaluate a / b without using division or mod operators is given below

```
#a, b: a is an integer >= 0. b is an integer > 0
#Return values: quotient and remainder
def integer_division(a, b) :
    max_bit_pos = 31

    if (b == 0) :
        raise ZeroDivisionError

    quotient = 0
    remainder = 0
    for  i in range(max_bit_pos, -1, -1):
        remainder = remainder << 1 #Double the remainder

        #Find the value of the next bit in the dividend a.
        #In first iteration, we find value of the Most Significant Bit.
        next_bit = 0
        if ((a & (1 << i)) != 0) :
                next_bit = 1

        #Copy the value of the next bit into the least significant
        #bit of remainder
        if (next_bit == 1):
                remainder = remainder | 1

        #If the remainder is now greater than the divisor b,
        #then subtract the divisor b from the remainder and
        #set the appropriate quotient bit
        if (remainder >= b) :
                remainder = remainder - b
                quotient = quotient | (1 << i)

    return quotient, remainder
```

1.6 Bitmaps

15. In a list of integers, all integers are repeated even number of times except one integer which is repeated odd number of times. Find the integer that occurs odd number of times in O(n) time and O(1) space. For instance in the list [1, 4, 8, 4, 6, 8, 1], 6 occurs once (odd number of times) while the remaining integers occur even number of times

---

For this problem we make use of the XOR operator. For any integer A, the XOR operator has the following properties

A XOR A = 0

A XOR 0 = A

To find the integer that occurs odd number of times, we XOR all the integers in the list. By doing this, all the integers that are repeated even number of times will cancel each other out (since A XOR A = 0). So the result of XORing all the integers in the list will give us the integer that occurs odd number of times.

```
#a: list consisting of numbers, where one element occurs odd number of times
#   while remaining elements occur even number of times
#Return value: element that occurs odd number of times
def find_odd_occurrence(a) :
    #XOR all the elements
    result = 0
    for cur_value in a :
        result = result ^ cur_value

    return result
```

The Big Book of Coding Interviews

16. In a list of integers, all integers are repeated even number of times except **two** integers which are repeated odd number of times. Find the two integers that occur odd number of times in O(n) time and O(1) space. For instance in the list [1, 4, 3, 8, 4, 7, 8, 1], 3 and 7 occur once (odd number of times) while the remaining integers occur even number of times

---

To solve the problem we do the following:

1. XOR all the integers in the list. The integers that occur even number of times will cancel each other out since A XOR A = 0. So the result of the XOR is actually the XOR of the two integers that occur odd number of times

2. Choose any bit position in the result of the XOR whose bit value is 1. This represents the bit where the two integers that occur odd number of times differ. For instance in the example list [1, 4, 3, 8, 4, 7, 8, 1], the result of the XOR of all elements is 4 (100 in binary). This implies that the two odd occurring integers differ at bit position 2 (the least significant bit is treated as bit 0). We can verify this. 3 and 7 occur odd number of times. 3 (011 in binary) and 7 (111 in binary) indeed differ at bit position 2.

3. We initialize result0 and result1 to 0. Then we iterate through all the elements in the list. If the element has 0 at the chosen bit position, then we XOR it with result0, otherwise we XOR it with result1. In this way we are partitioning the elements into two groups. Note that a repeated element will always go into the same group and if it occurs even number of times then it cancels out due to the XOR operation. So at the end, result0 will contain one integer that occurs odd number of times and result1 will contain the other integer that occurs odd number of times.

```
#a: input list where 2 elements occur odd number of times and the remaining
#   occur even number of times
#Return value: the two numbers that occur odd number of times
def find_odd_occurrences(a):
    #XOR all the values
    all_xor = 0
    for val in a:
        all_xor = all_xor ^ val

    #Find the first bit in the XOR result that is set to 1. The two odd
    #occuring numbers will differ at this bit position. So if difference
    #is at bit position 3, then mask will be ...00001000
    mask = all_xor & ~(all_xor - 1)

    #Separate out values in list a such that, values that have a 1 at the
    #different bit will be XORed with x and values that have a 0 at the
```

1.6 Bitmaps

```
#different bit will be XORed with y
x = y = 0
for val in a:
    if ( (val & mask) != 0):
        x = x ^ val
    else:
        y = y ^ val

#x and y will now contain the two numbers that occur odd number of times
return x, y
```

1.7 Application of Data Structures

1. What data structure would you choose for implementing priority queues?

In a priority queue, the node with the highest priority is processed first. If two nodes have the same priority, then they are processed in the order in which they are stored in the queue. A priority queue should support the following operations

1. Insert an element with a given priority into the priority queue
2. Process/Remove the element with the highest priority in the priority queue

A heap is the ideal data structure for representing a priority queue. If higher numeric value indicates higher priority, then a max-heap should be used to represent the priority queue. If lower numeric value indicates higher priority, then a min-heap should be used to represent the priority queue.

1.7 Application of Data Structures

2. What data structure would you choose for implementing an English dictionary?

An English dictionary can be represented using a Python dictionary (hash table) or a trie or a binary search tree. Each data structure has its own pros and cons.

If we use a Python dictionary, the access time to find the meaning of a word is O(1). However the drawback is that the Python dictionary doesn't store the information about the neighboring words. So if we want to display a word and its adjacent neighbors, we can't achieve it by using a Python dictionary alone. One alternative is to have an additional linked list that stores the words in dictionary sequence order. This increases the memory usage. Python has the OrderedDict class that supports order in dictionaries.

We can use a trie, where each node has 26 children corresponding to the 26 characters in the English alphabet. The access time depends on the number of characters in the word. We can display the neighboring words using the trie. However the memory consumed by the trie would be quite huge since each node has to maintain 26 references.

We can use a binary search tree to store the words in the English dictionary. The access time would be O(logn) where n is the number of words. So if we are storing 100,000 words then we will need about 17 accesses on an average to find a particular word. So the access time is more than the Python dictionary and the trie. However the memory requirements of a binary search tree are much smaller than a trie and it is also possible to find the adjacent neighbors of a word by traversing the binary search tree.

So in conclusion, we prefer to use the OrderedDict for implementing the English dictionary.

The Big Book of Coding Interviews

3. Design a data structure which can perform each of the following operations in O(1): insert, delete, fetch and get_random

---

The insert, delete and fetch operations can be performed in O(1) using a dictionary.

To perform the get_random operation in O(1) we use an extra doubly linked list along with the dictionary. The dictionary will store the references to the nodes and the nodes will be connected to each other in the doubly linked list. The operations are described below:

- Insert: the node is added to the dictionary. The node is then randomly connected either to the head of the doubly linked list or to the tail of the doubly linked list. This can be done in O(1). This way we can randomize the order of nodes in the doubly linked list

- Delete: the node is removed from the dictionary and the node is also deleted from the doubly linked list. This can be done in O(1).

- Fetch: the fetch operation is performed on the dictionary and the reference to the node is returned

- Get_Random: A separate iterator is maintained for traversing the linked list. It is initialized to the head of the doubly linked list. When get_random() is invoked, the node that the iterator refers to is returned and the iterator is advanced to the next member in the doubly linked list. This can be done in O(1). Since the order of nodes in the linked list is random, we will be returning random nodes.

1.7 Application of Data Structures

4. Design a data structure for an LRU cache?

A Least Recently Used cache has a fixed number of slots in it. Once all the slots in the LRU cache are used up and we need to store a new node in the LRU cache, then the least recently used node is removed and the new node is added to the LRU cache.

An LRU cache can be implemented using two data structures: a dictionary (given the key for the node, the dictionary returns the node) and a doubly linked list (the most recently used node is maintained at the head and the least recently used node is maintained at the tail of the doubly linked list)

The operations that the LRU cache will support are

lru_add – adds a node to the cache. If the LRU cache is already full, then the least recently used node which is present at the tail of the doubly linked list is removed from the doubly linked list and the node is also removed from the dictionary. The new node is then added to the head of the doubly linked list and the new node is added to the dictionary

lru_get – returns the node given the key. The key is used to access the dictionary and obtain the node. The node is then removed from the doubly linked list and added to the front of the doubly linked list since it is now the most recently accessed node.

The LRU cache and the implementation of lru_add and lru_get are given below

```
class LruCache(object):

    def __init__ (self, max_size):
        self.max_size = max_size #Max number of nodes that cache can hold
        self.count = 0 #current number of nodes in the cache
        self.ht = {} #dictionary
        self.head = None #Head of the doubly linked list
        self.tail = None #Tail of the doubly linked list


    #self - LRU cache
    #key - key for the node that should be fetched from the cache
    def lru_get(self, key):
        #Get the node from the key using the dictionary
        cur_node = self.ht.get(key)

        if (not cur_node):
                return None
```

```
#If the node being fetched is at the head of the linked list,
#then simply return
if (self.head == cur_node):
        return cur_node

#The node being fetched is not at the front. So detach it from
#the linked list and add it to the beginning.
#If the node was removed from the tail, then update the tail
if (self.tail == cur_node):
        self.tail = cur_node.prev

cur_node.prev.next = cur_node.next
if (cur_node.next):
        cur_node.next.prev = cur_node.prev

cur_node.prev = None
cur_node.next = self.head
self.head.prev = cur_node
self.head = cur_node

return cur_node



#self - the LRU cache
#new_item - new node to be added to the LRU cache
def lru_add(self, new_item):
    if (self.count == self.max_size) :
            #The cache is full. So remove the last node from
            #linked list
            temp = self.tail

            self.tail = self.tail.prev

            if (not self.tail):
                    self.head = None
            else:
                    self.tail.next = None

            self.count -= 1

            #Remove the last node from the dictionary
            del self.ht[temp.key]


    #Add the new node to the front of the linked list
    new_item.prev = None
    new_item.next = self.head

    if (self.head):
            self.head.prev = new_item

    self.head = new_item
```

1.7 Application of Data Structures

```
if (not self.tail):
        self.tail = new_item

self.count += 1

#Add the new node to the dictionary
self.ht[new_item.key] = new_item
```

5. What data structure will you use for finding out if a person is connected to another person on LinkedIn/Facebook?

A graph data structure can be used to find out if a person is connected to another person. The graph can be represented using any of the following:

- Incidence matrix: the rows of the matrix represent persons and the columns of the matrix represent edges. If the edge k connects person i with person j, then matrix[i][k] = 1 and matrix[j][k] = 1
- Adjacency matrix: the rows and columns represent persons. If person i is connected to person j, then matrix[i][j] and matrix[j][i] will be set to 1.
- Adjacency list: for each person, a list of his/her friends is maintained.

The problem with incidence matrix and adjacency matrix is that they are sparse and this leads to a lot of wasted memory. So the preferred data structure is the adjacency list. We can perform depth first search or breadth first search on the adjacency list to find if two persons are connected.

2. Sorting and Searching

The summary of different sorting techniques is given below. A **stable** sorting algorithm will preserve the relative order between two equal elements even after sorting

	Average case	Best case	Worst Case	Stability
Bubble sort	$O(n^2)$	$O(n)$	$O(n^2)$	Stable
Insertion sort	$O(n^2)$	$O(n)$	$O(n^2)$	Stable
Heap sort	$O(n\log n)$	$O(n\log n)$	$O(n\log n)$	Not stable
Merge sort	$O(n\log n)$	$O(n\log n)$	$O(n\log n)$	Stable
Quick sort	$O(n\log n)$	$O(n\log n)$	$O(n^2)$	Stable

Counting sort is an integer sorting algorithm that can be applied only if the range of integers present is small. The time complexity is $O(n)$.

2. Sorting and Searching

Radix sort is also an integer sorting algorithm where the individual digits of the integers are sorted either from most significant to least significant digit or vice versa. The time complexity is O(kn), where k is the number of digits in the integer. Although radix sort has a better time complexity compared to quicksort, quicksort is preferred since radix sort requires additional memory.

If all the elements to be sorted can't fit into the main memory at once, then external storage devices must be used for sorting. Sorting done using external storage is referred to as external sorting.

2.1 Searching

1. Find the smallest and second smallest numbers in a list

We can find the smallest and second smallest numbers in a single scan of the list. We will maintain another list called min_values for storing the 2 smallest numbers. min_values[0] will store the smallest value and min_values[1] will store the second smallest value. min_values[0] and min_values[1] are initialized to MAX_INT. As we traverse the main list, we do the following:

- If the current element is smaller than min_values[0], then we move min_values[0] to min_values[1] and store the current element in min_values[0]
- If the current element is larger than min_values[0] but smaller than min_values[1], then we store the current element in min_values[1]

The code is given below

```
#a:input list
#Return value: the two smallest values will be returned
def find_two_smallest(a) :
    length = len(a)

    min_value = [MAX_INT, MAX_INT]

    for  cur_val in a:
        if (cur_val < min_value[0]) :
             min_value[1] = min_value[0]
             min_value[0] = cur_val
        elif (cur_val  < min_value[1]) :
             min_value[1] = cur_val

    return min_value[0], min_value[1]
```

The Big Book of Coding Interviews

2. Find the maximum and minimum elements in a list using the least number of comparisons

In the simple approach, we will compare each element of the list with the maximum value and minimum value obtained so far. So for every element, we need 2 comparisons.

In the efficient approach, we pick all pairs of consecutive numbers in the list and first compare the numbers within each pair. Then we compare the highest in the pair with the maximum value and the lowest in the pair with the minimum value. So we need 3 comparisons for 2 elements instead of 4 comparisons needed by the simple approach.

Since we will be picking pairs of consecutive numbers, if we have odd number of elements in the list, the last element will be left unpaired. To avoid this problem, if we have odd elements, we will initialize the max value and the min value to the first element in the list and then go on picking pairs of numbers from the second element onwards.

```
#a: input list
#Returns: the minimum value and maximum value in list are returned
def find_min_max(a) :
    max_value = MIN_INT
    min_value = MAX_INT

    i = 0
    if (len(a) % 2 == 1) :
        #If there are odd number of elements, then initialize
        #max_value and min_value with a[0]
        max_value = min_value = a[0]
        i = 1

    while ( i < len(a) ) :
        if (a[i] > a[i+1]) :
            if (a[i] > max_value) :
                max_value = a[i]
            if (a[i+1] < min_value):
                min_value = a[i+1]
        else :
            if (a[i] < min_value):
                min_value = a[i]
            if (a[i+1] > max_value):
                max_value = a[i+1]

        i += 2

    return min_value, max_value
```

2.1 Searching

3. Find the first occurrence of a number in a sorted list without using the Python index function

---

Consider the sorted list A = [10, 10, 20, 20, 30, 30, 30]. If we are asked to return the first occurrence of 30, then we return the index 4. If we are asked to return the first occurrence of a number not present in the list such as 15, then we return -1.

We can do this using modified binary search in O(logn). In normal binary search, we stop as soon as we find the element being searched. In the modified binary search, we continue the binary search if we find the element but the found element is not the first occurrence of the element in the list. The code is given below

```
#a: list being searched
#x: element being searched
#Return value: first position of x in a, if x is absent -1 is returned
def find_first(a, x) :
    start = 0
    end = len(a) - 1

    while (start <= end) :
        mid = (start + end) // 2

        if (a[mid] == x) :
                if (mid == 0 or a[mid - 1] != x):
                    return mid
                else:
                    end = mid - 1

        elif (a[mid] > x) :
                end = mid - 1
        else :
                start = mid + 1

    return -1
```

4. Find the first element larger than k in a sorted list

Consider the sorted list A = [10, 20, 20, 30, 40, 50]. The first element larger than 25 is 30. In normal binary search, we search for a particular element and stop when we find the element. When we are trying to find the first element larger than k, k may not even exist in the list. So we instead use a modified form of binary search where we keep track of the first element larger than k that we have encountered so far as we search the list. The time complexity is O(logn). The code is given below

```
#a: sorted list containing elements in non-decreasing order
#k: we are searching for the number immediately above k
#Returns: the number immediately greater than k in the list if it exists,
#         MAX_INT otherwise
def find_next_higher(a, k) :
    low = 0
    high = len(a) - 1

    result = MAX_INT
    while (low <= high) :
        mid = (low + high) // 2

        if (a[mid] > k) :
            result = a[mid] #update the result and continue
            high = mid - 1
        else :
            low = mid + 1

    return result
```

2.1 Searching

5. Consider the sorted list of strings A= ["", "apple", "", "", "ball", "cat", "", "dog", "", "", "", "egg", ""]. The list has empty strings interspersed in it. How will you efficiently search for strings in such a list?

We can use binary search to search the list of sorted strings. However since the list has empty strings in it, suppose we hit an empty string during binary search, we won't know how to continue the search. To solve this problem we slightly modify the binary search and use the following strategy:

1. Binary search will occur between indexes low and high. If A[high] is an empty string, then we go on decrementing high until A[high] is a non-empty string. (Suppose we don't find a non-empty string and we reach A[low], then all elements between low and high are empty strings. So we simply return indicating the search string was not found.)

2. We then find the mid element between low and high. If A[mid] is a non-empty string, then we proceed with the usual binary search. If A[mid] however is an empty string, then we go on incrementing mid until A[mid] is a non-empty string. Since A[high] already has a non-empty string, we will surely find a non-empty string when we keep incrementing mid.

```
#strings: sorted list of strings in which some of the strings can be empty ('')
#x: string to be searched
#Returns: index of x in the list strings if found, -1 otherwise
def search(strings, x) :
    low = 0
    high = len(strings) - 1

    while (low <= high) :
        #If we hit an empty string at position high, then keep decreasing
        #high till we get a non-empty string
        while (low <= high and strings[high] == '') :
            high -= 1

        #If we have only empty strings between low and high, then return
        #not found
        if (low > high):
            return -1

        mid = (low + high) // 2

        #If we get an empty element at mid, then keep incrementing mid.
        #We are guaranteed to find a non-empty string since strings[high]
        #is non-empty
        while (strings[mid] == ''):
            mid += 1
```

```
        #Compare the mid element with the element being searched
        if (strings[mid] == x) :
                return mid
        elif (strings[mid] < x) :
                low = mid + 1
        else :
                high = mid - 1

    return -1
```

Note that we can use this approach for any sorted list that is interspersed with elements that can be skipped. So if we are given a list of positive integers interspersed with -1, then we can use the same strategy.

2.1 Searching

6. How will you search for an element in a sorted list of unknown length?

If we don't know the length of a list, we may access an element outside the list bounds. In this case an exception is raised. We should catch the exception and continue the search. We use the following approach to search an element:

1. First we find the upper bound on the length of the list using exponential search. So say a list has 20 elements in it and we don't know its length beforehand. We first check element at position 0, followed by position 1, position 2, position 4, position 8, position 16 and position 32. When we access position 32, we will be outside the list and an exception is raised. So we know that the upper bound on length is 32 and the actual list length must be less than 32.

2. Once we know the upper bound, we use normal binary search to find the element. While doing binary search, we may still try to access an element outside the list bounds. In such a case, we again catch the exception, reduce the index range being searched and continue the search.

```
#Helper function that performs binary search on a list of unknown length
#a: list which should be searched
#x: element which we are trying to find
#low: start position of region in list for searching
#high: end position of region in list for searching
def binary_search(a, x, low, high) :
    mid = 0
    while (low <= high) :
        try:
            mid = (low + high) // 2

            #if mid is greater than actual list length, then
            #an exception is raised
            value = a[mid]

            if (value == x):
                return mid
            elif (value > x):
                high = mid - 1
            else :
                low = mid + 1
        except IndexError as e:
            #mid has crossed the boundary of the list. So reduce
            #the search region to (low, mid - 1)
            high = mid - 1

    return -1
```

```python
#Main function for performing search on list whose length is not known
#a: input list
#x: item to be searched
#Returns: if x is found, the index of x is returned, otherwise -1 is returned
def search(a, x) :
    #Perform exponential search to first find the upper bound. Start with
    #high = 0 and then increase high to 1, 2, 4, 8, 16 and so on
    low = high = 0
    while (True) :
        try:
            value = a[high]

            if (value == x) :
                return high #We found the element x
            elif (value > x):
                break   #Found range (low, high) where element exists

            low = high + 1

            if (high == 0):
                high = 1
            else:
                high = high * 2

        except IndexError as e:
            #We have crossed the boundary of the list. So we have found
            #the upper bound for high.
            break

    #Perform binary search in range(low, high). Note that high may still be
    #outside the list bounds
    return binary_search(a, x, low, high)
```

2.1 Searching

7. Given a two dimensional matrix M in which each row contains 0's and 1's in sorted order, efficiently find the row with the maximum number of 1's

---

Suppose the matrix below is provided, then we should return that row 2 has the maximum number of 1's. If the matrix doesn't have any 1's, then we should return -1.

row 0	0	0	0	1	1
row 1	0	0	0	0	0
row 2	0	1	1	1	1

The algorithm is as follows:

1.) Find the first location of 1 in each row. To find the first location of 1, we use the find_first function described earlier on page 187. Then subtract the first location of 1 from the total number of columns to get the number of 1's in each row. For instance, in row 0 of above matrix, the first 1 is present at index 3 and the total number of columns is 5. So the total number of 1's = 5 – 3 = 2.

2.) Now that we know the number of 1's in each row, we can easily find the row with the most 1's

If there are n columns, we can find the first 1 in a row and thereby the number of 1's in a row in $O(\log n)$. Since there are m rows, the complexity of the algorithm is $O(m \log n)$.

```python
#a: list where each row is sorted and has only 0's and 1's
#Return value: row number that has most ones, if no row has 1's then return -1
def find_row_with_most_ones(a) :
    ncols = len(a[0])

    max_row = -1
    max_num_ones = 0

    for  i, inner_list in enumerate(a):
        #Find the position of the first 1 in the row
        first_one_index = find_first(inner_list, 1)

        #Compute number of 1's in row based on position of the first 1
        if (first_one_index == -1):
            cur_num_ones = 0 #there are no 1's in the row
        else:
            cur_num_ones = ncols - first_one_index

        if (cur_num_ones > max_num_ones) :
            max_num_ones = cur_num_ones
            max_row = i

    return max_row
```

2.1 Searching

8. Given a matrix in which the elements in any row or column are in sorted order, efficiently find if an element k is present in the matrix.

Let the elements in the matrix be sorted in non-decreasing order in each row and column. To solve the problem, we start from the rightmost top corner of the matrix and apply the following logic to solve the problem in O(m+n)

- If element in matrix is less than the searched value, then go to the row below
- If element in matrix is greater than the searched value, then go to the previous column

Let us take an example. Consider the following matrix M, which is sorted in non-decreasing order along both rows and columns and we have to find 72 in it.

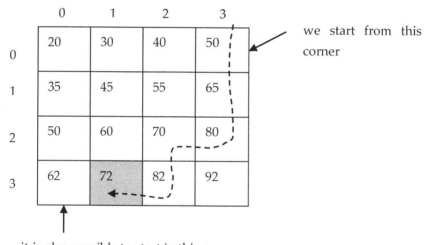

it is also possible to start in this corner

In our case, we start with M[0][3] and compare with 72.

- M[0][3] = 50 which is less than 72. So we go to the row below
- M[1][3] = 65 which is less than 72. So we go to the row below
- M[2][3] = 80 which is greater than 72. So we go to the previous column
- M[2][2] = 70 which is less than 72. So we go to the row below
- M[3][2] = 82 which is greater than 72. So we go to the previous column
- M[3][1] = 72 which matches our search key and we have found the element

```
#m: matrix to be searched
#x: element to search
#Return value:  True if element is present, False otherwise
def search_matrix(m, x):
    num_rows = len(m)
    num_cols = len(m[0])

    i = 0
    j = num_cols - 1
    is_found = False
    while (i < num_rows and j >= 0) :
        if (m[i][j] == x) :
                is_found = True
                break
        elif (m[i][j] < x):
                i += 1 #go to the row below
        else :
                j -= 1 #go to the previous column

    return is_found
```

Note that it is also possible to search for the value from the opposite corner (the bottom leftmost corner). In this case, the logic we should use to search is

- If element in matrix is less than the searched value, then go to the next column
- If element in matrix is greater than the searched value, then go to the row above

2.1 Searching

9. The elements of a list first continually increase in value and then continually decrease in value. All elements in the list are unique. Efficiently find the maximum element in the list.

Let the size of the list be N. Since we want to find the maximum element as efficiently as possible, we are not going to use the Python max function. To solve the problem we first initialize start to 0 and end to N-1. Then

1. Find the middle element in the list between start and end.

2. If the middle element is greater than the previous element and also greater than the next element, then we have found the maximum element in the list. Otherwise modify the search range indexes (start and end) and repeat the process.

Consider list A = [1, 4, 9, 16, 25, 36, 5, 0]

(start, end)	middle	A[middle]	Compare A[middle] with neighbors and take action
(0, 7)	3	16	9 < 16 < 25. The maximum element should be after 16. So start = middle + 1 = 4, end = 7
(4, 7)	5	36	25 < 36 > 16. Since 36 is greater than previous and next element, the maximum element is 36

The time complexity of this approach is $O(\log n)$.

```
#a: list where elements first increase and then decrease
#Return value: maximum element in the list
def find_max(a) :
    start = 0
    end = len(a) - 1
    max_element = MIN_INT

    while (start <= end) :
        #If only one element is left, then it is the max element
        if (start == end)       :
                max_element = a[start]
                break

        #If two elements are left, find the maximum of the two
        if (start + 1 == end) :
                max_element = a[start]
                if (a[start+1] > max_element):
                        max_element = a[start+1]
                break

        #If there are more than two elements left, then inspect the
        #middle element in between start and end
        mid = (start+end) // 2

        #If middle element is greater than previous element and also
        #greater than the next element, then it is the maximum element
        if (a[mid - 1] < a[mid] and a[mid] > a[mid + 1]) :
                max_element = a[mid]
                break

        #We have not yet been able to find the max_element. So modify the
        #range in which to search in the next iteration
        if (a[mid - 1] < a[mid] and a[mid] < a[mid + 1]) :
                start = mid + 1
        else :
                end = mid - 1

    return max_element
```

2.1 Searching

10. A sorted list has been rotated an unknown number of times. Efficiently find the maximum element in the list and the number of times the list has been rotated. All elements in the list are unique

Since we want to find the maximum element as efficiently as possible, we are not going to use the Python max function.

Consider the list A = [10, 20, 30, 40, 50] with unique elements that is sorted in ascending order. When we rotate the list, we end up with two sequences of numbers in ascending order. For instance, if we rotate A two times to the right, we get $A_{Rotated}$ = [40, 50, 10, 20, 30]. So the two ascending order sequences are [40, 50] and [10, 20, 30]. Similarly if we rotate A 4 times to the right we get $A_{Rotated}$ = [20, 30, 40, 50, 10] in which case the ascending order sequences are [20, 30, 40, 50] and [10]. Note that any number in the first sequence is always greater than any number of the second sequence. The maximum element will be the last element of the first sequence. Sometimes the maximum element in the list is also referred to as pivot element.

We use binary search to locate the largest element. When we choose the middle element in the range (start, end), there are three possibilities:

1. the middle element is greater than the next element. In this case, the middle element is the largest element in the sequence

2. the middle element is present in the first sequence. In this case the middle element will always be > than the ending element because ending element is present in the second sequence and elements in the first sequence are always greater than elements in the second sequence. For instance consider, $A_{Rotated}$ = [20, 30, 40, 50, 10]. Middle element is 40 which is greater than 10. In this case, the maximum element will lie between the middle element and the last element.

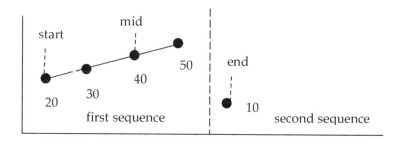

3. the middle element is present in the second sequence. In this case the middle element will always be < than the ending element since the second sequence has elements in ascending order. In this case we can ignore the range (middle, end) and search the range (start, middle − 1). For instance, consider $A_{Rotated}$ = [40, 50, 10, 20, 30]. The middle element is 10 which lies in the second sequence. So we can ignore (middle, end) which is [10, 20, 30] and search only (start, middle − 1) which is [40, 50] in the next iteration

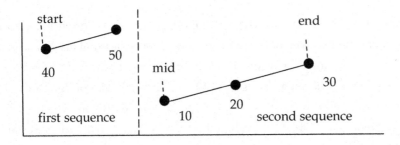

Based on these observations, given a list of size N, to solve the problem we first initialize start to 0 and end to N-1. Then

- Find the middle element in the list between start and end.
    - If the middle element is greater than next element, middle element is the largest element
    - If middle element is greater than the last element, then repeat the search in the range (middle, end).
    - Otherwise repeat the search in the range (start, middle − 1).

We put in one more optimization to the code. If a[start] < a[end], then we have found the exact starting and ending locations of the first sequence. In this case, we stop searching any further and return the last element a[end] as the maximum element. Note that this condition will also cover the case where the list has had 0 rotations (no shift has been performed on the list)

2.1 Searching

```
#a: non-empty list that has been sorted and rotated.
#   There should NOT be any duplicates in the list
#Return value: maximum element in the list
def find_max(a) :
    start = 0
    end = len(a) - 1

    while (a[start] > a[end]) :
        mid = (start + end) // 2

        if (mid < len(a) - 1 and a[mid] > a[mid + 1]):
            return a[mid]

        if (a[mid] > a[end]) :
            start = mid    #max is in the region (mid, end)
        else :
            end = mid - 1 #max is in the region (start, mid - 1)

    return a[end]
```

In some cases, we may be asked to find the number of times the list has been rotated. In this case, (index of the maximum element in the list + 1) gives the number of rotations. For instance, if A = [10, 20, 30, 40, 50] is rotated twice, we get [40, 50, 10, 20, 30]. The maximum element 50 is present at position 1 in the rotated list. So the number of times the list has been rotated = 1+1 = 2.

Note that this solution will work only if the list has unique elements in it. If there are duplicates, for instance [2, 2, 3, 3, 1, 1, 2, 2, 2], then the above solution will give the wrong result. If there are duplicates then we can perform a linear search.

The Big Book of Coding Interviews

11. A sorted list has been rotated an unknown number of times. Efficiently search if a particular value is present in the list. All elements in the list are unique.

Since we want to search as efficiently as possible, we are not going to use the Python in operator or the Python index function.

Consider the list A = [10, 20, 30, 40, 50] with unique elements that is sorted in ascending order. When we rotate the list, we end up with two sequences of numbers in ascending order. For instance, if we rotate A two times to the right, we get $A_{Rotated}$ = [40, 50, 10, 20, 30]. So the two ascending order sequences are [40, 50] and [10, 20, 30]. Similarly if we rotate A 4 times to the right we get $A_{Rotated}$ = [20, 30, 40, 50, 10] in which case the ascending order sequences are [20, 30, 40, 50] and [10]. <u>Note that any number in the first sequence is always greater than any number of the second sequence.</u>

We use binary search to locate a particular element X. When we choose the middle element during binary search, if A[mid] is equal to X then we have found the element we are looking for. Otherwise there are two possibilities:

1. Mid is in first sequence	2. Mid is in second sequence

$A_{Rotated}$ = (20, 30, 40, 50), (10)
              ↗
     mid
	$A_{Rotated}$ = (40, 50), (10, 20, 30)
	              ↖
	              mid

Region (start, mid) is perfectly sorted in ascending order and is used to decide	Region (mid, end) is perfectly sorted in ascending order and is used to decide

1.) Here the middle element lies in the first ascending order sequence of the rotated list. So A[start] <= A[mid]. We are guaranteed that all elements in the region (start, mid) are perfectly sorted. So we use this region for taking a decision. So if the search element lies between A[start] and A[mid], then search (start, mid - 1) in the next iteration else search (mid +1, end) in the next iteration

2.) Here the middle element lies in the second ascending order sequence. So A[start] > A[mid]. We are guaranteed that all elements in the region (mid, end) are perfectly sorted.

2.1 Searching

So we use this region for taking a decision. If the search element lies between A[mid] and A[end], then search (mid + 1, end) in the next iteration else search (start, mid -1)

```
#a: non-empty list that has been sorted and rotated
# There should NOT be any duplicates in the list
#x: element to be searched in the list
#Return value: location of the element in list if found, -1 if not found
def find_element(a, x) :
    start = 0
    end = len(a) - 1

    while (start <= end) :
        mid = (start+end) // 2

        if (x == a[mid]) :
            return mid

        #Check which portion of the list has elements in sorted order
        if (a[start] <= a[mid]) :
            #The lower portion (start, mid) is still sorted even after
            #rotations. So use this portion for taking decisions
            if (a[start] <= x and x < a[mid]) :
                end = mid - 1 #search in region (start, mid-1)
            else:
                start = mid + 1      #search in region (mid+1, end)
        else :
            #The upper portion (mid, end) is sorted even after
            #rotations. So use this portion for taking decisions
            if (a[mid] < x and x <= a[end]) :
                start = mid + 1 #search in region (mid+1, end)
            else:
                end = mid - 1 #search in region (start, mid-1)

    return -1
```

Note that the above solution can't be applied to a list with duplicates. For instance, the above solution will not be able to find 2 in the list [3, 3, 2, 2, 3, 3, 3, 3, 3]. If there are duplicates, then we can perform linear search.

The Big Book of Coding Interviews

12. Find the largest k numbers out of a list of a trillion unsorted numbers

Since we have to find only the largest k numbers, we don't need to sort all the elements of the list. We can use a simple technique where-in the largest number in the list is found in each iteration and is marked so that it is not used in the subsequent iterations. If N is the size of the list we can find the k largest numbers in k iterations and the maximum number of operations needed is k*N. However there are better methods to solve the problem.

The preferable way to solve the problem is to use a min-heap of size k. Notice that to find the largest k numbers, min-heap is used and not max-heap. Using the first k numbers in the list, construct a min-heap. The root will contain the smallest element among the first k elements. Then compare the $(k+1)^{th}$ element in the list with root. If the $(k+1)^{th}$ element is greater than the root of the min-heap, then remove the root from the heap and add the $(k+1)^{th}$ element to the heap. Continue this procedure for all the remaining elements in the list. So at each stage if the next element in the list is greater than the smallest of our top k numbers, the smallest element is removed from the heap and the next element is added to the heap. This way we store only the largest k elements in the heap.

For instance, suppose we have to find the 5 largest numbers in the list of size 1 trillion. Let the list consist of the elements [80, 90, 60, 40, 20, 50, 10, ...]

We construct a min-heap using the first 5 numbers to get the following heap.

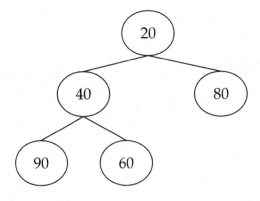

2.1 Searching

The next element is 50 which is greater than the root of the heap (20). So 20 is first removed from the heap and 50 is added in its place. The heap is then re-adjusted using the heapify procedure to form the heap shown below

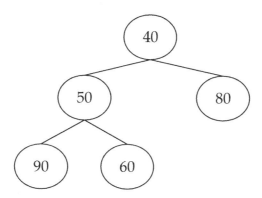

The next element is 10. 10 can't be added to the heap since it is smaller than the root of the heap (40).

Removing the root and adding 1 element to the heap of size k has a time complexity of O(logk). So worst case complexity for N elements is O(Nlogk).

Suppose instead of finding the largest k numbers, we are asked to find the smallest k numbers, then we can use a similar procedure using a max-heap instead of a min-heap.

```
#Helper function to perform heapify
#heap: min heap.  Maximum number of elements in heap is k
#pos: position of the heap that may need to be fixed
#heap_size: current number of nodes in the heap
def heapify(heap, pos, heap_size) :
    left = 2 * pos
    right = (2 * pos) + 1
    ix_of_smallest = pos

    #Find which of the three are the smallest - value at pos OR left child
    #OR right child
    if (left < heap_size and heap[pos] > heap[left]):
        ix_of_smallest = left
    if (right < heap_size and heap[ix_of_smallest] > heap[right]):
        ix_of_smallest = right

    if (ix_of_smallest != pos) :
        #If pos doesn't contain the smallest value,
        #then swap the smallest value into pos
        heap[pos], heap[ix_of_smallest] = heap[ix_of_smallest], heap[pos]
```

```
        #Recursively readjust the heap
        heapify(heap, ix_of_smallest, heap_size)


#Main function to find the k largest elements
#a: non-empty list in which we have to find the k largest elements
#k: the number of largest elements that we need to find. k <= len(a)
#Return value: the k largest elements will be returned in a list
def find_k_largest(a, k):
    heap = []

    #Store the first k elements of the list in the heap
    for i in range(k):
        heap.append(a[i])

    #Construct the initial min-heap
    for i in range(k - 1, -1,-1):
        heapify(heap, i, k)

    for i in range(k, len(a)):
        #The root of heap will have the smallest item in the heap
        #If current item in list is greater than root of the heap, then
        #place current item into root of the heap and re-adjust the heap
        if (a[i] > heap[0]) :
            heap[0] = a[i]
            heapify(heap, 0, k)

    return heap
```

Suppose we are asked to find the k largest/smallest elements in a stream, we can use the same technique.

2.1 Searching

13. Given a list, find the maximum element for each window of size k

In the brute force approach, we look at all possible windows of size k and compute the maximum element for each window separately. If n is the size of the list, then there are (n − k + 1) windows of size k. To find the maximum in one window, we need k operations. So the total time complexity is O(k * (n-k+1)). We can do much better by using a double ended queue (also called dequeue or deque) wherein we can insert and remove elements at both ends of the queue.

The **indexes** of the elements of the list that are relevant for the neighboring windows are stored in the dequeue. The index of the maximum element for the current window will always be at the front of the dequeue. The maximum size of the dequeue at any point of time is equal to the length of the window k.

Consider the list A = [20, 40, 70, 60, 30, 40, 50] with a window size of 4. While processing the list, when we pick the element 70, 70 is greater than all the elements **before** it in the current window. So we no longer need to store 20 and 40 in the dequeue and we can discard them.

The solution is as follows:

1. From the front of the dequeue, remove all indexes that are outside the current window

2. Pick the next element (also called chosen element) in the list. Remove all the indexes from the rear of the dequeue if the elements corresponding to the indexes are <= the chosen element.

3. Store the index of the chosen element in the dequeue

4. If we have processed at least k items in the list, then output the element corresponding to the index at the front of the dequeue as the maximum for the current window

The Big Book of Coding Interviews

The operations of the dequeue are shown for list A = [20, 40, 70, 60, 30, 40, 50] and k = 4

1. Pick 20 and store its index

2. Pick 40 and store its index

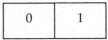

3. Pick 70. Remove index of 40 and 20 since 70 > 40 and 70 > 20. Store index of 70

4. Pick 60 and store its index

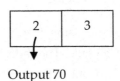

Output 70

5. Pick 30 and store index of 30

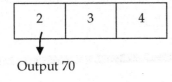

Output 70

6. Pick 40 and store its index

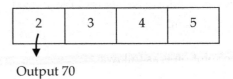

Output 70

7. 70 is out of the window. So remove its index. Pick 50. Remove index of 30 and 40 since 50 > 30 and 50 > 40. Store index of 50

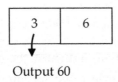

Output 60

2.1 Searching

```
#a: list for which we have to find the maximum in every window of size k
#k: size of the window
#dq: double ended queue that stores list indices
#Return value: list that contains the result (maximum in every window of size k)
def find_window_max(a, k, dq) :
    result = []
    for  i in range(len(a)):
        #Remove the elements outside the current window from
        #front of dequeue
        while (len(dq) > 0 and (peekleft(dq) + k <= i)):
                dq.popleft()

        #Remove all elements that are smaller than or equal to current
        #element from the rear of the dequeue
        while (len(dq) > 0 and a[i] >= a[peek(dq)] ):
                dq.pop()

        #Push the index of the current element into the end of dequeue
        dq.append(i)

        if (i >= k-1) :
                #Front of dequeue has index of maximum element for the
                #current window
                pos = peekleft(dq)
                result.append(a[pos])

    return result
```

The Big Book of Coding Interviews

14. Find the median in a stream of data

When we have a stream of data, the entire data will not be available immediately. Each time the next member in the stream will be available to us, we will have to recompute the median of the stream.

If the data is sorted, then the median is the middle element. So we can sort the stream each time a new member of the stream is available. If we perform merge sort, the complexity of one sort is O(nlogn) and we have to perform n such sorts. So the total complexity will be O(n^2logn). We can do better using insertion sort. When a new member of stream is available, we add the new item into a sorted list and find the median. The time complexity of insertion sort is O(n^2).

We can efficiently solve the problem using heaps in O(nlogn) (n items will be added to the heap and adding each item to heap has a time complexity of O(logn)). We will be using O(n) additional space. The idea is to maintain a max_heap for storing the smaller half of the elements in the stream and a min_heap for storing the larger half of the elements in the stream. The median of the stream will be stored in the root of the heaps. So let us say that the stream of data we have seen so far is 1, 5, 3, 6, 8, 2, then the two heaps that we construct will be as shown below

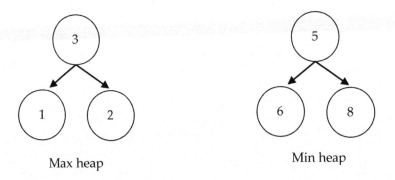

Max heap   Min heap

The smaller half of the numbers are [1, 2, 3] and they are stored in the max_heap. The larger half of the numbers are [5, 6, 8] and they are stored in the min_heap. Since the heaps are equal in size, the median of the stream is the average of the roots of the heaps (($3 + 5$)/ 2 = 4).

2.1 Searching

To construct the heaps in this manner, we do the following:

1. If the min_heap is empty, then we add the new item in the stream to the min_heap

2. If the min_heap is not empty, then if the new item in the stream is greater than the root of the min_heap, we will add the new item to the min_heap otherwise we will add it to the max_heap.

So min_heap takes the larger elements and max_heap takes the smaller elements. Note that one heap can grow much faster than the other. But our intention is to keep half the elements in each heap. To achieve this, whenever the size of one heap exceeds the size of the other heap by more than one element, we remove the root of the heap with more elements and add it to the heap with fewer elements. So the difference between the number of elements in the two heaps will never exceed 1.

To find the median at any time we do the following:

1. If the two heaps are of equal size, then the total number of elements in the stream are even. We calculate the median as the average of the roots of the two heaps

2. If one heap has 1 more element than the other heap, then root of the heap having more elements is the median of the stream.

```python
#min_heap: heap for storing the larger half of numbers in the stream
#max_heap: heap for storing the smaller half of numbers in the stream
#cur_value: value of the current item in the stream
#Return value: Median of the stream
def get_median(min_heap, max_heap, cur_value):
    #If min_heap is empty, add the current value to min_heap.
    #If min_heap is non-empty, the top of min_heap will contain the smallest
    #among the larger half of numbers in the stream. If current value is
    #larger than the top of min_heap, then add it to min_heap otherwise
    #add it to max_heap
    if (len(min_heap) == 0) :
        heappush(min_heap, cur_value)
    elif (cur_value >= min_heap[0]):
        heappush(min_heap, cur_value)
    else:
        #Python has only a min heap implementation. So to mimic a
        #max heap using a min heap we are multiplying -1 to cur_value
        #and adding it to the heap
        heappush(max_heap, -1 * cur_value)


    #If min_heap has more than 1 element than the max_heap, move the top
    #of min_heap into the max_heap and vice versa.
    if (len(min_heap) > len(max_heap) + 1) :
        min_top = heappop(min_heap)
        heappush(max_heap, -1 * min_top)
    elif (len(max_heap) > len(min_heap) + 1):
        max_top = heappop(max_heap)
        heappush(min_heap, -1 * max_top)
    else:
        pass


    #If both heaps are of the same size, then the median will be the average
    #of the top element in the two heaps. Otherwise the median is the top of
    #the heap with more elements
    if (len(min_heap) == len(max_heap)) :
        median = (min_heap[0] + (-1 * max_heap[0])) / 2
    elif (len(min_heap) > len(max_heap)):
        median = min_heap[0]
    else :
        median = -1 * max_heap[0]

    return median
```

Note that Python has only the min heap implementation. To convert the min heap into a max heap, we are reversing the sign of the current value and adding it to the heap that acts as the max heap.

2.2 Sorting

1. Re-arrange the elements in a list like a wave so that the values of the list alternately increase and decrease. The elements in the list are unique. For instance, if A = [50, 10, 20, 30, 40], after re-arranging A can be [10, 30, 20, 50, 40] where the value of consecutive elements alternately increases and decreases

---

This problem can be solved in O(nlogn) without additional memory as follows:

1. First sort the entire list in ascending order. So [50, 10, 20, 30, 40] becomes [10, 20, 30, 40, 50]

2. Then starting from index 1 in the list, swap the neighboring elements. So [10, 20, 30, 40, 50] becomes [10, 30, 20, 50, 40]

```
#a: non-empty list that has to be sorted so that the values in it
#   alternatively increase and decrease. The elements should be unique
def wave_sort(a) :
    #Sort the elements in ascending order
    a.sort()

    #Swap the neighboring elements
    for  i in range(1, len(a) - 1, 2):
        a[i], a[i+1] = a[i+1], a[i]
```

The Big Book of Coding Interviews

2. Given a small list of size n having n sorted elements and a big list of size m+n having m sorted elements at the beginning of the big list, merge the two lists and store them in the big list.

There is just enough free space in the big list to accommodate the elements of the small list. The two sorted lists can be merged in O(m+n). The trick is to start filling up the big list from the end where the free space is present. The code for this is given below

```
#a: list of size m+n which has m elements at beginning
#b: list of size n with n elements
#m: number of elements in list a
#n: number of elements in list b
def merge_lists(a, b, m, n) :
    i = m - 1
    j = n - 1
    fill_pos = m + n - 1 #Start filling from the rear of list a

    while (i >= 0 and j >= 0) :
        if (a[i] > b[j]) :
            a[fill_pos] = a[i]
            fill_pos -= 1
            i -= 1
        else :
            a[fill_pos] = b[j]
            fill_pos -= 1
            j -= 1

    #Fill up the remaining elements of list a if any
    while (i >= 0):
        a[fill_pos] = a[i]
        fill_pos -= 1
        i -= 1

    #Fill up the remaining elements of list b if any
    while (j >= 0):
        a[fill_pos] = b[j]
        fill_pos -= 1
        j -= 1
```

2.2 Sorting

1. Re-arrange the elements in a list like a wave so that the values of the list alternately increase and decrease. The elements in the list are unique. For instance, if A = [50, 10, 20, 30, 40], after re-arranging A can be [10, 30, 20, 50, 40] where the value of consecutive elements alternately increases and decreases

---

This problem can be solved in O(nlogn) without additional memory as follows:

1. First sort the entire list in ascending order. So [50, 10, 20, 30, 40] becomes [10, 20, 30, 40, 50]

2. Then starting from index 1 in the list, swap the neighboring elements. So [10, 20, 30, 40, 50] becomes [10, 30, 20, 50, 40]

```
#a: non-empty list that has to be sorted so that the values in it
#   alternatively increase and decrease. The elements should be unique
def wave_sort(a) :
    #Sort the elements in ascending order
    a.sort()

    #Swap the neighboring elements
    for  i in range(1, len(a) - 1, 2):
        a[i], a[i+1] = a[i+1], a[i]
```

The Big Book of Coding Interviews

2. Given a small list of size n having n sorted elements and a big list of size m+n having m sorted elements at the beginning of the big list, merge the two lists and store them in the big list.

There is just enough free space in the big list to accommodate the elements of the small list. The two sorted lists can be merged in O(m+n). The trick is to start filling up the big list from the end where the free space is present. The code for this is given below

```
#a: list of size m+n which has m elements at beginning
#b: list of size n with n elements
#m: number of elements in list a
#n: number of elements in list b
def merge_lists(a, b, m, n) :
    i = m - 1
    j = n - 1
    fill_pos = m + n - 1 #Start filling from the rear of list a

    while (i >= 0 and j >= 0) :
        if (a[i] > b[j]) :
            a[fill_pos] = a[i]
            fill_pos -= 1
            i -= 1
        else :
            a[fill_pos] = b[j]
            fill_pos -= 1
            j -= 1

    #Fill up the remaining elements of list a if any
    while (i >= 0):
        a[fill_pos] = a[i]
        fill_pos -= 1
        i -= 1

    #Fill up the remaining elements of list b if any
    while (j >= 0):
        a[fill_pos] = b[j]
        fill_pos -= 1
        j -= 1
```

2.2 Sorting

3. Given m sorted lists each of which has a size n, merge the lists in sorted order into a single list of size m*n

---

To efficiently solve the problem we use a heap which has a maximum size of m (number of sorted lists). If the lists are sorted in non-decreasing order, then we maintain a min heap otherwise we maintain a max heap. The algorithm is as follows:

1. Pick the first element from each list, add it to the heap and construct the heap using the heapify function

2. Add the topmost element in the heap to the result list. Then replace the topmost element of the heap with the next element from the same list as the topmost element. Re-adjust the heap using the heapify function. Suppose all elements in the same list are over, then add MAX_INT for non-decreasing order (MIN_INT for non-increasing order) into the root of the heap and re-adjust the heap using heapify. Repeat this step until all elements in all the lists are processed.

Inserting an element into a heap of size m takes O(logm). Since we have n*m elements, the time complexity of this approach is O(nm * logm).

The code for merging k sorted lists is given below. The code for the heapify function has been described on page 205

```
#lists:  the lists to be merged. lists[0] has the first list, lists[1] has
#        the second list and so on
#Return value:  the merged results are passed back in this list
def merge_k_sorted_lists(lists) :
    k = len(lists)      #number of lists
    n = len(lists[0])   #number of elements in each list
    heap = []
    arr_pos = []

    #Store the first element in each list into the heap
    for  i in range(k):
        new_node = Node()
        new_node.value = lists[i][0]
        new_node.list_no = i
        heap.append(new_node)
        arr_pos.append(1)

    #Construct the initial heap using the heapify procedure
    for  i in range(k - 1, -1,-1):
        heapify(heap, i, k)

    #Process the remaining elements in the lists. When all elements in
```

```
#the lists have been processed, MAX_INT will be present at root of heap
result = []
while (heap[0].value != MAX_INT) :
    #root of the heap will have the lowest value. So store
    #it into the result
    result.append(heap[0].value)

    list_no = heap[0].list_no
    pos = arr_pos[list_no]

    #If the root belongs to list x, then replace the root with
    #the next element in list x
    if (pos >= n) :
            #If we have exhausted all elements in the list,
            #then insert MAX_INT into the heap
            heap[0].value = MAX_INT
            heap[0].list_no = list_no
    else :
            heap[0].value = lists[list_no][pos]
            heap[0].list_no = list_no


    #Re-adjust the heap after replacing the root
    heapify(heap, 0, k)

    arr_pos[list_no] += 1

return result
```

4. Given a linked list where the nodes can have the values 0 or 1 or 2, sort it in a single pass. For instance 2->1->0->0->2->0>1 should be sorted as 0->0->0->1->1->2->2

To sort the linked list in a single pass, we make use of the fact that there are only 3 possible values for the nodes in the linked list. So as we traverse the linked list, we can remove the nodes from the original linked list and append them into 3 separate linked lists based on the value of the nodes. At the end we can merge the 3 linked lists. The procedure we can use to solve the problem is as follows:

1. Maintain the head and tail for linked list-0 (will contain nodes with value 0), linked list-1 (will contain nodes with value 1) and linked list-2 (will contain nodes with value 2)

2. As we traverse through the original linked list, remove each node from the original linked list and add it to linked list-0 or linked list-1 or linked list-2 based on the value of the node.

3. At the end connect the tail of linked list-0 to the head of linked list-1 and the tail of linked list-1 to the head of linked list-2

The function used to add a node to a linked list is given below

```
#head: list having head nodes of all the separated linked lists
#tail: list having tail nodes of all the separated linked lists
#cur_node: current node being processed
#i: data value of the node
@staticmethod
def add_node(head, tail, cur_node, i) :
    cur_node.next = head[i]
    head[i] = cur_node
    if (not tail[i]):
        tail[i] = cur_node
```

The main function to sort the list is given below

```python
#first_node:  first node in the linked list to be sorted
#num_distinct_values: number of distinct values
#Return value: head of the sorted linked list
@staticmethod
def sort_linked_list(first_node, num_distinct_values) :
    head = [None] * num_distinct_values
    tail = [None] * num_distinct_values
    result = None

    if (not first_node):
        return None

    #Partition the input linked list into separate linked lists
    #(0-list, 1-list and 2-list) based on the data in the node
    cur_node = first_node
    while (cur_node) :
        next_node = cur_node.next
        LinkedListNode.add_node(head, tail, cur_node, cur_node.data)
        cur_node = next_node

    #Connect the tail of first linked list with head of second linked list
    #and so on
    result = head[0]
    last_element = tail[0]
    for  i in range(1, num_distinct_values):
        if (not result):
                result = head[i]

        #Link last element of previous linked list with head of
        #current linked list
        if (last_element):
                last_element.next = head[i]

        #update the last element to the tail of current linked list
        if (tail[i]):
                last_element = tail[i]


    return result
```

5. Sort a linked list

To sort a linked list, we use the following recursive technique

- Traverse to the middle of the linked list and divide the linked list into two smaller linked lists.
- Recursively sort the two smaller linked lists
- Now merge the two sorted smaller linked lists into a single linked list

The procedure is shown in the diagram below:

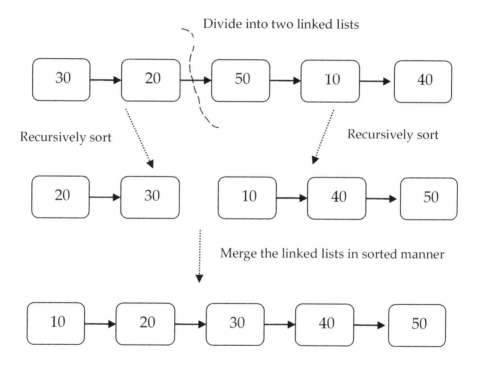

The source code for the merge sort is shown below. We are reusing the function for merging two sorted linked lists that has been described in page 23. One important point to note is that when we recursively divide the linked list and reach a single node, we have to make the next field of the node None in order to disconnect it from the original linked list and form a separate linked list that contains only that single node.

```
#first_node: head of the linked list to be sorted
#num_elements: number of elements in the linked list
#Return value: head of the merged and sorted linked list
@staticmethod
def sort_linked_list(first_node, num_elements) :
    if (num_elements == 0):
        return None

    #If there is only a single node in linked list, then disconnect next
    #and return the node as the result without any further recursive calls
    if (num_elements == 1) :
        first_node.next = None
        return first_node

    #Divide into two linked lists. linked list1 has count1 elements and
    #linked list2 has count2 elements
    linked_list1 = first_node
    count1 = num_elements // 2

    cur_node = first_node
    for  i in range(count1):
        cur_node = cur_node.next

    linked_list2 = cur_node
    count2 = num_elements - count1

    #Call sort_linked_list recursively on the two linked lists
    linked_list1 = LinkedListNode.sort_linked_list(linked_list1, count1)
    linked_list2 = LinkedListNode.sort_linked_list(linked_list2, count2)

    #The two linked lists are now sorted. So merge them into a single
    #sorted linked list and return its head node
    return LinkedListNode.merge(linked_list1, linked_list2)
```

2.2 Sorting

6. Given an unsorted list A and a pivot element in the list, re-arrange the elements so that elements less than pivot occur first, followed by elements equal to pivot followed by elements greater than pivot.

When we perform quicksort, we pick a pivot and move all the elements that are < than pivot to one side and all elements that are > than pivot to the other side. But the problem is that if there are multiple elements with the same value of the pivot, then these elements are not guaranteed to be next to each other. So for instance consider the list = [5, 5, 2, 30, 10, 5]. If we pick the pivot value of 5 and perform quicksort then after the first set of operations we end up with [2, 5, 5, 30, 10, 5]. Note that all the 5's are not grouped together. So default quicksort is not efficient in dealing with duplicates. In fact the worst case for quicksort is $O(n^2)$ and occurs when there are all identical values in the list. If quicksort is modified to store all values of the pivot together, quicksort can be speeded up. So if we rearrange the list as [2, 5, 5, 5, 30, 10] in the first pass of modified quicksort, then we can skip all the consecutive 5's and sort the remaining regions [2] and [30, 10].

Dijkstra suggested the modification to quicksort to speed it up. He posed the Dutch National Flag Problem and used the solution of the problem to speed up quicksort. The Dutch National Flag has 3 colors: red, white and blue. So he asked if there was a way to rearrange a random bunch of red, white and blue balls so that all the red balls appear first, followed by white balls followed by blue balls. He came up with a $O(n)$ solution that doesn't use extra space. If we map the red balls to elements less than the pivot, white balls to elements equal to the pivot and blue balls to elements greater than the pivot, we end up with the same problem we are trying to solve. So we can apply Dijkstra's solution to our problem as well.

In Dijkstra's solution, we maintain two markers: a left marker (initialized to 0) and a right marker initialized to n-1 where n is the number of elements in A. The current position i in A is initialized to 0. We pick A[i] as the pivot. As the algorithm runs we maintain the elements in the following manner

- All elements that are less than pivot are stored from A[0] to A[left – 1]
- All elements equal to the pivot are stored from A[left] to A[current position - 1]
- All elements that still need to be processed will be in the region A[current position] to A[right]
- All elements that are greater than pivot are stored from A[right + 1] to A[n-1]

The code for solving the problem is given below

```
#a: input list that has to be sorted.
#pivot_value: after sorting, all elements smaller than pivot will lie to the
#left of the pivot and all values that are greater than pivot will lie to the
#right of the pivot. If there are many pivot values, then they will occur
#together in the middle
def dutch_sort(a, pivot_value) :
    cur_pos = 0
    left_pos = 0
    right_pos = len(a) - 1
    while (cur_pos <= right_pos) :
        if (a[cur_pos] < pivot_value) :
            #swap a[left_pos], a[cur_pos]
            a[left_pos], a[cur_pos] = a[cur_pos], a[left_pos]

            left_pos += 1
            cur_pos += 1

        elif (a[cur_pos] > pivot_value) :
            #swap a[cur_pos], a[right_pos]
            a[cur_pos], a[right_pos] = a[right_pos], a[cur_pos]

            #Advance the right fill location. Since we have newly
            #brought in an element from right_pos to cur_pos, we
            #have to process the new element. So don't advance cur_pos
            right_pos -= 1

        else :
            cur_pos += 1
```

Suppose a list consists of random numbers and we need to re-arrange it so that we first have negative numbers followed by 0, followed by positive numbers, then we can use the same strategy.

2.2 Sorting

7. Find the kth smallest element in a list

We can solve the problem by completely sorting the list and then finding the kth element in the sorted list. However for just finding one element, sorting the entire list is expensive.

We can solve the problem using a heap of k elements. As we process the elements in the list, we will maintain the k smallest elements in the heap. The problem with this approach is that if k is large, then we will need a large amount of space. So even though we need to find only one element, we will have to allocate space for k elements.

The other approach is to use quick sort. In each iteration of quicksort, we will pick a pivot and move all the elements that are smaller than the pivot to the left of the pivot and move all the elements greater than the pivot to the right of the pivot. Let the region on which the current iteration of quicksort has operated on be (left_index, right_index). Then based on the location of the pivot, we do the following:

1. If the index of the pivot at the end of the quick-sort iteration matches with k, then we have found the kth smallest element.

2. If the index of the pivot is less than k, then we reduce the region to be searched in the next iteration to (index of pivot + 1, right_index)

3. If the location of the pivot is greater than k, then we reduce the region to be searched in the next iteration to (left_index, index of pivot – 1)

The worst case time complexity is $O(n^2)$. However in practice, the algorithm is expected to run in linear time $O(n)$ and the space complexity is $O(1)$.

```
#Helper function for finding the kth smallest element in a list
#This function, picks a pivot and arranges all numbers smaller than pivot to
#the left of the pivot and all numbers greater than pivot to the right of pivot
#a: list on which the partition operation should be performed
#left: index of the starting element of the partition in the list
#right: index of the ending element of the partition in the list
#Return value: index of the pivot element of the partition
def partition(a, left, right):
    num_elements = right - left + 1
    rand_pos = left + (random.randint(0, num_elements - 1))

    #pick a random element and swap it with the last element
    a[rand_pos], a[right] = a[right], a[rand_pos]
```

```python
#The last element is treated as the pivot
pivot = a[right]

i = left
for  j in range(left, right - 1+1):
    if (a[j] <= pivot) :
            #If i is not equal to j, then a[i] has a value
            #greater than pivot and a[j] has a value less than
            #pivot. So swap a[i] and a[j]
            if (i != j) :
                    a[i], a[j] = a[j], a[i]

        i += 1

#Swap a[i] and the pivot that is at a[right]
a[i], a[right] = a[right], a[i]

return i #the pivot is now at i. So return i


#Finds the kth smallest element in a list
#a: list in which the kth smallest element should be found
#k: value of k (can range from 0 to number of elements in list - 1)
#Returns: the kth smallest element in the list
def find_kth_smallest(a, k) :
    left = 0
    right = len(a) - 1

    while (k >= left and k <= right) :
        pivot_pos = partition(a, left, right)

        if (pivot_pos == k):
                return a[pivot_pos]
        elif (pivot_pos < k):
                left = pivot_pos + 1
        else :
                right = pivot_pos - 1

    return MAX_INT #incorrect k value was specified
```

2.2 Sorting

8. Sort a list which is almost sorted. An almost sorted list is one in which each element is at most k positions away from its position in the fully sorted list. For instance, the list [3, 2, 1, 5, 4] is almost sorted and k = 2 since the maximum distance an element has to be moved to get the fully sorted list in ascending order is 2.

To sort an almost sorted list where an element is at most k positions from its position in the sorted list, we will make use of a heap of size k+1. To sort in non-decreasing order, we will make use of a min_heap. We apply the following steps:

1. Store the first k elements in the list into the min_heap. Initialize write_pos to 0. write_pos is used to write the sorted values back into the list.

2. Add the next element in the list into the min_heap. The root of the min_heap will now contain the smallest element in the current window of size k+1. Remove the root and store the value of the root into the location write_pos in the list. Increment the write_pos

3. Repeat step 2 for all the remaining elements in the list

4. Once we have finished processing the list, the heap will still be containing elements in it. So go on removing the root from the heap and adding it to the list until the heap becomes completely empty. The list will now be completely sorted.

```
#a: almost sorted list that should be fully sorted
#k: max distance that any element should be moved so that list becomes sorted
def sort_almost_sorted_list(a, k) :
    min_heap = []

    read_pos = write_pos = 0

    #Fill in the first k values into the min_heap. If length is less than k
    #then we have to fill in only length number of elements
    while (read_pos < min(k, len(a))):
        heappush(min_heap, a[read_pos])
        read_pos += 1

    #Add the element a[read_pos] to the heap and then pop out a value.
    #Value popped from heap will contain the next smallest value. Add the
    #value popped from the heap back into the list at the write position
    while (read_pos < len(a)) :
        heappush(min_heap, a[read_pos])
        a[write_pos] = heappop(min_heap)

        read_pos += 1
        write_pos += 1
```

```
#Pop out the remaining elements in the heap and store them back into
#the list
while (len(min_heap) > 0) :
    a[write_pos] = heappop(min_heap)
    write_pos += 1
```

2.2 Sorting

9. Sort a list of words so that the anagrams are grouped together. For instance, if the words are ["tar", "phone", "rat"], after sorting we should get ["tar", "rat", "phone"] (since "tar" and "rat" are anagrams, they are grouped together)

We will maintain a class called the AnagramHelper as shown below

```
class AnagramHelper(object):

    def __init__(self, word, index):
        self.word = word
        self.index = index
```

Let the original word_list passed by user consist of ["tar", "phone", "rat"]

1. First copy the words and their index locations in the original word_list into an AnagramHelper list. So the AnagramHelper list will look like

word	"tar"	"phone"	"rat"
index	0	1	2

2. Sort each word in the AnagramHelper in the non-decreasing order of the characters in the word. After the sort, the AnagramHelper list will look like

word	"art"	"ehnop"	"art"
index	0	1	2

3. Now sort all the words in the AnagramHelper list. After the sort, the AnagramHelper list will be as shown below. Note that when we swap elements during sorting, both word and index will be moved together.

word	"art"	"art"	"ehnop"
index	0	2	1

Now the words in the AnagramHelper list have been modified ("rat" has become "art"). To get back the original word, we will use the index. The index will give us the location of the actual word in the original word_list. So if we lookup original word_list[2] we will get "rat" and so we conclude that the second "art" is actually "rat".

4. We now have to move the words in the original word_list so that anagrams occur together. If we use the AnagramHelper and directly write to the original word_list, then we will overwrite contents in the original word_list leading to an incorrect result. So we instead use a scratchpad list and fill it up using the information in the AnagramHelper list. So the scratchpad is filled up as shown below

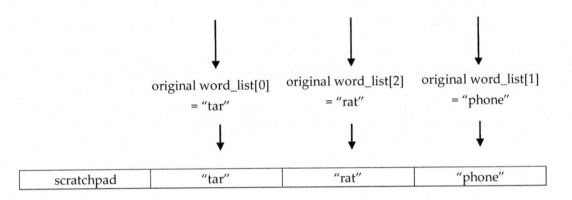

5. Finally we copy the contents of the scratchpad into the original word_list. So original word_list will now have ["tar", "rat", "phone"]

The code for sorting the anagrams together is given below

```
#word_list: list of words that should be sorted so that the anagrams occur
#   together
#num_words: Number of elements in the word_list
def anagram_sort(word_list) :
    num_words = len(word_list)
    helper = []

    for i, cur_word in enumerate(word_list):
        #Sort the characters of the word
        sorted_word = ''.join(sorted(cur_word))

        #Copy the original word into the helper
        #Store the original index (i) of the word in the helper
        obj = AnagramHelper(sorted_word, i)

        helper.append(obj)

    #Sort all the words in the helper
    helper.sort(key = lambda x: x.word )
```

2.2 Sorting

```
#We need to move the words in word_list based on the indexes in
#the helper. We can't directly move the strings in the word_list.
#First we will copy the strings into a scratchpad list
#based on the indexes in the helper and then copy the scratchpad
#list into the word_list.
scratchpad = []
for  i in range(num_words):
    index = helper[i].index
    scratchpad.append(word_list[index])

#copy word by word from scratchpad to word_list since when we
#return from the function, the original word_list should be
#modified
for  i, cur_word in enumerate(scratchpad):
    word_list[i] = cur_word
```

3. Algorithms

Some of the popular algorithm techniques used for solving problems are divide and conquer, greedy approach and dynamic programming.

In the divide and conquer approach, the main problem is broken into sub-problems recursively until the sub-problem can be easily solved. The solutions for the sub-problems are collected and used to find the solution for the main problem. Some of the problems where divide and conquer approach is used are: binary search, merge sort and Strassen's matrix multiplication.

In the greedy approach, at each stage of the algorithm, the local optimum is chosen hoping that this will result in the globally optimum solution. Some of the problems where the greedy approach is used are: the fractional knapsack problem, Huffman coding, finding minimum spanning trees and finding the shortest path from a single source (Dijkstra's algorithm)

The dynamic programming approach breaks the main problem into sub-problems that can be easily solved such that overlapping sub-problems are computed only once. Some of the problems where the dynamic programming approach is used are: the 0/1 knapsack problem, computing edit distance between two strings and longest common subsequence.

While solving algorithmic problems, sometimes we will have to make use of our knowledge of data structures. The other tools we can use for algorithmic problems include sorting, binary search, recursion and back tracking.

3.1 Greedy Algorithms

1. Given a list of stock prices over a period of time, find the maximum profit possible by buying and selling the stocks. For instance, if the stock prices are 100, 90, 200, 20, 70, 150, 10 and 40, then the maximum profit = 150 − 20 = 130

If we use a brute force approach, then we will compare every pair of numbers to find the maximum profit possible. This requires $O(n^2)$ operations. However using the greedy approach we can solve the problem in $O(n)$. The main idea of the greedy approach is that it is sufficient to maintain the minimum stock price that we have encountered so far as we traverse the stock prices.

The procedure is as follows: as we traverse the stock price list, subtract the minimum stock price seen so far from the current stock price to figure out the profit. If the profit is greater than the maximum profit so far, then update the maximum profit.

The working of the algorithm on the stock prices [100, 90, 200, 20, 70, 150, 10, 40] is given below. The minimum stock price is initialized to the first element 100. The max profit is initialized to 0. We start from the second stock price onwards.

Index	Current stock price	Minimum stock price so far	Current Profit	Max profit
1	90	100	90 − 100 = −10	0
2	200	90	200 − 90 = 110	110
3	20	90	20 − 90 = −70	110
4	70	20	70 − 20 = 50	110

5	150	20	150 − 20 = 130	130
6	10	20	10 − 20 = -10	130
7	40	10	40 − 10 = 30	130

```python
#stock_price: list of stock price values
#Return value: maximum profit possible
def find_max_profit(stock_price) :
    n = len(stock_price)

    max_profit = 0
    if (n <= 1):
        return max_profit

    min_stock_price = stock_price[0]

    for  i in range(1, n):
        cur_profit = stock_price[i] - min_stock_price

        if (cur_profit > max_profit):
            max_profit = cur_profit

        if (stock_price[i] < min_stock_price):
            min_stock_price = stock_price[i]

    return max_profit
```

3.1 Greedy Algorithms

2. Given the start time and end time of N activities, find the maximum number of activities that can be performed (Activity Selection problem)

We can find the maximum number of activities using the greedy approach as indicated below

1. Sort the activities based on their end times so that an activity with a smaller end time is placed before an activity with a larger end time.

2. Traverse through the sorted list and choose the activities that can be completed without any conflicts (the start and end time of a chosen activity should not overlap with the start and end time of another chosen activity)

```
#a: list of activities, where each activity has a start time and end time
#Return value: list having the index of the selected activities
def activity_selection(a) :
    #Sort the activities in non-decreasing order of their end time
    a.sort(key = lambda x: x.end_time)

    selected = []

    #Keep a track of the current time as we process the activities
    cur_time = 0

    for  i, cur_activity in enumerate(a):
        #Pick the activity whose start time is on or after current time
        if (cur_activity.start_time >= cur_time) :
            selected.append(i)

            #Update the current time to the end time of the activity
            cur_time = cur_activity.end_time

    return selected
```

Note that if instead of start time and end time, we are given start time and duration of each activity, then we must compute the end time (end time = start time + duration) and then apply the above algorithm

The Big Book of Coding Interviews

3. Given the arrival time and the departure time of N trains, find the minimum number of platforms needed to accommodate the trains

---

To find the minimal number of platforms needed for N trains, we do the following:

1. Sort the arrival time of the N trains so that an earlier arrival time is placed before a later arrival time

2. Sort the departure time of the N trains so that an earlier departure time is placed before a later departure time. Note that we independently sort the arrival time and the departure time of the trains.

3. Traverse through the arrival time and departure time of the trains as indicated below

- If the current arrival time is less than the current departure time, then we need an extra platform for the incoming train. So increment the number of platforms needed and advance to the next arrival time.
- If the current arrival time is equal to the current departure time, then we don't need an extra platform. So simply advance to the next arrival time and next departure time
- If the current departure time is less than the current arrival time, then a platform will be freed up. So decrement the number of platforms needed and advance to the next departure time.

As we do this, keep track of the maximum number of platforms needed at any given time. This will give us the minimum number of platforms needed to accommodate the trains.

```
#arrival: list containing the arrival time of the trains
#departure: list containing the departure time of the trains
#Return value: minimum number of train platforms needed
def find_min_platforms(arrival, departure) :
    n = len(arrival)
    if (n == 0):
        return 0

    #Sort the arrival and departure time independently in non-decreasing order
    arrival.sort()
    departure.sort()

    cur_num_platforms = min_num_platforms = 1
    i = 1 #i is used for traversing arrival
    j = 0 #j is used for traversing departure
```

3.1 Greedy Algorithms

```
while (i < n and j < n) :
    if (arrival[i] < departure[j]) :
            #A new train is coming in before a train departs. So
            #we need an extra platform
            cur_num_platforms += 1
            if (cur_num_platforms > min_num_platforms):
                    min_num_platforms = cur_num_platforms
            i += 1
    elif (arrival[i] == departure[j]):
            #A train arrives at the same time as a departing train.
            #So we don't need an extra platform
            i += 1
            j += 1
    else :
            #A train departs before the new train arrives.
            #So a platform is freed up
            cur_num_platforms = cur_num_platforms - 1
            j += 1

return min_num_platforms
```

The Big Book of Coding Interviews

4. There are N gas stations around a circular path. Each gas station i has a finite amount of fuel gas[i] in it. The fuel tank of the car has an unlimited size. The sum of the fuel available at all the gas stations is sufficient for the driver to complete the journey on the circular path. Note however that an individual gas station might not have enough gas to reach the next gas station. Find out if the driver can finish one complete circular trip in the car using the fuel available in the gas stations

---

It is always possible to find a circular trip around the N gas stations if the sum of the fuel in all the stations is >= to the fuel needed for the whole trip irrespective of the distribution of the fuel in the individual gas stations. We can find the starting station in $O(n^2)$ using the brute force approach: start from each of the N station and check if it is possible to complete the journey around all gas stations. However there is a faster $O(n)$ solution. Let gas[i] be the gas available at station i. Let distance[i] be the distance between the ith station and $(i+1)^{th}$ station. The algorithm is as follows:

1. Starting from the first gas station, fill up all the gas available in the current gas station and proceed to the next station. On reaching each station, before refueling the car, compute the gas present in the car tank. Allow for negative amount of gas in the car tank

2. The station where the gas available in the tank before refueling is the least, is the station from where to start the journey.

To illustrate the algorithm, consider the following diagram

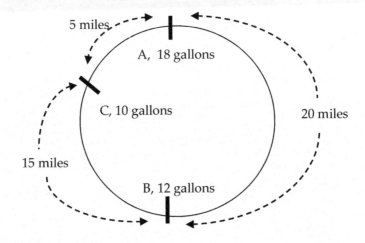

3.1 Greedy Algorithms

Let us start from gas station A. The initial amount of fuel in the tank is 0. The table below shows the sequence of events. Note that we allow the amount of gas in the fuel tank to become negative. Let the mileage be 1 mile per gallon.

Journey	Fuel in tank after filling up from starting gas station	Distance to next gas station	Fuel needed to reach next station = distance / mileage	Fuel left in tank after reaching next station
A -> B	18 gallons	20 miles	20 / 1 = 20 gallons	18-20 = -2 gallons
B -> C	-2 + 12 = 10 gallons	15 miles	15 / 1 = 15 gallons	10–15 = **-5 gallons**
C -> A	-5 + 10 = 5	5 miles	5 / 1 = 5 gallons	5 - 5 = 0 gallons

When we reach station C, before we refuel at station C, we have the lowest amount of gas in the entire trip (-5 gallons). So suppose we start the journey from gas station C, the amount of gas in the car will never fall below the lowest amount of gas. We will always have sufficient amount of gas or surplus gas in the fuel tank. Think of it this way: by starting from station C, we start with 0 gas in the car. Since the lowest amount of gas occurs when we reach station C, we are assured that the amount of gas when we reach other stations will always be >= 0.

```
#gas: the amount of gas available at each gas station. The total gas in all
#    stations should be sufficient to complete the circular trip
#distance: distance[i] has the distance between gas station i and i+1
#mileage: how much distance can the car travel for 1 unit of gas consumed
#Return value: station from where to start so that we don't run out of fuel and
#    complete the circular trip around all stations
def find_starting_gas_station(gas, distance, mileage) :
    num_stations = len(gas)
    assert(num_stations)

    #Station from where to start the journey so that we don't run out of fuel
    starting_station = 0

    least_gas = 0 #Tracks the least amount of gas in fuel tank
    gas_in_tank = 0 #Tracks how much fuel is currently present in fuel tank
    for i, (gas_in_station, cur_distance) in enumerate(zip(gas, distance)):
        gas_required = cur_distance // mileage

        #At station 1, we fill up gas_in_station and then as we drive,
        #we consume gas_required to reach the destination station =
        #(i+1) % num_stations
        gas_in_tank += gas_in_station - gas_required
        if (gas_in_tank < least_gas) :
            least_gas = gas_in_tank
            #The starting station is the station where we have
```

```
            #the least amount of gas in the tank just before we fill up
            starting_station = (i+1) % num_stations

    return starting_station
```

3.2 Dynamic Programming

1. Find the maximum continuous sum in a list

A list can have positive and negative elements in it. We have to find a subset of contiguous elements in the list whose sum is the maximum. Let the maximum continuous sum be represented as MCS

In the brute force approach, we pick an element and then go on adding its right neighbors one by one to find the maximum contiguous sum starting at that element. We then repeat the process for all elements in the list to find the MCS across all elements. The time complexity of the brute force approach is $O(n^2)$.

However it is possible to find the MCS in $O(n)$ time using Kadane's algorithm. This algorithm works for all cases (including the case where all the elements are negative). We maintain the variable max_local which will store the sum of the neighboring elements in the current window. The algorithm is described below:

1. Choose the first element and initialize max_local to the first element.

2. Traverse through the remaining elements. If the result of adding max_local to the current element is greater than current element, then add the current element to max_local and keep continuing the window. If however the result of adding max_local to the current element is less than the current element, then start a fresh window that starts at the current element and initialize max_local to the current element.

3. The maximum value of max_local across all elements will be the MCS of the list.

Let A = [4, -9, 5, 6, 1]. max_local is initialized to 4. The remaining calculations are shown in the table below

i	max_local	A[i]	A[i] + max_local	Action max_local = max(A[i], A[i] + max_local)
1	4	-9	-5	max_local = max(-9, -5) = -5
2	-5	5	0	max_local = max(5, 0) = 5
3	5	6	11	max_local = max(6, 11) = 11
4	11	1	12	max_local = max(1, 12) = 12

The maximum value of max_local is 12. So the MCS is 12.

```
#a: list of numbers for which MCS should be found. size of a >= 1
#Return value: 1. Maximum continuous sum of the elements ,
#         2. the starting list index of the MCS
#         3. the ending list index of the MCS
def kadane_mcs(a) :
    mcs_start_pos = mcs_end_pos = 0
    cur_start_pos = 0 #store the start position of the current window

    max_local = max_global = MIN_INT

    for i, cur_value in enumerate(a):
        max_local = max(cur_value, cur_value + max_local)
        if (max_local == cur_value):
            cur_start_pos = i #start a new window here

        #Find the global maximum
        if (max_local > max_global) :
            max_global = max_local
            mcs_start_pos = cur_start_pos
            mcs_end_pos = i

    return max_global, mcs_start_pos, mcs_end_pos
```

3.2 Dynamic Programming

2. Given a list of coin denominations, find the change for a given amount using the least number of coins. For instance, suppose the coin denominations are 4¢, 5¢ and 7¢, then to get 13¢ using the least number of coins, we need to pick two 4¢ coins and one 5¢ coin.

Let us say that coin denominations are 1¢, 5¢ and 25¢. We can use a greedy approach as follows - Pick the maximum possible number of coins with the highest denomination and then the maximum possible number of coins with the next highest denomination and so on. So if we have to pick the change for 58¢, we pick two 25¢, then one 5¢ and finally three 1¢. So we use a total of 6 coins. Greedy approach produces the optimal result for this set of coin denominations. However, given any arbitrary set of coin denominations, the greedy approach will fail for many cases. For instance let the denominations be 1¢, 3¢, 4¢ and 5¢. If we use the greedy approach to get 7¢, we use one 5¢ and two 1¢ thereby requiring three coins. However the optimal solution needs only two coins (one 3¢ and one 4¢).

To solve the problem for any possible coin denominations, we use dynamic programming. We first solve the minimum number of coins needed for the amount of 1¢, then for the amount of 2¢ and so on until we reach the required amount. To compute the minimum number of coins for a higher amount, we make use of the already computed minimum number of coins for lower amounts. The formula used is:

1. If amount = 0, min_num_coins(0) = 0

2. If amount > 0, min_num_coins(amount) = minimum of { 1 + min_num_coins(amount - denomination)} for all denominations which are less than or equal to the amount

For instance, let the denominations be 1¢, 3¢, 4¢ and 5¢. Using the formula above, min_num_coins[0¢] = 0 coins. The table below shows how the calculation is done for min_num_coins for 1¢, 2¢ and 3¢.

Amount	Denominations that are <= amount	1 + min_num_coins(amount - denomination)	min_num_coins
1¢	1¢	(1 + min_num_coins(1¢ - *1¢*)} = 1 + min_num_coins(0¢) = 1 + 0 = 1	min(1) = 1
2¢	1¢	(1 + min_num_coins(2¢ - *1¢*) = 1 + min_num_coins(1¢) = 1 + 1 = 2	min(2) = 2

Amount	Denominations that are <= amount	1 + min_num_coins(amount - denomination)	min_num_coins
3¢	1¢, 3¢	(1 + min_num_coins(3¢ - *1¢*) = 1 + min_num_coins(2¢) = 1 + 2 = 3 (1 + min_num_coins(3¢ - *3¢*) = 1 + min_num_coins(0) = 1 + 0 = 1	min(3, 1) = 1

So min_num_coins(1¢) = 1, min_num_coins(2¢) = 2 and min_num_coins(3¢) = 1. Similarly we find that min_num_coins(4¢) = 1 and min_num_coins(5¢) = 1. The calculations for 6¢ and 7¢ are shown below

Amount	Denominations that are <= amount	1 + min_num_coins(amount - denomination)	min_num_coins
6¢	1¢, 3¢, 4¢, 5¢	(1 + min_num_coins(6¢ - *1¢*) = 1 + min_num_coins(5¢) = 1 + 1 = 2 (1 + min_num_coins(6¢ - *3¢*) = 1 + min_num_coins(3¢) = 1 + 1 = 2 (1 + min_num_coins(6¢ - *4¢*) = 1 + min_num_coins(2¢) = 1 + 2 = 3 (1 + min_num_coins(6¢ - *5¢*) = 1 + min_num_coins(1¢) = 1 + 1 = 2	min(2, 2, 3, 2) = 2
7¢	1¢, 3¢, 4¢, 5¢	(1 + min_num_coins(7¢ - *1¢*) = 1 + min_num_coins(6¢) = 1 + 2 = 3 (1 + min_num_coins(7¢ - *3¢*) = 1 + min_num_coins(4¢) = 1 + 1 = 2 (1 + min_num_coins(7¢ - *4¢*) = 1 + min_num_coins(3¢) = 1 + 1 = 2 (1 + min_num_coins(7¢ - *5¢*) = 1 + min_num_coins(2¢) = 1 + 2 = 3	min(3, 2, 2, 3) = 2

So the minimum number of coins for 7¢ is 2 coins. If the final amount is m and there are n denominations, the time complexity of this approach is $O(mn)$.

3.2 Dynamic Programming

```
#denom: list having the coin denominations. Should have at least 1 element
#final_amount: amount for which change has to be obtained
#Return value: Minimum number of coins needed to represent final_amount
def find_min_coins(denom, final_amount) :
    #List for storing the minimum number of coins for an amount
    min_num_coins = [0] * (final_amount + 1)

    #List for storing the coin denomination chosen for an amount
    chosen_denom = [0] * (final_amount + 1)

    min_num_coins[0] = 0
    for  cur_amt in range(1, final_amount+1):
        min_num_coins[cur_amt] = MAX_INT_VALUE
        for  cur_denom in denom:
            if (cur_denom <= cur_amt) :

                smaller_amt = cur_amt - cur_denom

                if (1 + min_num_coins[smaller_amt] <
                        min_num_coins[cur_amt]) :
                    min_num_coins[cur_amt] = (1 +
                            min_num_coins[smaller_amt])
                    chosen_denom[cur_amt] = cur_denom


    result = min_num_coins[final_amount]
    print('Minimum number of coins = {}'.format(result) )

    #print the chosen denominations to get the amount
    cur_amt = final_amount
    while (cur_amt > 0) :
        print('{} '.format(chosen_denom[cur_amt]) , end='')
        cur_amt = cur_amt - chosen_denom[cur_amt]
    print(' = {}'.format(final_amount) )

    return result
```

The Big Book of Coding Interviews

3. Find the longest increasing subsequence in an unsorted list of numbers

Consider the sequence A = [30, 40, 20, 70, 10]. The longest increasing subsequence is [30, 40, 70]. Here we are considering a strictly increasing longest subsequence and so a number can be present only once in the longest increasing subsequence even if it occurs several times in the original sequence. To solve the problem, we use dynamic programming as follows:

1.) We make use of a list called seq_length where seq_length[i] stores the length of the longest increasing subsequence ending at the position i. For instance seq_length[3] stores the length of longest subsequence from 0th to 3rd position, i.e. for the region [30, 40, 20, 70] in the above example. We initialize seq_length list with 1 at each position since each number itself forms a sequence of size 1 by itself.

2. We then compute the seq_length[i] from position 1 onwards using the formula:

seq_length[i] = 1 + max(seq_length[j]) where j < i and A[j] < A[i]

position	value	calculation	seq_length
0	30		seq_length [0] = 1
1	40	1 +seq_length[0] = 1+1 = 2	seq_length [1] = 2
2	20	can't consider seq_length[0] since A[0] > A[2] can't consider seq_length[1] since A[1] > A[2]	seq_length [2] = 1
3	70	1 + seq_length[0] = 1 + 1 = 2 1 + seq_length[1] = 1 + 2 = 3 1 + seq_length[2] = 1 + 1 = 2	seq_length [3] = 3
4	10	can't consider seq_length[0] since A[0] > A[4], can't consider seq_length [1] since A[1] > A[4] can't consider seq_length [2] since A[2] > A[4] can't consider seq_length [3] since A[3] > A[4]	seq_length [4] = 1

3. Once we have computed sequence lengths for all positions, then the maximum value in the seq_length list gives the length of the longest increasing subsequence. In our example, the maximum value in the seq_length list is 3. So length of longest increasing subsequence is 3.

The time complexity of this approach is $O(n^2)$.

```
#a: list in which we need to find the longest increasing sequence
#   should have at least 1 element
#Return value: list having the longest increasing sequence is returned
def find_lis(a) :
    n = len(a)

    #seq_length stores length of LIS for each position of list a
    #Each element by itself forms a sequence of length 1
    seq_length = [1 for i in range(n)]

    #prev_ix stores the index of previous element in the LIS sequence
    prev_ix = [0] * n

    #Find the LIS for each position in list a
    for  i in range(1, n):
        for  j in range(i):
            if ( a[j] < a[i] and seq_length[i] < seq_length[j] + 1 ) :
                seq_length[i] = seq_length[j] + 1
                prev_ix[i] = j

    #The longest LIS amongst all positions of list a will be the LIS
    #for the whole list
    lis_length = 1
    lis_end = 0
    for  i in range(1, n):
        if (lis_length < seq_length[i]) :
            lis_length = seq_length[i]
            lis_end = i

    lis = [0] * lis_length

    #Use the prev_ix list to reconstruct the LIS for the whole list
    #lis_end has the index of the last element in the LIS for whole list
    j = lis_end
    for  i in range(lis_length - 1, -1,-1):
        lis[i] = a[j]
        j = prev_ix[j]

    return lis
```

The Big Book of Coding Interviews

4. Find the least number of dice throws needed to complete the snake and ladders game

To find the least number of dice throws, we use the following dynamic programming technique:

1. Initialize the least number of throws needed to reach the positions 1-6 on the board as 1 since we can reach these positions with a single dice throw of a 6-sided dice

2. For any remaining position, we can either reach it from

   - any of the previous 6 positions with one dice throw. If there is a snake at a previous position, then we ignore that cell while calculating the least number of throws for the current position
   - or we can reach it by a ladder if present from some previous position. If there is a ladder from position I to position P, and we need N throws to reach I, then we can reach P also in N throws.

So we use the formula below to calculate the least number of throws for positions greater than 6.

least_throws[pos] = Minimum of
   1. least_throws[prev_pos] + 1

      where prev_pos refers to the positions from (pos − 1) to (pos − 6) that don't have a snake in them

   2. least_throws[i], if there is a ladder from i to pos, where i < pos

3. The least number of throws to reach the final position of the board gives the least number of throws needed to complete the game.

3.2 Dynamic Programming

```
#is_snake: if there is a snake at position 20, is_snake[20] is set to True
#ladder:  if there is a ladder from position 30 to 44, then ladder[44] = 30.
#   if there is no ladder at location 90 then ladder[90] = -1
#Return value:   1. least number of throws to reach the position on the board
#        2. predecessor list
def find_least_throws(is_snake, ladder) :

    #for a particular position pos on the board, least_throws[pos] will store
    #the least number of dice throws required to reach the position
    least_throws = [0] * (MAX_POSITIONS_ON_BOARD + 1)

    #predecessor list has the previous board position from where we came to
    #current position with least number of dice throws. If predecessor[100]
    # = 95, then we reached 100 from 95.
    predecessor = [0] * (MAX_POSITIONS_ON_BOARD + 1)

    #All positions from 1 to 6 can be reached from a single dice throw
    for  pos in range(1, 7):
        least_throws[pos] = 1
        predecessor[pos] = 0

    for  pos in range(7, MAX_POSITIONS_ON_BOARD+1):
        min_throws = MAX_POSITIONS_ON_BOARD

        #Find how many dice throws are needed to reach pos from any of
        #the 6 previous cells
        for  i in range(1, 7):
            prev_pos = pos - i

            if (is_snake[prev_pos]):
                continue

            #Pick the minimum throws needed from the 6 previous cells
            if (least_throws[prev_pos] + 1 < min_throws) :
                min_throws = least_throws[prev_pos] + 1
                predecessor[pos] = prev_pos


        #Suppose we are at pos = 14 and ladder[14] = 4, then there is a ladder
        #from 4 to 14. So number of dice throws needed to reach 14 = number of
        #dice throws needed to reach position 4
        ladder_start_pos = ladder[pos]
        if (ladder_start_pos != -1) :
            if (least_throws[ladder_start_pos] < min_throws) :
                min_throws = least_throws[ladder_start_pos]
                predecessor[pos] = ladder_start_pos

        least_throws[pos] = min_throws

    return least_throws[MAX_POSITIONS_ON_BOARD], predecessor
```

5.

A thief wants to steal from houses that are arranged in a line. The thief knows the value of the valuables in each house. If the thief steals from one house, then the owner of the house will alert the immediate left and right neighbors and the thief can't steal from the immediately neighboring houses. What is the maximum loot that the thief can steal?

We use dynamic programming to solve this problem. Let value[i] store the net worth of valuables in the ith house. Let max_loot[i] store the sum of values of the houses that the thief has stolen up to the ith house. When a thief encounters a house, he has only two choices: either he can steal from the house or he can skip the house.

Then we can use the following formula to compute the max_loot for each house

$$\text{max\_loot}[i] = \text{Maximum of} \begin{cases} 1.\ \text{max\_loot}[i-2] + \text{value}[i] \\ \quad \text{the thief has chosen to steal the current house} \\ \\ 2.\ \text{max\_loot}[i-1] \\ \quad \text{the thief has chosen to skip the current house} \end{cases}$$

The max_loot of the last house gives the maximum loot that the thief can steal from all the houses.

It is not necessary to maintain a complete list for storing max_loot. The max_loot of the two previous houses is sufficient to calculate the max_loot of the current house.

3.2 Dynamic Programming

```
#house_value: value that the thief can steal from each house
#Return value: maximum loot value that the thief can steal from all the houses
def find_max_loot(house_value) :
    n = len(house_value)

    if (n == 0):
        return 0

    if (n == 1):
        return house_value[0]

    if (n == 2):
        return max(house_value[0], house_value[1])

    #val1 has the max loot up to the previous house,
    #val2 has the max loot up to the second previous house
    val1 = max(house_value[0], house_value[1])
    val2 = house_value[0]

    cur_val = 0
    for  i in range(2, n):
        #cur_val stores the maximum loot up to the current house (i$^{th}$ house)
        cur_val = max(val2 + house_value[i], val1)

        #val2 now takes the value of val1 and val1 takes the current value
        val2 = val1
        val1 = cur_val

    return cur_val
```

6. Given a list A, where A[i] indicates the maximum number of positions we can jump from location i, find the minimum number of jumps needed to reach the end of the list from the beginning of the list.

Let the given list be A = [3, 5, 2, 2, 1, 1, 0]. This means that from A[0], the maximum number of locations we can jump is 3. So in a single jump from A[0], we can choose to land at A[1] or A[2] or A[3]. The minimum number of jumps needed to reach the end of the list in this example is 2: We can jump from A[0] to A[1] and then jump from A[1] to A[6].

To solve the problem, we make use of dynamic programming. Let min_jumps[i] indicate the minimum number of jumps needed to reach location i. We calculate min_jumps[i] = Min { min_jumps[j] + 1} where j < i and j + A[j] >= i

So to figure out the minimum number of jumps to reach location i, we are looking at all the previous locations (j < i). We can jump from location j to location i only if j + A[j] is >= i. Since we start at the list beginning, min_jumps[0] = 0. min_jumps [last location in the list] gives the minimum number of jumps needed to reach the end of the list

```
#a: a[i] contains the maximum number of locations we can jump from position i
#   list a should have at least 1 element
#Return value: minimum number of jumps needed to reach the end of the list
def find_min_jumps(a) :
    n = len(a)
    min_jumps = [MAX_INT] * n

    #Since we start from location 0, the number of jumps needed to
    #reach it is 0
    min_jumps[0] = 0

    for  i in range(1, n):
        #Compute the minimum number of jumps to reach location i by looking
        #at the previous locations 0 to i - 1
        for  j in range(i):
            if (j + a[j] >= i and min_jumps[j] + 1 < min_jumps[i]) :
                min_jumps[i] = min_jumps[j] + 1

    return min_jumps[n-1]
```

3.2 Dynamic Programming

7. If the number of nodes in a binary search tree (BST) is N, find the number of unique binary search trees that can be constructed with the N nodes.

If there is only one node in the BST, then only one unique BST can be constructed. If there are two nodes in the BST, then two unique BSTs can be constructed as shown below.

If there are more than 2 nodes in the BST, we make use of dynamic programming to solve the problem. Let num_bst[i] indicate the number of BSTs we can form with i nodes. num_bst[1] = 1 and num_bst[2] = 2. If there are N nodes, then one of the nodes will be the root. We can then distribute the remaining N-1 nodes between the left sub-tree and the right sub-tree. So we can have 0 nodes in the left sub-tree and N-1 nodes in the right sub-tree OR we can have 1 node in the left sub-tree and N-2 nodes in the right sub-tree ..... OR we can have N-1 nodes in the left sub-tree and 0 nodes in the right sub-tree. So if there are x nodes in the left sub-tree, there are $N - 1 - x$ nodes in the right sub-tree.

Now note that left sub-tree of a binary search tree is also a binary search tree by itself. Similarly the right sub-tree of a binary search tree is also a binary search tree by itself. So if there are x nodes in the left sub-tree, num_bst[x] will give the number of ways we can arrange the x nodes in the left sub-tree and num_bst[$N - 1 - x$] will give the number of ways we can arrange the remaining $N - 1 - x$ nodes in the right sub-tree. So the total number of ways we can arrange the nodes is num_bst[x] * num_bst[$N - 1 - x$].

If there are 0 nodes in the left sub-tree (x = 0), then remaining N-1 nodes will be in right sub-tree and the number of ways we can arrange the nodes = num_bst[$N - 1$]. So for the formula num_bst[x] * num_bst[N-1-x] to work for x = 0, we assume num_bst[0] = 1.

The formula for total number of BST's is then given by

num_bst[N] = $\sum$ num_bst[x] * num_bst[$N - 1 - x$], where x can range from 0 to N-1

The Big Book of Coding Interviews

Let us take an example. If N = 3, then

num_bst[3] = (num_bst[0] * num_bst[2]) + (num_bst[1] * num_bst[1]) + (num_bst[2] * num_bst[0])

num_bst[3] = (1 * 2) + (1 * 1) + (2 * 1) = 5

```
#n: total number of nodes in the binary search tree
#Return value: Number of unique binary search trees that can be constructed
#with n nodes
def find_num_unique_bst(n) :
    if (n <= 2):
        return n

    num_bst = [0] * (n+1)

    num_bst[0] = 1     #We are making this 1 to simplify the calculation
    num_bst[1] = 1
    num_bst[2] = 2

    for  i in range(3, n+1):
        #the left sub-tree size can vary from 0 to i-1
        #(one node has to be reserved for root)
        for   left_sub_tree_size in range(i):
                #Subtract the left subtree size and the root node to
                #get right subtree size
                right_sub_tree_size = i - 1 - left_sub_tree_size

                num_bst[i] += (num_bst[left_sub_tree_size] *
                                num_bst[right_sub_tree_size])

    return num_bst[n]
```

3.2 Dynamic Programming

8. We are given a rod of length L and a price list p, where p[i] indicates the price of a piece of the rod of length i. The rod can be sold as a single piece or by cutting into multiple pieces. Find the maximum value that can be obtained for the rod.

Consider the following price list p for the rod of length 5.

Length	0	1	2	3	4	5
Price	0	3	8	5	6	7

The best value that we can get is by cutting the rod into three pieces of length 2, 2 and 1. The value will be 8 + 8 + 3 = 19.

We can solve this problem using dynamic programming. We will construct a best_value list and store in it the best value that we can get for each length. To compute the best_value for the current length, we will break the rod into two pieces. The length of the first piece is i and this piece will not be broken down further. The remainder piece will have a length of (current length – i) and can be sub-divided. So the value for i can range from 1 to current length.

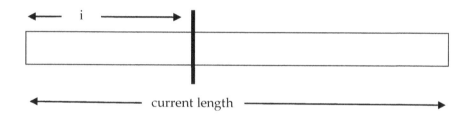

So best_value[current length] = max (price[i] + best_value[current length – i]) where i can range from 1 to current length.

If L is the total length of the rod, then best_value[L] will give the maximum value that we can obtain from the rod.

```
#price: price[i] gives the price of a rod of length i. price[0] is 0
#total_length: the total length of the rod given to us. Should be >= 1
#Return value: the best value that can be fetched from the rod
def cut_rod(price, total_length) :
    #Initialize best_value to 0
    best_value = [0] * (total_length + 1)

    #first_cut[i] will indicate the length of the first piece when we cut
    #the rod of length i. This is needed to print out where we should cut
    #so that we get the best value
    first_cut = [0] * (total_length + 1)

    for  cur_length in range(1, total_length+1):
        #We are cutting a rod whose length is cur_length
        #The length of the first piece after the cut can range from
        #1 to cur_length
        for  i in range(1, cur_length+1):
            if (price[i] + best_value[cur_length - i] >
                            best_value[cur_length]) :
                best_value[cur_length] = (price[i] +
                                best_value[cur_length - i])
                first_cut[cur_length] = i

    print_pieces(first_cut, total_length)

    return best_value[total_length]


#Helper function for printing out the sizes of the individual pieces
def print_pieces(first_cut, total_length) :
    print('The rod piece lengths are : ', end='')

    cur_length = total_length
    while (cur_length > 0 and first_cut[cur_length] > 0) :
        print('{} '.format(first_cut[cur_length]) , end='')
        cur_length = cur_length - first_cut[cur_length]


    print('')
```

3.2 Dynamic Programming

9. Find the maximum sum sub-matrix in a 2-D matrix. For instance, in the matrix

-10	20	30
-20	70	-10
10	-80	-60

the maximum sum sub-matrix is

20	30
70	-10

and the maximum sum is 20 + 30 + 70 − 10 = 110

The time complexity of the maximum sub-matrix sum problem can be reduced to $O(n^3)$ by using the Kadane's algorithm which we have already described in page 240.

Kadane's algorithm gives the maximum continuous sum in a 1-D (one dimensional) list in $O(n)$. To use Kadane's algorithm on a 2-D matrix, we sum up the elements in neighboring columns and store the result in a 1-D list. Kadane's algorithm is then applied on the 1-D list. Let us work out the procedure with an example.

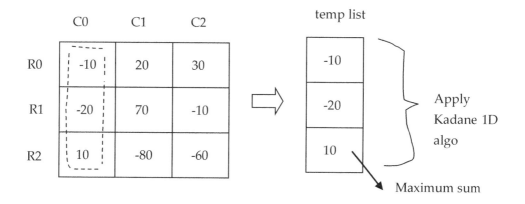

1. First we fix the start column to C0 and end column to C0. A 1-D temp list whose size is equal to the number of rows in the 2-D matrix is initialized to 0. The contents of column C0 are then added to the temp list and Kadane's algorithm is applied on the 1-D temp list. In this example, we get the result from Kadane's algorithm that 10 is the maximum

sum. This corresponds to row R2. Remember that our start column was C0, end column was C0. So the current maximum sum sub-matrix is the cell (R2, C0).

2. Then we keep start column at C0 and move end column to C1. The contents of column C1 are added to the temp list and Kadane's algorithm is applied on the 1-D temp list. We get the result from Kadane's algorithm that 60 (10 + 50) is the maximum sum. This corresponds to the rows R0, R1. The sum 60 is greater than the previous maximum of 10 and so 60 becomes the maximum submatrix sum and we update the current maximum sum sub-matrix to the region from cell (R0, C0) to the cell (R1, C1)

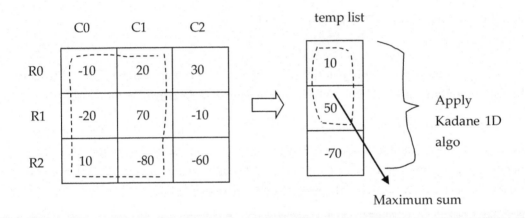

3. We then keep the start column at C0 and move the end column to C2 and add the contents of C2 to the temp list. Kadane's algorithm is applied to the temp list and we update the maximum sum sub-matrix if we get a higher value

4. We then change the start column to C1. When we change the start column, we re-initialize the temp list to 0. The end column is fixed at C1 and the above procedure is applied. Then the end column is moved to C2 and the same procedure is repeated.

5. Finally we change the start column to C2, reinitialize the temp list to 0, fix the end column to C2 and repeat the procedure to get the final result.

3.2 Dynamic Programming

The code for finding the maximum sum sub-matrix is given below. We are reusing the Kadane's algorithm explained in page 240.

```
#matrix: non-empty input matrix for which we have to find the maximum sum
#Return value: the sum of elements in the max sum sub-matrix in the input matrix
def find_max_sum_matrix(matrix) :
    n_rows = len(matrix)
    n_cols = len(matrix[0])

    max_sum = MIN_INT
    for  left_col in range(n_cols):
        #We have chosen a left column. Initialize the temporary list to 0
        #the temporary list will store the result of column additions
        a = [0 for i in range(n_rows)]

        #Iterate through the right side columns which are >= left column
        for  right_col in range(left_col, n_cols):

            #Add the elements in the current right column to list a
            for  i in range(n_rows):
                a[i] += matrix[i][right_col]

            #Find the maximum continuous sum of the 1-D list using
            #Kadane's algo. The start and end indices returned by Kadane's
            #algo will correspond to the start row and end row of the
            #2-D matrix
            cur_sum, start, end = kadane_mcs(a)

            if (cur_sum > max_sum) :
                max_sum = cur_sum

                #The maximum sum sub-matrix is bounded between
                #col1 = left_col, col2 = right_col, row1 = start
                #row2 = end

    return max_sum
```

The Big Book of Coding Interviews

10. Given a 2-D matrix with m rows and n columns, find the minimum cost path to reach the destination cell (m-1, n-1) starting from the source cell (0, 0). From any cell, the allowed moves are: right, down and diagonal

---

Consider the matrix A shown below. The minimum cost path is 5 ->2 ->3->1. The cost of the path is 5 + 2 + 3 + 1 = 11.

	0	1	2
0	5	3	1
1	2	6	5
2	9	3	1

To calculate the minimum cost path, we will use another 2-D matrix of the same dimensions called the cost matrix. The entries in the cost matrix are filled up in the following manner

1. cost[0][0] = A[0][0]

2. All cells in row 0 can be reached only by moving right from the starting cell (0, 0). So the cost reaching j^{th} cell in row 0 is cost[0][j] = cost[0][j-1] + A[0][j]

3. All cells in column 0 can be reached only by moving down from the starting cell (0, 0). So the cost of reaching the ith cell in column 0 is cost[i][0] = cost[i-1][0] + A[i][0]

4. The remaining cells can be reached by traversing down or right or diagonally from a preceding cell. So for the remaining cells, the minimum cost for reaching the cell is cost[i][j] = A[i][j] + min(cost[i-1][j], cost[i][j-1], cost[i-1][j-1])

3.2 Dynamic Programming

	0	1	2
0	5	5+3 = 8	8+1 = 9
1	5+2 = 7		
2	7+9 = 16		

Cost matrix after computing row 0 and column 0

	0	1	2
0	5	8	9
1	7	11	13
2	16	10	12

Final cost matrix

So in this example, cost[1][1] = 6 + min(5, 7, 8) = 6 + 5 = 11

If there are m rows and n columns, cost[m-1][n-1] will store the result. So in this example, cost[2][2] stores the cost of the minimum path which in this case is 12.

```
#a: non-empty 2D matrix in which we have to find the minimum cost path
#Return value: cost of the minimum path from (0, 0) to (num_rows-1, num_cols-1)
def find_min_path(a) :
    num_rows = len(a)
    num_cols = len(a[0])

    cost = [[0 for y in range(num_cols)] for x in range(num_rows)]
    cost[0][0] = a[0][0]

    for  i in range(1, num_rows):
        cost[i][0] = cost[i-1][0] + a[i][0]

    for  j in range(1, num_cols):
        cost[0][j] = cost[0][j-1] + a[0][j]

    for  i in range(1, num_rows):
        for  j in range(1, num_cols):
            cost[i][j] = a[i][j] + min(cost[i-1][j],
                                      cost[i][j-1], cost[i-1][j-1])

    return cost[num_rows - 1][num_cols - 1]
```

11. The strength of an egg can be found by dropping it from a floor in a building. For instance, if the egg doesn't break when dropped from floor 1, 2 and 3 but breaks when it is dropped from floor 4, then its strength is 3. Given N identical eggs and K floors in the building, find the minimum number of throws needed to find the strength of the egg.

We have to minimize the number of trials needed to find the strength of the egg. Let num_throws(N, K) represent the minimum number of throws needed to find the strength of the egg if we are given N eggs and K floors. Suppose we drop an egg from floor X, then there are two possibilities:

1. The egg breaks. In this case we are left with N-1 eggs and we have to find the strength of the egg in the X-1 floors. The number of throws needed will be 1 + num_throws(N-1, X-1). We have added 1 since we just used up 1 throw.

2. The egg doesn't break. In this case, we still have N eggs. We will have to try out the floors above floor X. There are K – X floors above floor X. The number of throws needed will be 1 + num_throws(N, K – X). We have added 1 since we just used up 1 throw.

We have to account for the worst case of the two possibilities since we don't know beforehand what we are going to encounter. So the number of throws needed from floor X is max(1 + num_throws (N-1, X-1), 1 + num_throws(N, K – X))

Now when we drop an egg, we have to intelligently pick which floor to drop from next. So given all K floors, each time we drop an egg, we need to pick the floor that needs the least number of throws. So

num_throws(N, K) = min (max(1 + num_throws (N-1, X-1), 1 + num_throws(N, K – X))
for all values of X from X = 1 to X = K)

To solve the problem, we make use of dynamic programming. If there is only 1 egg and there are K floors, then we need at least K throws to find the strength of the egg. If there are N eggs and only 1 floor, then we can perform only 1 throw. These details are filled up in the dynamic programming table below

3.2 Dynamic Programming

	floors					
eggs	0	1	2	3	4	5
0						
1		1	2	3	4	5
2		1				
3		1				
4		1				

Minimum number of throws needed

The remaining cells are filled up using the formula

num_throws(N, K) = min (max(1 + num_throws (N-1, X-1), 1 + num_throws(N, K – X))
  for all values of X from X = 1 to X = K)

At the end, the dynamic programming table will contain the result. Each cell in the table indicates the minimum number of throws needed for a particular number of eggs and a particular number of floors.

```
#num_eggs: total number of identical eggs available. should be >= 1
#num_floors: total number of floors available. should be >= 1
#Return value: minimum number of throws with which we can find egg strength
def find_min_egg_drops(num_eggs, num_floors) :
    min_throws = [[0 for y in range(num_floors + 1)] for x in
                                        range(num_eggs + 1)]

    #If there is only 1 floor, we need only 1 throw
    for  cur_egg in range(1, num_eggs+1):
        min_throws[cur_egg][1] = 1

    #If there is only 1 egg and k floors, we need k throws
    for  cur_floor in range(1, num_floors+1):
        min_throws[1][cur_floor] = cur_floor
```

```
for  cur_egg in range(2, num_eggs+1):
    for  cur_floor in range(2, num_floors+1):
            min_throws[cur_egg][cur_floor] = MAX_INT

            for  floor_iter in range(1, cur_floor+1):
                    #Find the number of throws needed from floor_iter
                    num_throws = max(
                            1 + min_throws[cur_egg - 1][floor_iter - 1],
                            1 + min_throws[cur_egg][cur_floor -floor_iter])

                    if (min_throws[cur_egg][cur_floor] > num_throws):
                            min_throws[cur_egg][cur_floor] = num_throws

return min_throws[num_eggs][num_floors]
```

3.2 Dynamic Programming

	floors	0	1	2	3	4	5
eggs	0						
	1		1	2	3	4	5
	2		1				
	3		1				
	4		1				

Minimum number of throws needed

The remaining cells are filled up using the formula

num_throws(N, K) = min (max(1 + num_throws (N-1, X-1), 1 + num_throws(N, K – X))
for all values of X from X = 1 to X = K)

At the end, the dynamic programming table will contain the result. Each cell in the table indicates the minimum number of throws needed for a particular number of eggs and a particular number of floors.

```
#num_eggs: total number of identical eggs available. should be >= 1
#num_floors: total number of floors available. should be >= 1
#Return value: minimum number of throws with which we can find egg strength
def find_min_egg_drops(num_eggs, num_floors) :
    min_throws = [[0 for y in range(num_floors + 1)] for x in
                                            range(num_eggs + 1)]

    #If there is only 1 floor, we need only 1 throw
    for  cur_egg in range(1, num_eggs+1):
        min_throws[cur_egg][1] = 1

    #If there is only 1 egg and k floors, we need k throws
    for  cur_floor in range(1, num_floors+1):
        min_throws[1][cur_floor] = cur_floor
```

```python
for cur_egg in range(2, num_eggs+1):
    for cur_floor in range(2, num_floors+1):
        min_throws[cur_egg][cur_floor] = MAX_INT

        for floor_iter in range(1, cur_floor+1):
            #Find the number of throws needed from floor_iter
            num_throws = max(
                1 + min_throws[cur_egg - 1][floor_iter - 1],
                1 + min_throws[cur_egg][cur_floor -floor_iter])

            if (min_throws[cur_egg][cur_floor] > num_throws):
                min_throws[cur_egg][cur_floor] = num_throws

return min_throws[num_eggs][num_floors]
```

3.2 Dynamic Programming

12. Given a dictionary of words, find if a string can be broken into the words in the dictionary. For instance, if the dictionary contains the words "play", "now", "will" and "i", then the string "nowiwillplay" can be broken into the words in the dictionary

---

To solve the problem, we make use of dynamic programming. We maintain a list is_break_possible. If the substring from position 0 to position i of the original string can be broken into words of the dictionary, then is_break_possible[i] will be set to True. Let the string be "nowiwillplay".

1. We will generate all the prefixes of the string namely "n", "no", "now", "nowi", "nowiw", "nowiwi", "nowiwil", "nowiwill", etc. and check if each prefix is present in the dictionary. If the prefix ending at position i is present in the dictionary, then is_break_possible[i] will be True. In this case, since "now" is present in the dictionary and the prefix "now" ends at position 2 in the original string, is_break_possible[2] will be True.

2. If is_break_possible[i] is True, we will check all the substrings that start from position i+1 if they are in the dictionary. If the substring starting at position i+1 and ending at position j is present in the dictionary, then we will make is_break_possible[j] True. Since is_break_possible[2] is True, we will check the substrings starting at position 3 of the original string, namely "i", "iw", "iwi", "iwil" and "iwill", etc. Only "i" is present in the dictionary. "i" ends at position 3 in the original string. So we will set is_break_possible[3] to True.

We apply steps 1 and 2 for the input string. At the end, if is_break_possible is set to True for the position of the last character in the input string, then we can say that the string can be broken into words in the dictionary. The position of the last character in the string "nowiwillplay" is 10. Since is_break_possible[10] is True, we conclude that it is possible to break the string into words in the dictionary.

Note that if the input word is "now", then the above algorithm will return True. If we want to return True only for the truly compound input words that can be broken into two or more dictionary words, then we add an additional check that the starting position of the word corresponding to the last character in the input string should not be 0. The code below returns True for words that can be broken into two or more dictionary words.

```python
#str1: string that we need to check if it can be broken
#dictionary: permitted words are stored in the dictionary
#Return value: True if we can break str1 into words in the dictionary
def word_break(str1, dictionary) :
    length = len(str1)

    if (length == 0):
        return False

    #if we can break the string from 0 to pos, then is_break_possible[pos]
    #will be True
    is_break_possible = [False] * length

    #if the substring from position i to position j of the original string
    #is a word in dictionary, then word_start[j] will be i
    word_start = [-1] * length

    for i in range(length):
        #Check if the substring from 0 to i is in the dictionary
        temp_str = str1[0:i+1]
        if (not is_break_possible[i] and temp_str in dictionary) :
            is_break_possible[i] = True
            word_start[i] = 0

        #If we can break the substring upto i into dictionary words,
        #then check if all substrings starting from i+1 can be broken
        #into dictionary words
        if (is_break_possible[i]) :
            for j in range(i + 1, length):
                temp_str = str1[i+1:j+1]
                if (not is_break_possible[j]
                    and temp_str in dictionary) :
                        #We can form a word from i+1 to j
                        is_break_possible[j] = True
                        word_start[j] = i+1

    #If is_break_possible[length-1] is True, then entire string can be
    #broken into dictionary words. If the word_start[length-1] is 0, then
    #it means the entire input word is present in the dictionary. But we
    #want a compound word that has 2 or more dictionary words in it.
    #So modify the result condition to check word_start[length-1] != 0
    if (is_break_possible[length-1] and word_start[length-1] != 0):
        print_result(str1, word_start)
        return True

    return False
```

3.2 Dynamic Programming

```python
#Helper function to print the words present in the string
#str1: input string
#word_start: if the substring from position i to position j of the original
#    string is a word in dictionary, then word_start[j] will be i
def print_result(str1, word_start) :
    pos = len(str1) - 1
    while (pos >= 0) :
        #The current word ends at pos in the input string and
        #starts at word_start[pos]
        start = word_start[pos]
        print( str1[start : pos + 1] + ' ', end='')
        pos = word_start[pos] - 1
```

The Big Book of Coding Interviews

13. Given a group of 3 dimensional boxes where length, breadth and height are specified, find the height of the tallest stack of boxes that can be constructed. Box B can be stacked on top of Box A only if the length **and** breadth of the base of Box B is **strictly smaller** than Box A. For each box, multiple instances of the box are available.

The length and breadth of the box will form the base of the box. Without loss of generality, we will pick the dimension with the greater value as length and the other dimension as breadth

Suppose we are given only one box A with the dimensions (10, 20, 30). Then there are 3 possible orientations of the box: A1 (height = 10, length = 30, breadth = 20), A2 (height = 20, length = 30, breadth = 10) and A3 (height = 30, length= 20, breadth = 10). Note that the problem states that multiple instances of the box are available. So we can pick all 3 possible orientations for the same box and check if one or more of them are feasible while constructing the stack of boxes. To construct the tallest stack, we place A1 at the bottom and then A3 on top of A1. Note that we can't place A2 on top of A1, since length of A2 (30) is not smaller than length of A1 (30). The height of the tallest stack = 10 + 30 = 40.

In general, given N boxes, to solve the problem we make use of dynamic programming.

1. For each box, generate all the 3 possible orientations and store them in a list. So if there are N boxes input, the list will store 3*N boxes. From now on we will be dealing with these 3*N boxes.

2. Sort the list so that boxes with larger base area are arranged earlier than those with smaller base area

3. Let best_height[i] be the height of the tallest stack built by placing box i on top of the stack. Initialize best_height[i] to the height of box i.

4. Use the formula below to update the best_height

best_height[i] = { Max(best_height[j] + height of box i} where j < i and length of box i < length of box j and breadth of box i < breadth of box j

So we are basically looking at boxes with larger area on top of whom box i can be placed

5. The maximum value in best_height list gives the height of the tallest stack of boxes.

3.2 Dynamic Programming

```
#a: list of boxes of different dimensions. Should contain at least one box
#Result: maximum height of the stack of boxes that can be constructed.
#Assumption is that multiple instances of each box are available
def max_stack_height(a) :
    num_input_boxes = len(a)
    boxes = []

    #For each box, all 3 orientations are possible. Length will always be
    #greater than breadth
    for  cur_box in a:
        new_box = Box()
        new_box.height = cur_box.height
        new_box.length = max(cur_box.length, cur_box.breadth)
        new_box.breadth = min(cur_box.length, cur_box.breadth)
        boxes.append(new_box)

        new_box = Box()
        new_box.height  = cur_box.length
        new_box.length  = max(cur_box.breadth, cur_box.height)
        new_box.breadth = min(cur_box.breadth, cur_box.height)
        boxes.append(new_box)

        new_box = Box()
        new_box.height  = cur_box.breadth
        new_box.length  = max(cur_box.length, cur_box.height)
        new_box.breadth = min(cur_box.length, cur_box.height)
        boxes.append(new_box)

    num_boxes = 3 * num_input_boxes

    #Sort the boxes so that the boxes with larger base area appear first
    boxes.sort(key = lambda x: -1 * x.length * x.breadth)

    best_height = []
    for  cur_box in boxes:
        best_height.append(cur_box.height)

    for  i in range(1, num_boxes):
        for  j in range(i):
            #We can place box i on box j, only if base of box i
            #is smaller than the base of box j
            if (boxes[i].length < boxes[j].length
            and boxes[i].breadth < boxes[j].breadth):
                    if (best_height[i] <
                    best_height[j] + boxes[i].height) :
                        best_height[i] = (best_height[j] +
                                                  boxes[i].height)

    #Find the stack with the maximum height
    result = max(best_height)

    return result
```

3.3 Miscellaneous Algorithms

1. There are n nuts and n bolts of distinct sizes in a box. For each bolt there is a matching nut and vice versa. We are allowed to compare only a nut with a bolt. Comparison of a nut with another nut or a bolt with another bolt is not allowed. Find the matching pairs of nuts and bolts.

If we are allowed to compare a nut with another nut or a bolt with another bolt, then we can solve the problem in O(nlogn) by sorting. We can sort all the nuts independently and all the bolts independently to find the matching pair of nuts and bolts. However direct comparison is not allowed.

In the brute force approach, we can pick a bolt and compare it with all the nuts until we find the matching nut and repeat this process for all the bolts. The time complexity will be $O(n^2)$.

There is a better approach that has an average time complexity of O(nlogn) similar to the quicksort algorithm. Let the bolts be stored in the list B and the nuts be stored in the list N. The procedure is as follows:

1.) Pick a bolt at random. This bolt acts as the pivot in quicksort. Compare the pivot bolt with each nut and partition the nuts into three groups: group N1 which has nuts smaller than the pivot bolt, group N2 which has the nut that exactly matches the pivot bolt and group N3 which has nuts that are larger than the pivot bolt.

2.) Pick the nut that exactly matched the pivot bolt. Now make this nut as the pivot nut. Compare the pivot nut with each bolt and partition the bolts into three groups: group B1 which has the bolts smaller than the pivot nut, group B2 which has the pivot bolt which matches the pivot nut and group B3 which has the bolts that are larger than the pivot nut.

3.) Recursively repeat steps 1 and 2 for the partitions N1 and B1. Then recursively repeat the steps 1 and 2 for the partitions N2 and B2.

At the end, we will have sorted the nuts and bolts without directly comparing a nut to a nut and a bolt to a bolt and we will know the matching pairs.

2. Place N queens on a chess board so that they can't attack each other

N queens on the chess board will be in non-attacking positions if:

1. Each row has only 1 queen.

2. Each column has only 1 queen

3. None of the queens are in the same diagonal.

To find the non-attacking positions of the queens, we make use of recursion and backtracking. In each row, we place a queen in a cell which is not attacking with the other queens placed so far and then move to the next row. Suppose we can't place the queen in any of the cells in the current row, then we back-track to the previous row and pick the next possible cell for the queen in the previous row.

To keep the storage requirements small, we will maintain a list col_for_row that stores the positions of the queens. If we place a queen at cell (row = i, column = j), then col_for_row[i] = j.

Consider two cells (x1, y1) and (x2, y2). The two cells are in the same diagonal if the absolute difference between their rows is equal to the absolute difference between their columns. So if abs(x2 – x1) is equal to abs(y2 – y1), then the cells are diagonal.

```
#Helper function which checks if it is possible to place queen in cur_row
#at position col_for_row[cur_row]
#cur_row: Row in which the current queen should be placed
#col_for_row: col_for_row[i] gives the column in which queen is placed in the
# ith row
#Return value: True if queen can be placed at col_for_row[cur_row], False
# otherwise
def check_placement(cur_row, col_for_row) :
    #Check if the queens placed in the rows before the current row conflict
    #with the queen placed in current row
    for  i in range(cur_row):
        #Check if two queens are present in the same column
```

```python
        if (col_for_row[i] == col_for_row[cur_row]):
            return False

        #Check if two queens are in the same diagonal
        col_diff = abs(col_for_row[cur_row] - col_for_row[i])
        row_diff = cur_row - i
        if (row_diff == col_diff):
            return False

    return True



#Main function for arranging the queens
#cur_row: current row in which the queen should be placed
#N: the number of cells in one row of the chess board
#col_for_row: col_for_row[i] is used for storing the column of the ith row queen
def arrange_queens(cur_row, N, col_for_row) :
    if (cur_row == N) :
        #We have found a successful arrangement. So print it
        for  i in range(N):
            print('Row = {}, Col =  {}'.format(i, col_for_row[i]) )

        print('_____')

        return #Terminate the recursion

    #Try out different columns in the current row
    for  i in range(N):
        col_for_row[cur_row] = i
        if (check_placement(cur_row, col_for_row)) :
            #The placements of queens looks good so far. Go to the next row
            arrange_queens(cur_row + 1, N, col_for_row)
```

3.3 Miscellaneous Algorithms

3. Given an equation in which only numbers are specified, fill in the operators + and − to get the required result. For instance, if equation without operators is 10 __ 20 __ 50 = 40, then we should fill in the operators as 10 − 20 + 50 = 40.

We use recursion and backtracking to solve the problem. The numbers of the equation will be stored in a list. We generate all possible combinations of operators between the numbers and check if we get the right hand side value of the equation.

```
#Helper function that evaluates the numbers and operators
#a: list of numbers. Should have at least one element
#operators: list of operators (+, -) to be applied on numbers
def evaluate(a, operators) :
    result = a[0]
    for  i in range(1, len(a)):
        if (operators[i-1] == '+'):
                result += a[i]
        else:
                result -= a[i]

    return result


#a: list of numbers. Should have at least one element
#rhs: right hand side of the equation
#operators: list for storing the operators to be applied on the numbers
#num_operators: number of operators that have been filled in so far
#Return value: True if we can get the rhs by placing operators between numbers
def fill_operators(a, rhs, operators, num_operators) :
    if (num_operators == len(a) - 1) :
        #We have filled in all the operators. So evaluate the result and
        #terminate the recursion
        result = evaluate(a, operators)
        if (result == rhs) :
                return True
        else:
                return False

    #Fill in + as the next operator and try out
    operators[num_operators] = '+'
    is_possible = fill_operators(a, rhs, operators, num_operators + 1)
    if (is_possible):
        return True

    #Fill in - as the next operator and try out
    operators[num_operators] = '-'
    is_possible = fill_operators(a, rhs, operators, num_operators + 1)

    return is_possible
```

4. Implement a Sudoku solver

The Sudoku grid is a square of size 9 * 9. The rules of Sudoku are as follows:

1. Each cell contains a number from 1 to 9

2. A number should not be repeated in the same row or the same column

3. The grid is further sub-divided into squares of 3*3 called boxes. A number should also not be repeated in the same box.

In the Sudoku puzzle, the puzzle writer fills up some of the cells with numbers and we have to fill up the remaining cells. To solve Sudoku, we make use of recursion and backtracking. Given a cell, we recursively try out all possible numbers that can be filled up in the cell. So we fill a cell with a possible number and then move to the next cell. Suppose we hit a dead-end at a cell and can't fill it with any number, then we back-track to the previous cell, try out the next possible number in the previous cell and proceed. To distinguish between the cells filled up by the puzzle writer and the other cells, we initialize the other cells with -1.

```python
#Helper function which checks if it is possible to place a number in a cell
#grid: the 2-D sudoku matrix
#row_nr: row number of the cell we are checking
#col_nr: column number of the cell we are checking
#num: the number which we want to place in the cell
#Returns: True if we can place num in the cell, False otherwise
def can_fill_cell(grid, row_nr, col_nr, num) :
    #Ensure that the number is not present in any row of requested column
    for i in range(NUM_ROWS):
        if (grid[i][col_nr] == num):
            return False

    #Ensure that the number is not present in any column of requested row
    for j in range(NUM_COLS):
        if (grid[row_nr][j] == num):
            return False

    #Ensure that the number is not present in the 3*3 box it belongs to
    region_start_row = (row_nr // 3) * 3
    region_start_col = (col_nr // 3) * 3
```

```python
        for i in range(region_start_row, region_start_row + 3):
            for j in range(region_start_col, region_start_col + 3):
                if (grid[i][j] == num):
                    return False

    return True


#Main function for solving the sudoku puzzle
#grid: the 2-D sudoku matrix
#row_nr: row number of the current cell being processed
#col_nr: column number of the current cell being processed
def solve_sudoku(grid, row_nr, col_nr) :
    if (row_nr >= NUM_ROWS) :
        #We have found a solution. print the grid and
        #terminate the recursion
        print_grid(grid, True)
        return

    #Pre-compute the row and column of the next cell
    next_row = row_nr
    next_col = col_nr + 1
    if (next_col >= NUM_COLS) :
        next_col = 0
        next_row = row_nr + 1

    if (grid[row_nr][col_nr] == -1) :
        #The puzzle writer has not assigned a number to this cell.
        #So try assigning numbers 1-9 to the cell
        for num in range(1, 10):
            if (can_fill_cell(grid, row_nr, col_nr, num)) :
                grid[row_nr][col_nr] = num
                solve_sudoku(grid, next_row, next_col)

        #Once we are done trying all numbers from 1-9, assign the cell
        #back to -1 to indicate puzzle writer has not assigned a number
        #to the cell
        grid[row_nr][col_nr] = -1

    else :
        #The puzzle writer has already assigned a value to the cell.
        #So proceed to the next cell
        solve_sudoku(grid, next_row, next_col)
```

The Big Book of Coding Interviews

5. Find the longest compound word in a given list of words. For instance, in the list [box, big, toybox, toy, bigbox, bigtoybox], the longest compound word is bigtoybox

---

We have already solved the problem of breaking a compound word into simple words in page 264. To find the longest compound word, we again make use of this algorithm as described below:

1. Take each word in the list and add it into a dictionary. So the dictionary consists only of the words in the given list

2. Sort the words in the list in the descending (non-increasing) order of length so that longer words appear first.

3. Pick each word in the sorted list and check if the word can be broken into two or more simple words in the dictionary using the word_break algorithm in page 264. If yes, then we have found the longest compound word.

```
#words: the input list of words
#Return value:  the longest compound word if it exists, None otherwise
def find_longest_compound_word(words) :
    dictionary = {}

    #Create the dictionary from the input list of words
    for cur_word in words :
        dictionary[cur_word] = 1

    #Sort the words so that the longest word appears first
    words.sort(key = lambda x: -1 * len(x))

    #Starting from the longest word, check if the word can be broken into
    #two or more words present in the dictionary. If yes, then we have
    #found the longest compound word
    for cur_word in words :
        if (word_break(cur_word, dictionary)):
            return cur_word

    #There is no compound word in the input
    return None
```

Note that instead of a dictionary we could have used a set. But the word_break function operates on a dictionary. So we are using a dictionary here.

3.3 Miscellaneous Algorithms

6. A person has travelled from city A to city B by transiting through one or more cities. Each ticket indicates the start city and the end city for each leg of the journey. However the tickets have been jumbled up. Reconstruct the travel path taken by the person using the jumbled tickets. There are no cycles in the path. For instance, if the tickets are [Tokyo -> Beijing], [LA -> San Francisco], [Hawaii -> Tokyo] and [San Francisco -> Hawaii], then the travel path is LA -> San Francisco -> Hawaii -> Tokyo -> Beijing.

To solve the problem, we need to do two things:

1. Given the current city, we quickly need to find the next city that the person is going to visit. For this purpose, we make use of a dictionary called next_hop. The next_hop will store the current city as the key and the next city as the value. So if the person travels from Tokyo to Beijing, Tokyo will be the key and Beijing will be the corresponding value.

2. We need to find the starting city of the journey. For this, we make use of a set called destinations. If a person travels from city A to city B, then city B will be stored in destinations. To find the starting city, we check all cities in the destinations set and the city which is not present in it will be the starting city (since there are no cycles in the journey).

So using the destinations set, we find the starting city and then using the next hop dictionary, we go on finding the next city of the journey and reconstruct the travel path of the person.

```
#tickets: list which stores the information about the tickets bought.
#    ticket[i][0] stores the starting city of the i$^{th}$ ticket
#    ticket[i][1] stores the destination city of the i$^{th}$ ticket
#    There should be no loop in the trip
#    There should be at least 1 ticket
#Return value: list containing the names of cities in the order of travel
def reconstruct_trip(tickets) :
    num_tickets = len(tickets)
    next_hop = {}
    destinations = set()

    #Store the starting city (key) and destination city (value) in next_hop
    #dictionary. Store the destination cities in destinations set
    for  start, dest in tickets:
        next_hop[start] = dest
        destinations.add(dest)

    #Search the starting city of each ticket in the destinations
    #Only the first city of the entire trip will NOT be in destinations
```

```
start_index = -1
i = 0
for  start, dest in tickets:
    if (start not in destinations) :
            #We didn't find the city in the destinations.
            #So this must be the first city of the entire trip
            start_index = i
            break
    i += 1

if (start_index == -1):
    return None

result = []

#add the first city of entire trip into the result
result.append(tickets[start_index][0])

#Search for the first city of the entire trip in the next_hop dictionary
next_city = next_hop.get(tickets[start_index][0])

while (next_city) :
    #Store the destination city in the result
    result.append(next_city)

    #make the destination city as the next starting city
    #and search for it in the next_hop dictionary
    next_city = next_hop.get(next_city)

return result
```

3.3 Miscellaneous Algorithms

7. A 2-dimensional matrix consists of 0's and 1's. An island is defined as a contiguous occurrence of 1's that are adjacent to each other. Find the number of islands in the matrix

---

If there are two adjacent cells (left-right neighbors, top-down neighbors, diagonally adjacent neighbors) with a value 1, then the two cells belong to the same island. In the matrix below there are 3 islands. The cells A0, B1, C0, D0 and E0 form one island. The cells A3, B3, C3 and B4 form one island. The cell E3 forms the remaining island.

	0	1	2	3	4
A	1	0	0	1	0
B	0	1	0	1	1
C	1	0	0	1	0
D	1	0	0	0	0
E	1	0	0	1	0

To find the number of islands, we make use of recursion. Once we find a cell whose value is 1, we start with the neighbors of this cell and recursively visit all cells that are reachable from this cell. To prevent from going into loops, we keep track if a cell has been visited or not and once a cell has been visited, we don't visit it again.

A similar problem is the flood fill problem. The color at each pixel of an image is stored in a 2 dimensional matrix. Given the starting pixel and the new color, we have to change the color of all adjacent pixels that have the same color as the starting pixel. So if the starting pixel A[2][3] is red and the new color is blue, then we have to recursively find all red cells that are reachable from A[2][3] and change their color to blue.

In some cases, diagonal neighbors may not be considered as adjacent. It is better to clarify this with the interviewer.

```python
#Helper function that indicates if we can enter the cell or not
def can_enter_cell(matrix, is_visited, cur_row, cur_col) :
    n_rows = len(matrix)
    n_cols = len(matrix[0])

    #If we are outside the bounds of the matrix or
    #if the cell is already visited or if the value in cell is 0
    #then we shouldn't enter the cell
    if (cur_row < 0 or cur_row >= n_rows
        or cur_col < 0 or cur_col >= n_cols
        or is_visited[cur_row][cur_col]
        or matrix[cur_row][cur_col] == 0) :
        return False


    return True


#Helper function to count the number of islands of 1's
#matrix: 2-D matrix consisting of 0's and 1's
#is_visited: if cell (i, j) has been visited, is_visited[i][j] is set to True
#cur_row: row of the current cell being processed
#cur_col: column of the current cell being processed
def expand_search(matrix, is_visited, cur_row, cur_col) :
    n_rows = len(matrix)
    n_cols = len(matrix[0])

    is_visited[cur_row][cur_col] = True

    #For the current cell, find out if we can continue the island of 1's
    #with its neighbors. Each cell has 8 neighbors. The rows
    #of neighbors will vary from cur_row - 1 to cur_row + 1
    #The columns of the neighbors will vary from cur_col - 1
    #to cur_col + 1
    for i in range(-1, 2):
        for j in range(-1, 2):
            is_safe_cell = can_enter_cell(matrix, is_visited, cur_row+i,
                                                    cur_col+j)

            if (is_safe_cell) :
                expand_search(matrix, is_visited, cur_row+i, cur_col+j)
```

3.3 Miscellaneous Algorithms

```python
#Main function to find the number of islands of 1's
#matrix: 2-D matrix consisting of 0's and 1's. Should not be empty
def find_islands(matrix) :
    n_rows = len(matrix)
    n_cols = len(matrix[0])
    is_visited = [ [False for x in range(n_cols)] for x in range(n_rows)]

    #Search all the cells in matrix that are not yet visited
    count = 0
    for  i in range(n_rows):
        for  j in range(n_cols):
            if (matrix[i][j] == 1 and not is_visited[i][j]) :
                    #We have found an island. Now expand the island
                    #in all directions
                    expand_search(matrix, is_visited, i, j)
                    count += 1

    return count
```

8. Find the number of inversions in a list. If i < j and A[i] > A[j], then this constitutes an inversion.

We can use the brute force technique to find the number of inversions by comparing every pair of elements in the list. This can be done in $O(n^2)$. We can improve the time complexity to $O(n\log n)$ using the divide and conquer technique. We perform merge sort on the list and as we sort the list we calculate the number of inversions in it.

Let merge_sort(A, x, y) be the function that sorts the list A between index x and y and returns the number of inversions between indices x and y. Let merge(A, x, y, z) be the function that merges two sorted regions (x, y) and (y+1, z) in list A and returns the number of inversions between the two regions. Then we can recursively calculate the number of inversions between index low and index high as: number of inversions = merge_sort(A, low, mid) + merge_sort(A, mid+1, high) + merge(A, low, mid, high), where mid = (low + high) / 2

We need to now figure out how to calculate the number of inversions we encounter when we merge two sorted regions in the list. Let us say that we are merging region-1 (A[2] to A[5]) with region-2 (A[6] to A[7]). Index i is used to access region-1 and index j is used to access region-2.

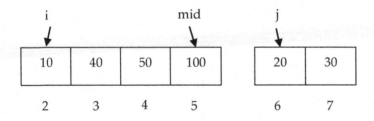

Initially i= 2 and j = 6. Since A[i] is smaller than A[j] and the two regions are sorted, we are sure that A[i] will be smaller than all elements after j in region-2. So we will not have any inversions in this case. We will then advance i to the next index

3.3 Miscellaneous Algorithms

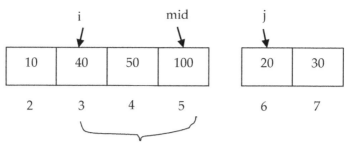

All these elements are > A[j]

Now i = 3 and j = 6. A[i] is greater than A[j]. Since region-1 is sorted, all elements in A from i onwards up to mid will be greater than A[j] and so these form inversions. The total number of elements from index i to index mid is mid + 1 – i. In this case mid = 5. So the total number of inversions = 5 + 1 – 3 = 3. The inversions are (40, 20), (50, 20) and (100, 20).

So while merging two sorted regions, each time we encounter an element at index i in the first region which is higher than the element at index j in the second region, we add mid + 1 – i to the number of inversions.

```
#Helper function that merges two sorted regions
#a: list where a[left] to a[mid] is sorted and a[mid+1] to a[right] is sorted
#   We now need to merge these two regions
#temp: temporary list used for sorting
#Return value: Number of inversions
def merge(a, temp, left, mid, right) :
   num_inversions = 0

   i = left
   j = mid + 1
   k = left #k is used for storing the merged values into temp
   while (i <= mid and j <= right) :
      if (a[i] <= a[j]) :
            temp[k] = a[i]
            k += 1
            i += 1
      else :
            temp[k] = a[j]
            k += 1
            j += 1
            num_inversions += mid + 1 - i

   #Handle any pending entries in first region
   while (i <= mid) :
      temp[k] = a[i]
      k += 1
      i += 1
```

```
        #Handle any pending entries in second region
        while (j <= right):
            temp[k] = a[j]
            k += 1
            j += 1

        #Restore the values from temp into a
        for  i in range(left, right+1):
            a[i] = temp[i]

        return num_inversions


#Helper function that performs merge sort
#a: list that should be sorted
#temp: temporary list used for sorting
#left: first index of the region in the list to be sorted
#right: last index of the region in the list to be sorted
#Return value: Number of inversions
def merge_sort(a, temp, left, right) :
    if (left >= right):
        return 0

    mid = (left + right) // 2

    num_inversions = merge_sort(a, temp, left, mid)

    num_inversions += merge_sort(a, temp, mid + 1, right)

    num_inversions += merge(a, temp, left, mid, right)

    return num_inversions


#a: list of numbers. should have at least one number
#Return value: number of inversions
def find_inversions(a) :
    num_elements = len(a)

    temp = [0] * num_elements

    num_inversions =  merge_sort(a, temp, 0, num_elements - 1)

    return num_inversions
```

3.3 Miscellaneous Algorithms

9. Calculate the maximum amount of water that can be trapped in a histogram

Consider the histogram below. The water that can be stored in the histogram is shaded.

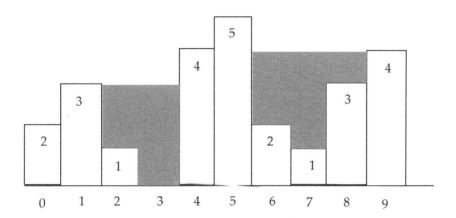

To efficiently find the amount of water that can be trapped in the histogram, we make use of the technique below and solve the problem in O(n).

1. We maintain two additional lists: left_max and right_max

2. Traverse from the left of the histogram to the right and for each index i, store the height of the tallest bar encountered so far in left_max[i]. So left_max[i] will store the tallest bar in the region (0, i). Note that the height of the ith bar is also considered while computing left_max[i]

3. Traverse from the right of the histogram to the left and for each index i, store the height of the tallest bar encountered so far in right_max[i]. So right_max[i] will store the tallest bar in the region (i, n-1) where n is the total number of histogram bars. Note that the height of the ith bar is also considered while computing right_max[i]

The amount of water that can be stored above the ith bar in the histogram = min(left_max[i], right_max[i]) – height of the ith bar. The sum of the amount of water over each bar will give the total amount of water that can be trapped in the histogram

The Big Book of Coding Interviews

The table below gives the calculation for the amount of water that can be stored above each bar in the histogram

index i	left_max[i]	right_max[i]	min(left_max[i], right_max[i])	height of ith bar	Amount of water
0	2	5	2	2	2 – 2 = 0
1	3	5	3	3	3 – 3 = 0
2	3	5	3	1	3 - 1 = 2
3	3	5	3	0	3 - 0 = 3
4	4	5	4	4	4 – 4 = 0
5	5	5	5	5	5 – 5 = 0
6	5	4	4	2	4 – 2 = 2
7	5	4	4	1	4 – 1 = 3
8	5	4	4	3	4 – 3 = 1
9	5	4	4	4	4 – 4 = 0

The total amount of water that can be stored = 2 + 3 + 2 + 3 + 1 = 11

```
#histogram: histogram[i] contains the height of the bar at location i
#   histogram should consist of at least one bar
#Return value: amount of water that can be trapped by the histogram
def water_trap(histogram) :
    n = len(histogram) #number of bars in the histogram
    left_max = [0] * n
    right_max = [0] * n

    #The left max of bar i is the height of the tallest bar in the
    #region (0, i). Note that region (0, i) includes 0 and i
    left_max[0] = histogram[0]
    for  i in range(1, n):
        left_max[i] = max(left_max[i-1], histogram[i])


    #The right max of bar i is the height of the tallest bar in the
    #region (i, n-1). Note that region (i, n-1) includes i and n-1
    total_water = 0
    right_max[n-1] = histogram[n-1]
    for  i in range(n - 2, -1,-1):
        #Compute the right max and simultaneously calculate the
        #amount of water that can be trapped
        right_max[i] = max(right_max[i+1], histogram[i])

        smaller_max = min(left_max[i], right_max[i])

        #calculate the amount of water that can be stored
        #on top of the histogram bar i
        total_water += smaller_max - histogram[i]

    return total_water
```

3.3 Miscellaneous Algorithms

10. Calculate the area of the largest rectangle possible in a histogram

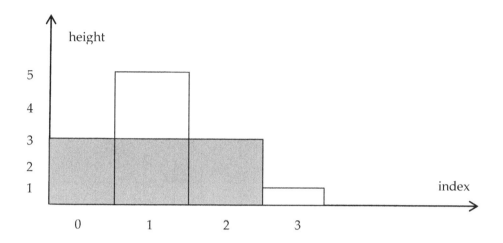

The largest possible rectangle in the histogram above has been shaded. The area of the largest rectangle is 9. To find the area of the largest rectangle in O(n) we make use of two stacks: one stack for storing the height of a histogram bar and another stack for storing the index of the histogram bar. We pick up each bar in the histogram and perform the following steps:

1. If the height of the current bar is > than the topmost element in the height stack, then push the height of the current bar into the height stack and push the index of the current bar into the index stack

2. If the height of the current bar is equal to the topmost element in the height stack, then do nothing

3. If the height of the current bar is < than the topmost element in the height stack, then keep popping the elements from the height stack and index stack until the height of the current bar becomes >= the topmost element in height stack. For each popped bar, compute the area of rectangle from the popped bar to the current bar. The length of the rectangle = (index of current bar − index of popped bar). The breadth of rectangle = height of the popped bar. Finally push the height of the current bar into the height stack and index of the last popped element into the index stack (not the index of the current bar). This is because all the popped bars are taller than the current bar and we can form a rectangle from current bar to the last popped element where the height of rectangle is

equal to the height of the current bar. For instance, for the histogram shown in the diagram, we perform the following steps

1. Push height and index of first bar

| 3 | height stack

| 0 | index stack

2. Height of 2nd bar (5) is > top of stack(3). So push height and index of 2nd bar

| 5 |
| 3 | height stack

| 1 |
| 0 | index stack

3. Height of 3rd bar (3) is < top of stack(5). So pop the height and index stack until top of stack is <= height of current bar. The height of the popped element (5) and the difference in index of popped element from current bar (2 – 1 = 1) is used to calculate the area of rectangle (5 * 1 = 5)

| 3 | height stack

| 0 | index stack

4. Height of 4th bar (1) is < top of stack(3). So pop the height and index stack until top of stack is <= height of current bar. The height of the popped element is 3. Current bar index - popped bar index = 3 – 0 = 3. So the area of rectangle (3 * 3 = 9). Then push the height of current bar (1) onto height stack and last popped index (0) onto the index stack

| 1 | height stack

| 0 | index stack

So area of rectangle is 9

3.3 Miscellaneous Algorithms

At the end we have to empty out the contents of the stack. We have processed a total of 4 bars. The height in the height stack is 1. The numbers of bars processed − index in the index stack = 4 − 0 = 4. The area of the rectangle that can be formed = 4 * 1 = 4.

The area of the largest rectangle that can be formed = max (5, 9, 4) = 9.

```
#histo_height: histo_height[i] has height of ith bar. Should not be empty
#Return value: returns the area of the largest rectangle in the histogram
def find_max_area(histo_height) :
    max_area = 0
    n = len(histo_height)
    height_stack = queue.LifoQueue() #stack stores the height of the bars
    index_stack = queue.LifoQueue() #stack stores the index of the bars

    for i in range(n):

        if ( height_stack.empty() or
        histo_height[i] > peek(height_stack) ) :
                #push height and index of current bar
                height_stack.put(histo_height[i])
                index_stack.put(i)

        elif (histo_height[i] < peek(height_stack)):

                while (not height_stack.empty() and
                histo_height[i] < peek(height_stack)) :
                    # keep popping from index and height stacks
                    popped_index = index_stack.get()
                    popped_height = height_stack.get()

                    # calculate the area from popped bar to
                    #the current bar.
                    #Area = popped height * difference of index of
                    #current bar and popped bar
                    area =  popped_height * (i - popped_index)

                    if (area > max_area):
                            max_area = area

                #push the height of the current bar into the height stack
                height_stack.put(histo_height[i])

                #push the LAST POPPED INDEX into the index stack,
                #since we can form a rectangle from the LAST POPPED INDEX
                #to the current bar (where the height of the rectangle is
                #height of current bar)
                index_stack.put(popped_index)
```

```
#Process the remaining elements in the stacks
while (not height_stack.empty() ) :
    popped_index = index_stack.get()
    area = height_stack.get() * (n - popped_index)

    if (area > max_area):
        max_area = area

return max_area
```

3.3 Miscellaneous Algorithms

11. Evaluate a mathematical expression consisting of +, -, *, /, parenthesis and integers. For instance, when we evaluate (150 − 100) * 10 + 100 we should return the value 600.

To solve the problem, we make use of two stacks: an operator_stack for storing the operators +, -, *, /, (,) and a num_stack for storing the integers.

First we will define the compute operation as follows:

1. Pop the operator from the operator_stack

2. First pop the topmost element in num_stack into value2 and then pop the topmost element from the num_stack into value1

3. Apply the operator on value1 and value2. Then push the result onto the num_stack.

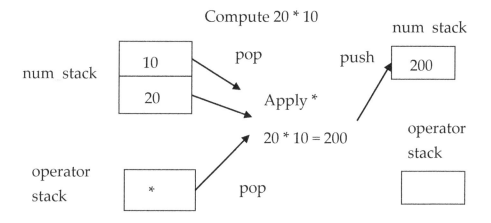

The mathematical expression will be stored in a string. To evaluate the expression, we parse the string and as we obtain tokens which may be operators or integers, we do the following:

1. If the current token is an integer, we push the integer onto the num_stack

2. If the current token is '(', then we push it onto the operator_stack

3. If the current token is ')', then we go on computing values using the num_stack and operator_stack until we get the '(' operator in the operator_stack. We then pop out '(' as we no longer need it.

4. If the current token is '+', '-', '*', '/', then as long as the operator on top of the operator_stack has a higher precedence than the current token, we go on computing values using the num_stack and operator_stack. Then we push the current token onto the operator_stack. The operators * and / have higher precedence than + and − as shown in the table below.

Operator	Precedence
*, /	2
+, -	1

5. After parsing the expression, if the operator_stack is not empty, then we go on computing values using the operator_stack and num_stack until the operator_stack becomes empty.

6. The top of the num_stack will contain the result.

```
#Helper function that picks the operator from the top of operator stack
#and applies them on the two values at the top of the num_stack. The result
#will then be pushed back onto the num_stack
def compute(num_stack, operator_stack) :
    c = operator_stack.get()

    #Since stack is LIFO we will first pop value2 and then pop value1
    value2 = num_stack.get()
    value1 = num_stack.get()

    if (c == '+') :
        num_stack.put(value1 + value2)
    elif (c == '-'):
        num_stack.put(value1 - value2)
    elif (c == '*'):
        num_stack.put(value1 * value2)
    elif (c == '/'):
        num_stack.put(value1 // value2)


#Helper function to check priority of operators
#stack_operator: operator that is at the top of the operator stack
#exp_operator: operator that is currently being examined in the expression
#Return value: True if operator in the stack is higher priority than operator
#being examined in the expression
def is_higher_precedence(stack_operator, exp_operator) :
    if ((stack_operator == '*' or stack_operator == '/') and
        (exp_operator == '+' or exp_operator == '-')) :
        return True

    return False
```

3.3 Miscellaneous Algorithms

```
#Main function for evaluating the expression
#expression: string containing the expression to be evaluated
#Return value: the integer result value obtained by evaluating the expression
def evaluate_expression(expr) :
    num_stack = queue.LifoQueue()
    operator_stack = queue.LifoQueue()

    i = 0
    while (i < len(expr)) :
        #Skip the white space characters
        if (expr[i] == ' ' or expr[i] == '\t' or expr[i] == '\n') :
                i += 1
                continue

        #If we encounter an integer, then parse out the digits in it
        if (expr[i] >= '0' and expr[i] <= '9') :
                start_pos = i
                while (i < len(expr) and expr[i] >= '0' and expr[i] <= '9') :
                    i += 1

                cur_value = int(expr[start_pos:i])
                num_stack.put(cur_value)

        elif (expr[i] == '(') :
                operator_stack.put(expr[i])
                i += 1

        elif (expr[i] == ')'):
                #Till we encounter '(', process the two stacks
                while (peek(operator_stack) != '(') :
                    compute(num_stack, operator_stack)
                operator_stack.get() #pop out '('
                i += 1

        elif (expr[i] == '+' or expr[i] == '-' or
              expr[i] == '*' or expr[i] == '/'):
                #As long as the operator in the stack is of higher
                #priority than the operator in the expression, keep processing
                #the two stacks
                while (not operator_stack.empty() and
                    is_higher_precedence(peek(operator_stack), expr[i])):
                        compute(num_stack, operator_stack)

                operator_stack.put(expr[i])
                i += 1

    #If there are still operators in the operator stack, then process them
    while ( not operator_stack.empty()):
        compute(num_stack, operator_stack)

    #The result will be present at the top of the num_stack
    return num_stack.get()
```

The Big Book of Coding Interviews

12. Find the number of connected components in an undirected graph

In the graph below, there are two connected components in it. The nodes (0, 1, 2, 3) form one connected component and the nodes (4, 5, 6) form the other connected component.

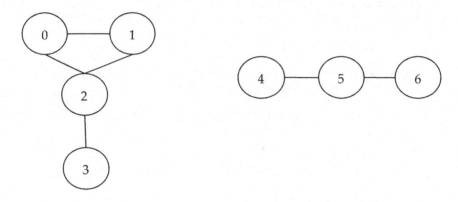

To simplify the implementation, the nodes in the graph will be represented by integers. For each node in the graph, we will keep a track of its neighboring nodes as shown in the table below:

Node	Adjacent nodes
0	1, 2
1	0, 2
2	0, 1, 3
3	2

To find the number of connected components, we will perform a depth first search on the graph as indicated below.

1. Initially all nodes will be marked as not visited.

2. Start with a node that has not been visited, and recursively traverse the node's neighbors and their neighbors and so on using depth first search. Once we traverse a node, it will be marked as visited. After we have finished traversing all nodes that are reachable from the starting node, we increment the number of connected components

3. Repeat step 2 until all the nodes in the graph have been visited.

3.3 Miscellaneous Algorithms

```python
#Helper function that performs depth first search on the graph
#cur_node: the current node that we are searching
#adjacency_table: a list of lists. If there is an edge between node 0
#   and node 5, then adjacency_table[0] is a list which will store 5 in it.
#is_visited: this list indicates if a node has already been visited or not
#num_nodes: total number of nodes in the graph
def dfs(cur_node, adjacency_table, is_visited, num_nodes):
    neighbors = adjacency_table[cur_node]

    is_visited[cur_node] = True

    #Go through all the neighbors of the current node
    for  cur_neighbor in neighbors:
        #If the current neighbor has not been visited, then recursively
        #call dfs on it
        if (not is_visited[cur_neighbor]):
            dfs(cur_neighbor, adjacency_table, is_visited, num_nodes)



#Main function to find the number of connected components in an undirected graph
#adjacency_table: a list of lists. If there is an edge between node 0 and
#   node 5, then adjacency_table[0] is a list which will store 5 in it.
#num_nodes: total number of nodes in the graph
#Return value: number of connected components in the graph
def connected_components(adjacency_table, num_nodes) :
    is_visited = [False] * num_nodes

    #Traverse through all the nodes in the graph and perform Depth First
    #Search. Each time we perform DFS on a node that has not been visited
    #so far, increment the number of connected components
    count = 0
    for  i, visited in enumerate(is_visited):
        if (not visited) :
            dfs(i, adjacency_table, is_visited, num_nodes)
            count += 1

    return count
```

The Big Book of Coding Interviews

13. Find if a directed graph has a cycle

Suppose we are given an undirected graph and asked to find a cycle in it, then all we need to do is the following

1. Initialize all nodes in the graph as unvisited.

2. Pick a node that has not been visited and recursively traverse its neighbors and their neighbors and so on using depth first search. Once we traverse a node, we will mark it as visited.

3. Repeat step 2 until all the nodes in the graph are visited.

While traversing the graph, if we encounter a node that has already been visited, then there is a cycle in the undirected graph.

We can't apply the same procedure for a directed graph. Consider the diagram below:

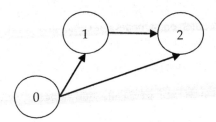

Suppose we start from node 0 and apply DFS. We first traverse the edge from node 0 to node 1. Then from node 1 we reach node 2. So nodes 0, 1 and 2 have been visited. Then we traverse the edge from 0 to 2. But node 2 has already been visited. Since we encounter a node that we have already visited, we conclude that there is a cycle in the directed graph. However this is incorrect since there is no directed cycle in this directed graph. If we had an edge from node 2 to node 0 instead of an edge from node 0 to node 2, then the graph has a directed cycle in it.

3.3 Miscellaneous Algorithms

To overcome this problem, instead of just maintaining two states whether the node has been visited or not, we maintain 3 states that are identified using colors

- White: the node has not yet been processed
- Gray: the node is currently being processed. This means that the node's neighbors and their neighbors and so on are still being expanded
- Black: the node has been completely processed. This means that all the nodes that are reachable from this node have been traversed

During depth first search, if we encounter a node whose color is already gray, then it means that there is a cycle in the directed graph.

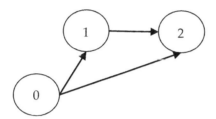

Using this approach, let us traverse the above directed graph. Initially all nodes are white. When we start with node 0, we change the color of 0 to gray. From 0 we move to 1. So node 1 now becomes gray. From 1 we reach 2. The color of 2 becomes gray. From 2 we try to traverse further. But there are no nodes reachable from 2. So we have finished processing node 2 and change its color to black. Then we check if we can reach another node from node 1. There are no new nodes that we can reach from node 1. So we change color of 1 to black and come back to node 0. From node 0 we can reach node 2. The color of node 2 is black. If color of 2 was still grey, then it means that there is a loop in the graph. In this case, since color of 2 is black, there is no loop in the graph.

To simplify the implementation, the nodes in the graph will be represented by integers. For each node in the graph, we will be storing its neighboring nodes as shown in the table below:

Node	Adjacent nodes
0	1, 2
1	2

```
#Helper function that performs depth first search on the graph
#cur_node: the current node that we are searching
#adjacency_table: a list of lists. If there is an edge between node 0 and
#   node 5, then adjacency_table[0] is a list which stores 5 in it.
#color: this list indicates color assigned to the node
#num_nodes: total number of nodes in the graph
#Return value: True if cycle is present in directed graph, False otherwise
def dfs(cur_node, adjacency_table, color, num_nodes) :
    does_cycle_exist = False
    neighbors = adjacency_table[cur_node]

    #Assign the gray color to the node indicating that we have started
    #processing this node
    color[cur_node] = GRAY
    for  cur_neighbor in neighbors:
        #If we find a neighboring node with the gray color, then we
        #have found a loop
        if (color[cur_neighbor] == GRAY) :
            return True

        #If the neighboring node has a white color, then perform
        #DFS on it
        if (color[cur_neighbor] == WHITE) :
            does_cycle_exist = dfs(cur_neighbor, adjacency_table,
                                    color, num_nodes)
            if (does_cycle_exist):
                return True

    #Assign the node the black color to indicate that we have finished
    #processing it
    color[cur_node] = BLACK
    return False

#Main function that checks if cycle is present or not
#adjacency_table: a list of lists. If there is an edge between node 0 and
#   node 5, then adjacency_table[0] is a list which stores 5 in it.
#num_nodes: total number of nodes in the graph
#Return value: True if cycle is present in directed graph, False otherwise
def is_cycle_present(adjacency_table, num_nodes) :
    does_cycle_exist = False

    #Assign the white color to all the nodes to indicate that we have not
    #started processing the nodes
    color = [WHITE] * num_nodes

    #Go through all the nodes in the graph and perform DFS on the
    #nodes whose color is white
    for  i, cur_color in enumerate(color):
        if (cur_color == WHITE) :
            does_cycle_exist = dfs(i, adjacency_table,
                                    color, num_nodes)
            if (does_cycle_exist) :
                break

    return does_cycle_exist
```

3.3 Miscellaneous Algorithms

14. Given an alien dictionary comprising of a few **words** in sorted order, find out the sorted order of occurrence of **characters** in the alien language

---

Let the sorted words in the alien dictionary be "aba", "abb", "abd", "ac", "ad" and "pq". The first step is to compare adjacent words and look at the first mis-matching character. (Note that it is not necessary to compare all possible word pairs. Just comparing neighboring words is sufficient.). So when we compare "aba" and "abb", the two words mismatch at the last character. Add a directed edge in a graph from the mismatching character of the first word to the mismatching character of the second word. So we will add an edge from a to b. This procedure is shown below

Word 1	Word 2	First Mismatching char in word 1	First Mismatching char in word 2	Action
"aba"	"abb"	'a'	'b'	Add edge a -> b
"abb"	"abd"	'b'	'd'	Add edge b -> d
"abd"	"ac"	'b'	'c'	Add edge b -> c
"ac"	"ad"	'c'	'd'	Add edge c->d
"ad"	"pq"	'a'	'p'	Add edge a->p

The graph would look like this

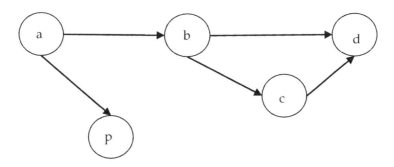

To represent the graph, we will use the adjacency information. So for each node, we will store the adjacent nodes as shown in the table

Node	Adjacent nodes
a	b, p
b	d, c
c	d

Then we perform topological sort on the graph with the help of a stack. In topological sorting, we first push all the adjacent nodes of the current node recursively onto the stack and then push the current node onto the stack. A node will be pushed onto the stack only once. So if we encounter the same node again while traversing the graph, we will not process it. Then at the end, when we pop out the contents of the stack, we will get the order of characters in the alien language. Note that topological sort is different from depth first search (in DFS, we first push the node to the stack and then push all its children to the stack recursively).

Let us say that, we start processing from node 'a'. Its adjacent nodes are 'b' and 'p'. Before placing 'b' on the stack, we first check its adjacent nodes 'd' and 'c'. 'd' has no adjacent nodes and so is pushed on to the stack. We then check the adjacent nodes of 'c'. Since 'd' is adjacent to 'c' and 'd' is already on the stack, we don't process 'd' again. Then we place 'c' on to the stack. Then we place 'b' onto the stack since all the nodes reachable from 'b' have been processed. Then we place 'p' on the stack. Finally we place 'a' on the stack. So the stack will look like this.

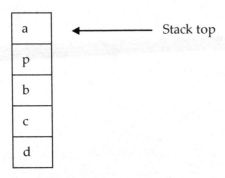

When we pop out the characters in the stack, we will get 'a', 'p', 'b', 'c', 'd'. This is the order of characters in the alien language. Note that 'p' comes ahead of 'b', 'c' and 'd'. From the words in the alien dictionary, we don't know the relationship between 'p' and 'b', 'c', 'd'. In such a case, topological sort will give us one possible order of characters that is consistent with the information available. Also note that although we started the topological sort with 'a', it is possible to start topological sort with any node in the graph.

3.3 Miscellaneous Algorithms

```
#Helper function for performing topological sorting
#cur_char: current character that we are processing
#adjacency_table: a list of lists. if there is an edge from 'a' to 'b' then
#adjacency_table['a'] contains list which will store b
#is_visited: indicates if a character has already been visited or not
#s: stack for storing the result of the topological sort
def topological_sort_helper(cur_char, adjacency_table, is_visited, s):
    if (is_visited[ord(cur_char)]):
        return

    #make is_visited to True here so that we don't run into loops
    is_visited[ord(cur_char)] = True

    #Process all the characters that are neighbors of the current
    #character (ie adjacent to current character) in the graph
    neighbor_list = adjacency_table[ord(cur_char)]

    for neighbor_char in neighbor_list:
        if (not is_visited[ord(neighbor_char)]):
            topological_sort_helper(neighbor_char, adjacency_table,
                            is_visited, s)

    #Push the current character onto the stack only after all the
    #characters reachable from it have been recursively added to the stack
    s.put(cur_char)


#Function that performs topological sorting
#adjacency_table:a list of lists. if there is an edge from 'a' to 'b' then
#adjacency_table['a'] contains list which will store b
def topological_sort(adjacency_table) :
    is_visited = [False] * MAX_NUM_CHARACTERS
    s = queue.LifoQueue()

    #Process all the characters
    for  i, neighbor_list in enumerate(adjacency_table):
        if (len(neighbor_list) ):
            topological_sort_helper(chr(i), adjacency_table,
                            is_visited, s)

    #Pop out the contents of the stack to get the result of topological
    #sort. This is the order of characters in the alien language
    while (not s.empty()) :
        cur_char = s.get()
        print(cur_char)
```

```python
#Main function to find the order of characters in an alien language
#words: the words present in the dictionary
def get_alphabet_order(words) :
    #adjacency_table is a list of lists
    #For each character in the language we maintain a list
    adjacency_table = [[] for x in range(MAX_NUM_CHARACTERS)]

    num_words = len(words)

    #Go through the consecutive pairs of words in dictionary
    for  i in range(0, num_words - 1):
        word1 = words[i]
        word2 = words[i+1]

        for c1, c2 in zip(word1, word2):
             #Find first mismatching characters between the two words
             if (c1 != c2) :
                    #In the graph, we have an edge from c1
                    #to c2. Fetch the list for c1
                    #and store c2 in it, since
                    #c2 is adjacent to c1
                    neighbor_list = adjacency_table[ord(c1)]
                    neighbor_list.append(c2)
                    break


    #Perform the topological sort
    topological_sort(adjacency_table)
```

3.3 Miscellaneous Algorithms

15. Given a beginning word and an ending word, find out if there is a sequence of words in a dictionary using which we can transform the beginning word to the ending word by changing only one character at a time. For instance, we can transform the beginning word 'bell' to the ending word 'walk' using the following word sequence: bell -> ball -> tall -> talk -> walk

---

To solve the problem, we perform breadth first search. We make use of

- a queue for storing the words generated while performing the search,
- a set called visited which stores the words visited until now so that we don't go into loops while doing the search
- a dictionary called reverse_path which stores the mapping from a word with its previous word. So if we generate the word ball from bell (bell -> ball), then we store ball as the key and bell as the value in the reverse_path dictionary (ball -> bell). This is needed to generate the word transformation sequence at the end

The procedure for solving the problem is:

1. Store the beginning word in the queue

2. Pick the current word from the front of the queue. If the current word is the same as the ending word, then we have found a successful word sequence to transform the words. Use the reverse_path to print out the word sequence.

If the current word at the front of the queue is not the same as the ending word, then generate all possible words that can be obtained by changing a single character in the current word. So if the current word is bell, we will generate *ell (from aell to zell), b*ll (from ball to bzll), be*l (from beal to bezl) and bel* (bela to belz). If the generated word is present in the dictionary and the generated word has not been visited so far, then add the generated word to the queue.

3. Repeat step 2, until we find the ending word or the queue becomes empty (in which case the word transformation is not possible)

```python
#begin_word: starting word in the word transformation
#end_word: ending word in the word transformation
#dictionary: contains the permitted words that can be used in the transformation
#Result:  the list that contains the sequence of words if word transformation
#  is possible, None if word transformation is not possible
def transform_word(begin_word, end_word, dictionary):
    q = queue.Queue()

    visited = set()   #Contains the words that have already been visited

    #If we can transform word a to word b, then we store b -> a mapping in
    # the reverse_path. b is the key and a is the value.
    reverse_path = {}

    q.put(begin_word)
    visited.add(begin_word)
    while (not q.empty()) :
        #Get the word at the beginning of the queue
        cur_word = q.get()

        #If the current word matches the ending word, we have found
        #the word transformation. Store the sequence of transformation
        #in the result list
        if (cur_word == end_word):
            result = []
            result.insert(0, cur_word) #Add to beginning of list

            #Find the previous word from where we reached the current
            #word and add the previous word to the result list
            cur_word = reverse_path.get(cur_word)
            while (cur_word) :
                result.insert(0, cur_word) #Add to beginning of list
                cur_word = reverse_path.get(cur_word)

            return result

        #Look at all possible words that can be generated from the
        #current word by changing a single character
        for  i in range(len(cur_word)):
            char_list = list(cur_word)

            #Generate new word by changing the character at position i
            for c in range(ord('a'), ord('z') + 1) :
                char_list[i] = chr(c)
                new_word = ''.join(char_list)

                #If the new word is present in dictionary and has
                #not been visited so far, then add it to the queue
                if (new_word in dictionary and
                  new_word not in visited ):
                      q.put(new_word)
                      visited.add(new_word)
                      reverse_path[new_word] = cur_word

    return None #transformation is not possible
```

4. Math

In this section, we will cover math topics such as arithmetic, random numbers, probability and co-ordinate geometry.

A small note about random numbers: the best method to generate random numbers is to make use of a physical process that is random (it is difficult to say if a physical process is truly random!). Computers generate pseudo-random numbers. One of the techniques used is the Linear Congruential Generator where

$X_{n+1} = (AX_n + C) \mod M$

where X_{n+1} is the $(n+1)^{th}$ random number and X_n is the nth random number.

A, C and M are constants whose values are pre-decided.

To obtain a good random number generator, C and M should be relatively prime. The seed specified during random number generation determines the value of X_0

1. Find the Greatest Common Divisor of two numbers

The Greatest Common Divisor (GCD) of two numbers a and b is the largest number that divides a and b without leaving a remainder. For instance, the GCD of 12 and 20 is 4. It is also called Greatest Common Factor, Highest Common Factor, etc. To find the GCD we use Euclid's algorithm which is as follows:

gcd(a, 0) = a

gcd(a, b) = gcd(b, a mod b)

So, suppose we have to calculate gcd(12, 20) then we get

gcd(12, 20) = gcd(20, 12 mod 20) = gcd(20, 12)

gcd(20, 12) = gcd(12, 20 mod 12) = gcd(12, 8)

gcd(12, 8) = gcd(8, 12 mod 8) = gcd(8, 4)

gcd(8, 4) = gcd(4, 8 mod 4) = gcd(4, 0) = 4

```
#a, b: Two integers. a may be greater than, equal to or less than b
#Return value: Greatest common divisor
def gcd(a, b) :
    if (b == 0):
        return a

    #Find the GCD of b and the remainder of a/b
    return gcd(b, a % b)
```

Variation: We may be asked to find the Least Common Multiple (LCM) of a and b. For instance, LCM of (20, 12) = 60. In this case, we first find the GCD of a and b and use the formula LCM(a, b) = a * b / GCD(a, b). So LCM(20, 12) = 20 * 12 / 4 = 60

2. Swap two variables without using a temporary variable

There are two ways to solve this problem. The first uses XOR and the second uses addition and subtraction. The XOR technique can be used for swapping any two variables whereas the addition and subtraction technique can only be used for numbers. The two techniques are described below:

Steps for the XOR procedure	Example: let x initially have the value a and y have the value b
x = x ^ y;	x = x ^ y = a ^ b
y = x ^ y;	y = x ^ y = (a ^ b) ^ b = a
x = x ^ y;	x = x ^ y = (a ^ b) ^ a = b;
	So x has b and y has a at the end

Steps for the addition, subtraction procedure	let x initially have the value a and y have the value b
x = x + y;	x = x + y = a + b
y = x - y;	y = x - y = (a + b) - b = a
x = x - y;	x = x - y = (a + b) - a = b;
	So x has b and y has a at the end

The Big Book of Coding Interviews

3. An unsorted list contains all integers from 1 to N except one integer. All the elements in the list are unique. Find the missing integer in O(n) time and O(1) space. For instance in the list [5, 1, 3, 2], the missing element is 4.

All integers from 1 to N are present in the list except one integer. To find the missing integer we do the following:

1. Calculate the expected_sum of integers from 1 to N. We know that the sum of integers from 1 to N is given by the formula N * (N+1) / 2

2. Calculate the total_sum of the N-1 elements in the list.

3. The difference between expected_sum and the total_sum will give the missing element.

So if N = 5, and list is [5, 1, 3, 2], then expected sum = 5 (5 + 1) / 2 = 15. The total sum of elements in the list = 5 + 1 + 3 + 2 = 11. So missing number = 15 – 11 = 4.

```
#a: list of unique numbers. A number can have a value between 1 to n
#n: maximum value that can be stored in the list. list has n-1 elements
#Return value: missing element in the list
def find_missing(a, n) :
    #Since 1 element is missing, there are only n-1 elements in the list
    total_sum = 0
    for  i in range(n - 1):
        total_sum += a[i]

    expected_sum = n * (n+1) // 2

    missing_num = expected_sum - total_sum
    return missing_num
```

4. Math

4. An unsorted list contains all integers from 1 to N except two integers. All the elements in the list are unique. Find the missing integers in O(n) time and O(1) space. For instance in the list [5, 1, 3], the missing elements are 2 and 4.

Since there are two missing numbers, we need two equations to solve the problem. Let the missing numbers be a and b.

1. Add up all the elements in the list and store the result in actual_normal_sum. Add up the squares of all elements in the list and store the result in actual_square_sum.

2. The sum of the first N numbers is given by the formula N * (N+1) / 2. Store this in expected_normal_sum.

actual_normal_sum + a + b = expected_normal_sum

So <u>a+b = expected_normal_sum – actual_normal_sum</u>

3. The sum of the squares of the first N numbers is given by the formula N * (N+1) * (2N + 1) / 6. Store this in expected_square_sum.

actual_square_sum + a^2 + b^2 = expected_square_sum

So <u>a^2 + b^2 = expected_square_sum - actual_square_sum</u>

4. Calculate 2ab using the formula 2ab = $(a+b)^2$ – (a^2 + b^2)

We can calculate 2ab since we know a+b and (a^2 + b^2)

5. Calculate a-b. We know that $(a - b)^2$ = a^2 + b^2 – 2ab.

So (a – b) = sqrt(a^2 + b^2 – 2ab)

We know (a^2 + b^2) and we know 2ab. So we can calculate a – b.

6. Now we have a + b and a – b.

So we can calculate a as a = ((a + b) + (a – b)) / 2

Using the value of a and (a+b), we can calculate b as b = (a + b) - a

```python
#values: list of unique numbers. A number can have a value between 1 to n
#n: maximum value in the list is n. list has n-2 elements
#Return value: the missing elements in the list are returned
def find_missing(values, n) :
    #Since 2 elements are missing, there are only n-2 elements in the list
    actual_normal_sum = 0
    actual_square_sum = 0
    for  i in range(n - 2):
        actual_normal_sum += values[i]
        actual_square_sum += values[i] * values[i]


    expected_normal_sum = n * (n+1) // 2
    expected_square_sum = n * (n+1) * (2*n + 1) // 6

    a_plus_b = expected_normal_sum - actual_normal_sum
    a_square_plus_b_square = (expected_square_sum - actual_square_sum)
    two_a_b =  ((a_plus_b * a_plus_b) - a_square_plus_b_square)
    a_minus_b = int (math.sqrt(a_square_plus_b_square - two_a_b))

    a = (a_plus_b + a_minus_b) // 2
    b = (a_plus_b - a)

    return a, b
```

5. Generate all the prime numbers that are less than or equal to N

To generate all prime numbers <= N, we make use of the sieve of Eratosthenes where we do the following:

1. We generate the numbers from 2 to N and for each number X, we mark all multiples of X up to N to indicate that these multiples can't be primes

2. If a number is not a multiple of any of the numbers preceding it, then it is a prime

We skip 0 and 1 as they are not considered to be prime. 2 is the first prime number. Then all multiples of 2 up to N are marked to indicate that these multiples can't be primes. The next number is 3. Since 3 is not a multiple of any number before it (note that we have skipped 1 and so we ignore the fact that 3 is a multiple of 1), 3 is a prime. We then mark all multiples of 3. The next number is 4. Since 4 has been marked to be a multiple, it can't be prime. We then mark all the multiples of 4 and this process continues up to N.

```
#n: Upto what number the primes should be generated
def generate_primes(n) :
    #is_multiple will be initialized with False since we have not yet
    #identified the multiples
    is_multiple = [False] * (n+1)

    #We don't consider 0 and 1 as prime. Start from 2
    for  i in range(2, n+1):
       if (is_multiple[i]) :
                continue #i is a multiple, so it can't be prime

       print('{} is prime '.format(i) )

       #Mark all multiples of i (2i, 3i, 4i, etc) starting from 2i
       for  j in range(2*i, n+1, i):
                is_multiple[j] = True
```

6. Compute x^y efficiently

We can compute x^y by multiplying x for y times. This will require y multiplications. However there is a faster method to compute x^y. The procedure is as follows:

1. Initialize result to 1. Let the position of the most significant bit in y be z

2. Compute x to the power of powers of 2 up to the 2^zth power. (x, x^2, x^4, x^8, x^{16}, etc.). This can be achieved by doubling the value of x every time.

3. If bit i is set in y, then multiply the 2^i power of x with the result.

For instance, if we have to evaluate 3^{22}, we do the following

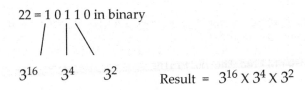

$$22 = 1\ 0\ 1\ 1\ 0 \text{ in binary}$$

$$3^{16} \quad 3^4 \quad 3^2 \qquad \text{Result} = 3^{16} \times 3^4 \times 3^2$$

So we need 3 multiplications to get the result. We have to also compute the powers of 3 which are 3^{16}, 3^8, 3^4, 3^2. So we need 4 multiplications. So the total number of multiplications needed to compute 3^{22} is 3+4 = 7 which is less than the 22 multiplications needed by the naïve solution. The source code is given below

```python
#x, y: two integers, x > 0, y >= 0
#Return value: x multiplied with itself y times
def power(x, y) :
    result = 1
    while (y > 0) :
        #look at the least significant bit of y
        if ((y & 0x1) == 0x1) :
            result = result * x
        y = y >> 1 #shift out the least significant bit of y
        x = x * x

    return result
```

5. Generate all the prime numbers that are less than or equal to N

To generate all prime numbers <= N, we make use of the sieve of Eratosthenes where we do the following:

1. We generate the numbers from 2 to N and for each number X, we mark all multiples of X up to N to indicate that these multiples can't be primes

2. If a number is not a multiple of any of the numbers preceding it, then it is a prime

We skip 0 and 1 as they are not considered to be prime. 2 is the first prime number. Then all multiples of 2 up to N are marked to indicate that these multiples can't be primes. The next number is 3. Since 3 is not a multiple of any number before it (note that we have skipped 1 and so we ignore the fact that 3 is a multiple of 1), 3 is a prime. We then mark all multiples of 3. The next number is 4. Since 4 has been marked to be a multiple, it can't be prime. We then mark all the multiples of 4 and this process continues up to N.

```python
#n: Upto what number the primes should be generated
def generate_primes(n) :
    #is_multiple will be initialized with False since we have not yet
    #identified the multiples
    is_multiple = [False] * (n+1)

    #We don't consider 0 and 1 as prime. Start from 2
    for  i in range(2, n+1):
        if (is_multiple[i]) :
                continue #i is a multiple, so it can't be prime

        print('{} is prime '.format(i) )

        #Mark all multiples of i (2i, 3i, 4i, etc) starting from 2i
        for  j in range(2*i, n+1, i):
                is_multiple[j] = True
```

The Big Book of Coding Interviews

6. Compute x^y efficiently

We can compute x^y by multiplying x for y times. This will require y multiplications. However there is a faster method to compute x^y. The procedure is as follows:

1. Initialize result to 1. Let the position of the most significant bit in y be z

2. Compute x to the power of powers of 2 up to the 2^zth power. (x, x^2, x^4, x^8, x^{16}, etc.). This can be achieved by doubling the value of x every time.

3. If bit i is set in y, then multiply the 2^i power of x with the result.

For instance, if we have to evaluate 3^{22}, we do the following

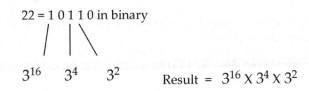

So we need 3 multiplications to get the result. We have to also compute the powers of 3 which are 3^{16}, 3^8, 3^4, 3^2. So we need 4 multiplications. So the total number of multiplications needed to compute 3^{22} is 3+4 = 7 which is less than the 22 multiplications needed by the naïve solution. The source code is given below

```python
#x, y: two integers, x > 0, y >= 0
#Return value: x multiplied with itself y times
def power(x, y) :
    result = 1
    while (y > 0) :
        #look at the least significant bit of y
        if ((y & 0x1) == 0x1) :
            result = result * x
        y = y >> 1 #shift out the least significant bit of y
        x = x * x

    return result
```

4. Math

7. Suppose you are given a random number generator that generates numbers uniformly in the range 1 to 5. How will you generate numbers uniformly in the range 1 to 7?

Let us say that we are provided with the rand5() function that generates values uniformly from 1 to 5. We can generate values uniformly from 0 to 4 by subtracting 1 from the result of rand5(). Now using rand5() we can uniformly generate numbers in the range 0 to 24 using the following formula

(rand5() – 1) + 5 * (rand5() – 1)

Now to generate numbers uniformly from 1 to 7, we use rejection sampling. If the above formula generates a random number in the range 0 to 20, we accept the number. If the formula generates a number in the range 21 to 24, then we reject the number and re-try the formula until we get a number in the range 0 to 20. We then find the remainder when the number in range 0 to 20 is divided with 7. The remainder will be uniformly distributed in the range 0 to 6. We then add 1 to the remainder to get the result which will be uniformly distributed in the range 1-7.

The rejection sampling in this case can be visualized with a 5 * 5 grid, wherein if we throw a dart and the dart randomly lands on a cell, the number in the grid is accepted for some cells and rejected for others.

	0	1	2	3	4
0	0	1	2	3	4
1	5	6	0	1	2
2	3	4	5	6	0
3	1	2	3	4	5
4	6	reject	reject	reject	reject

```
def rand7() :
    while(True) :
        result = (rand5() - 1) + (5 * (rand5() - 1))
        if (result <= 20):
            break

    result = 1 + (result % 7)
    return result
```

8. Suppose you are given a random number generator that generates numbers uniformly in the range 1 to 7. How will you generate numbers uniformly in the range 1 to 5?

Let's say that rand7() generates values in the range 1 to 7. The instinctive answer to generate random values from 1 to 5 is 1 + ((rand7() − 1) % 5). However this produces a wrong result.

rand7()	1 + ((rand7() − 1) % 5)
1	1
2	2
3	3
4	4
5	5
6	1
7	2

As can be seen from the table, 1 and 2 are generated twice whereas 3, 4 and 5 are generated only once. So this can't be a uniform distribution. To get the correct result, we once again use rejection sampling. If rand7() produces a value greater than 5, we reject the sample and call rand7() again. The code is given below

```
def rand5() :
    while(True) :
        result = rand7()
        if (result <= 5):
            break

    return result
```

4. Math

9. How would you "perfectly" shuffle a deck of cards?

A deck of cards consists of 52 cards. There are 52! possible orderings of cards in the deck. When a perfect shuffle is done, there is an equal likelihood for one of the 52! possible orderings to occur. A simple approach to shuffle a deck of cards is to swap the ith card with a randomly chosen card. The code for this approach is

```
def incorrect_shuffle(cards) :
    for  i in range(len(cards) - 1, -1,-1):
        rand_num = random.randint(0, len(cards) - 1)

        #Swap the card at the random position with the card at i
        cards[i], cards[rand_num] = cards[rand_num], cards[i]
```

While the above approach shuffles the cards, it does not produce a perfect shuffle. For a perfect shuffle, all cards should be shuffled equal number of times. However with the approach above, some cards are shuffled more times than others. To see this, consider a deck consisting of three cards A, B, C in that order.

In the first iteration we swap the first card with a random card (the random card position may be the same as the first card).

So [A, B, C] can give [A, B, C], [B, A, C] and [C, B, A]

In the second iteration, we swap the second card with a random card. So the set of states after the second iteration are

[A, B, C] can give [A, B, C], [B, A, C] and [A, C, B]

[B, A, C] can give [B, A, C], [A, B, C] and [B, C, A]

[C, B, A] can give [C, B, A], [B, C, A] and [C, A, B]

In the third iteration, we swap the third card with a random card. The set of states after the 3rd iteration are

[A, B, C] can give [A, B, C], [C, B, A] and [A, C, B]

[B, A, C] can give [B, A, C], [C, A, B] and [B, C, A]

[A, C, B] can give [A, C, B], [B, C, A] and [A, B, C]

[B, A, C] can give [B, A, C], [C, A, B] and [B, C, A]

[A, B, C] can give [A, B, C], [C, B, A] and [A, C, B]

[B, C, A] can give [B, C, A], [A, C, B] and [B, A, C]

[C, B, A] can give [C, B, A], [A, B, C] and [C, A, B]

[B, C, A] can give [B, C, A], [A, C, B] and [B, A, C]

[C, A, B] can give [C, A, B], [B, A, C] and [C, B, A]

We now count the number of outcomes for each ordering after the third iteration

[A, B, C] = 4. [A, C, B] = 5. [B, A, C] = 5. [B, C, A] = 5. [C, A, B] = 4. [C, B, A] = 4

So some outcomes are more likely than others. The problem becomes more severe when the deck contains more cards. To overcome this problem, Fish-Yates proposed a solution that was popularized by Knuth (sometimes the solution is also called Knuth shuffle). The idea used here is that in the first iteration, we pick a random card X out of 52 cards and swap it with the 51st card in the deck (last card in the deck, since the 0th card is the first card according to our convention). The card X continues to stay at the end of the deck and is not shuffled further. In the next iteration, we pick a random card Y out of 51 cards and swap it with the 50th card in the deck. The card Y continues to stay at its new position(50th position) and is not shuffled further. This process repeats. The code for this is given below

```python
#Performs a perfect shuffle of cards
def card_shuffle(cards) :
    for  i in range(len(cards) - 1, -1,-1):
        #Pick a random position from 0 to i
        rand_num = random.randint(0, i)

        #Swap the card at the random position with the card at i
        cards[i], cards[rand_num] = cards[rand_num], cards[i]
```

4. Math

Let the deck consist of 5 cards and the ordering of the cards be A, B, C, D, E. The table shows how the Knuth shuffle works

Iteration	Random number range	Chosen random number	Arrangement before swap	Arrangement after swap
1	0-4	2	A, B, **C**, D, **E**	A, B, **E**, D, **C**
2	0-3	0	**A**, B, E, **D**, C	**D**, B, E, **A**, C
3	0-2	1	D, **B**, **E**, A, C	D, **E**, **B**, A, C
4	0-1	0	**D**, **E**, B, A, C	**E**, **D**, B, A, C

The Big Book of Coding Interviews

10. Given a list with n values, pick m (m < n) random values from it such that each element has an equal probability of being chosen

---

We could generate m random indexes from 0 to n-1 and pick the items at the random indices. The problem with this approach is that we may generate the same random index multiple times. But we want each element to have an equal probability of being chosen. So to solve the problem, we have to prevent choosing an already chosen element. We can do this as follows:

1. Initialize the last index that we can choose to n-1.

2. Pick a random position rand_index between 0 to last index and store the element at rand_index in the result. Then swap the element at rand_index with the element at last index. Then decrement the last index by 1. Repeat step 2 to get all the m values.

This way all the chosen values get moved to the end of the list and never get chosen again. Note that since we move elements around, the original list will get modified. To avoid this, we will create another copy of the list and work with the copy instead of the original.

```
#a: input list of unsorted numbers
#k: number of random values to pick
#Return value: the k random values will be stored in result
def pick_random_values(a, k) :
    #We will need to rearrange the elements in list a. Since the user
    #may expect list a to remain unchanged, we are allocating memory
    #for another list b and copying elements of a into b
    b = a[:]
    result = []
    j = 0
    last_index = len(a) - 1
    while (j < k) :
        #Pick a random position from 0 to last_index
        rand_index = random.randint(0, last_index)

        #Store b[rand_index] in the result
        result.append(b[rand_index])

        #Let's say original value at b[rand_index] is x.
        #b[rand_index] is now overwritten with b[last_index].
        #So we cannot choose x again in the next iterations
        b[rand_index] = b[last_index]
        last_index -= 1
        j += 1

    return result
```

4. Math

11. You are given an unfair coin where the probability of getting one outcome (say heads) is more than the other (tails). What strategy will you use to ensure that the outcome of the biased coin is fair?

Let the probability of turning up heads be p. Then probability of turning up tails is 1-p. A fair coin will have an equal likelihood of turning up heads and tails. So p = 1-p = 0.5. In a biased coin, the likelihood of turning up heads and tails is different. So p is not equal to 1-p. To make the biased coin fair, we will have to use the biased coin to produce two events that have an equal likelihood of occurrence. Let the biased coin be tossed twice. The probabilities of the resulting outcomes is given below

Outcome	Probability
(Heads, Heads)	p*p
(Heads, Tails)	p*(1-p)
(Tails, Heads)	(1-p)*p
(Tails, Tails)	(1-p)*(1-p)

We notice that the probability of (Heads, Tails) is equal to the probability of (Tails, Heads). So if we consider (Heads, Tails) as one event and (Tails, Heads) as the other event, then they will have an equal probability of occurrence. The events (Heads, Heads) and (Tails, Tails) can be ignored. So the strategy to use so that the biased coin becomes fair is to toss the biased coin twice and do the following:

1. If the coin shows up (Heads, Tails) or (Tails, Heads), then take the result into account. (Heads, Tails) will represent one event (say actual Heads) and (Tails, Heads) will represent the other event (say actual Tails).

2. If the coin shows up (Tails, Tails) or (Heads, Heads) then ignore it and retry.

```
#Returns 0 with a probability of 0.5 and 1 with a probability of 0.5
def toss_fair_coin() :
    while (True) :
        x = toss_unfair_coin()
        y = toss_unfair_coin()

        if (x == 0 and y == 1):
            return 0
        elif (x == 1 and y == 0):
            return 1
```

The Big Book of Coding Interviews

12. You are given a function that generates either 0 or 1 with an equal likelihood. Using this function, generate numbers that are uniformly distributed in the range (a, b)

The number of possible outcomes (num_outcomes) that we have to produce is $b - a + 1$. Our approach will be to first generate a random number in the range (0 to num_outcomes − 1) and then add a to the generated random number so that it lies in the range (a, b)

The given function generates 0 and 1 with equal probability. We can call the given function i times and get i random bits. We can then concatenate these i bits. The largest number that we can form by concatenating i bits is $2^i - 1$. So we can generate a uniform distribution from (0 to $2^i - 1$) by concatenating i random bits. To generate a uniform distribution from (0 to num_outcomes − 1), we do the following:

1. Find the closest i value so that $2^i >=$ num_outcomes. For instance, if num_outcomes is 10, then nearest i is 4 ($2^4 > 10$)

2. Construct the random number using i random bits. If the random number < num_outcomes, then accept the random number. If the random number >= num_outcomes then reject the random number and try again (rejection sampling)

Now that we have a random number in the range (0, num_outcomes − 1), we add a to it to get a random number in the range (a, b)

```
#Returns number x where a <= x <= b and x is uniformly distributed
def get_random_num(a, b) :
    num_outcomes = b - a + 1

    while (True) :
        rand_num = 0
        i = 0
        while ( (1 << i) < num_outcomes) :
                #Append the random binary digit to the end
                rand_num = (rand_num << 1) | binary_rand()
                i += 1

        if (rand_num < num_outcomes):
                break
        #If rand_num >= num_outcomes, we try again

    return rand_num + a
```

13. Implement a function to calculate the square root of a number

One of the simplest techniques to calculate the square root of a number is to use binary search. Let us say that we have to find the square root of a positive number N, where N > 1. We know that the square root lies between 1 and N. We find the mid point M between 1 and N. We then compute M^2. If M^2 is greater than N, then we have to search for the square root in the region (1, M). If M^2 is less than N, then we have to search in the region (M, N). This process is repeated until we reach a mid point value with the required accuracy.

```
#n: number >= 1 whose square root has to be computed
#accuracy: how accurate should the result be
#Return value: square root of n
def find_sqrt(n, accuracy) :
    low = 1.0
    high = n * 1.0

    if (n == 1):
        return 1.0

    mid = (low + high) / 2

    while (low < high) :
        square = mid * mid

        #Find absolute difference between (mid * mid) and n
        difference =  square - n
        if (difference < 0):
            difference = difference * -1

        #If the absolute difference is within the required accuracy
        #then mid contains the square root. So break out of the loop
        if (difference < accuracy):
            break

        if (square > n) :
            high = mid
        else:
            low = mid

        mid = (low + high) / 2

    return mid #Return the square root
```

14.

There is a staircase with N steps. A person can climb up either one step at a time or two steps at a time. Find out the number of ways the person can climb the staircase

---

Suppose there is only 1 step. The person can climb it only in 1 way.

Suppose there are 2 steps. There are 2 ways to climb them: the person either climbed to step 1 and then climbed to step 2 or he directly climbed to step 2.

Let us say that the number of steps is N. He can reach the Nth step either from step N-1 or from step N-2 only (since he can climb up only one or two steps at a time). So the number of ways he can reach step N = number of ways he can reach $(N - 1)^{th}$ step + number of ways he can reach step N-2.

Let climb_steps(N) represent the number of ways a person can reach step N, then, climb_steps(1) = 1, climb_steps(2) = 2 and

climb_steps(N) = climb_steps(N-1) + climb_steps(N-2) when N > 2

Note that this gives us a sequence similar to the Fibonacci sequence where the current value is the sum of the two previous values. In the Fibonacci sequence, the first two numbers of the series are 1, 1 whereas here the first two numbers are 1 and 2.

The recursive solution to solve the problem is given below

```
#n: number of steps. n >= 1
#Returns: the number of ways to climb the steps using recursion
def climb_steps_r(n) :
    if (n <= 2):
        return n

    return climb_steps_r(n-1) + climb_steps_r(n-2)
```

The non-recursive solution to the problem is given below

```
#n: number of steps. n >= 1
#Returns: the number of ways to climb the steps
def climb_steps(n) :
    #Directly return the value for the first two numbers in the series
    if (n <= 2):
        return n

    x = 1
    y = 2
    for i in range(3, n+1):
        temp = x + y
        x = y
        y = temp

    return y
```

15. Find if two lines intersect

It is easy to figure out if two lines intersect if we consider the two lines in the slope-intercept form (Every line can be written in the form y = mx+c where m is the slope and c is the y-intercept). Two lines intersect if they have different slopes. Two lines will not intersect if they have the same slope but different y-intercepts. One boundary condition is what happens if we are given the same two lines (where-in the slopes and y-intercepts of the two lines are equal). In this case, we will consider that the lines intersect each other

```
#slope1: slope of the first line
#c1: y-intercept of the first line
#slope2: slope of the second line
#c2: y-intercept of the second line
#Return value: True if the lines intersect, False otherwise
def do_lines_intersect(slope1, c1, slope2, c2) :
    epsilon = 0.0001
    intersect = False

    if (abs(slope1 - slope2) < epsilon)  :
        #Both lines have the same slope. Check the y-intercept
        if (abs(c1 - c2) < epsilon) :
                #The y-intercepts are the same.
                #So both lines are the same lines.
                #We consider such lines to intersect with each other
                intersect = True
        else :
                #The lines are parallel and not coincident on each other
                #So these lines will not intersect
                intersect = False

    else :
        #The two lines have different slopes. They will intersect
        intersect = True

    return intersect
```

16. Find out if two rectangles overlap

It is easier to check if two rectangles don't overlap. Let each rectangle be specified by two points – its upper left corner (we will call this point left) and its lower right corner (we will call this point right). Each point has an x co-ordinate and a y co-ordinate.

Two rectangles will not overlap if any one of the two conditions below is satisfied:

- one of the rectangles lies completely to the right or left of the other

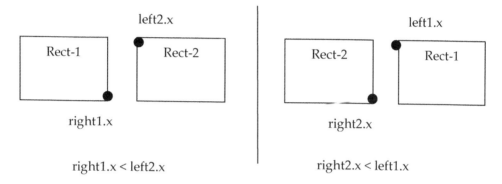

- one of the rectangles lies completely above or below the other

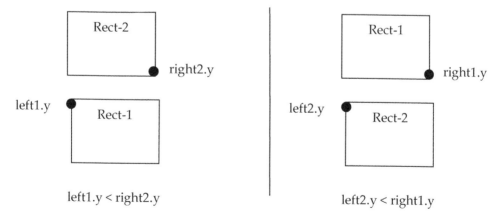

The code for checking if two rectangles overlap or not is given below

```
#left1: upper left corner of rectangle 1
#right1: lower right corner of rectangle 1
#left2: upper left corner of rectangle 2
#right2: lower right corner of rectangle 2
#Return value: True if rectangles overlap, False otherwise
def do_rectangles_overlap(left1, right1, left2, right2) :

    #one rectangle lies completely to the right or left of the other
    if (right1.x < left2.x or right2.x < left1.x):
        return False

    #one rectangle lies completely above or below the other
    if (left1.y < right2.y or left2.y < right1.y):
        return False

    #the rectangles overlap
    return True
```

4. Math

17. Find the area of overlap between two rectangles

First we find if the rectangles overlap or not. If the rectangles don't overlap, then the area of overlap is 0. If the rectangles overlap, then the overlapping region will also be a rectangle. In this case, we find the co-ordinates of the upper left corner of the overlap and the lower right corner of the overlap. Using these two corners, we find the length and breadth of the rectangular overlap and then compute area of overlap = length * breadth.

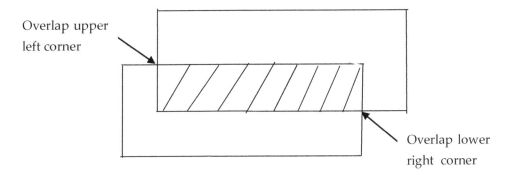

The code to find the area of overlap is given below

```
#left1: upper left corner of rectangle 1
#right1: lower right corner of rectangle 1
#left2: upper left corner of rectangle 2
#right2: lower right corner of rectangle 2
#Return value: area of the overlapping rectangles
def find_overlap_area(left1, right1, left2, right2) :

    #one rectangle lies completely to the right or left of the other
    if (right1.x < left2.x or right2.x < left1.x):
        return 0

    #one rectangle lies completely above or below the other
    if (left1.y < right2.y or left2.y < right1.y):
        return 0
```

```
#the rectangles overlap
result_left = Point()
result_right = Point()
result_left.x = max(left1.x, left2.x)
result_left.y = min(left1.y, left2.y)
result_right.x = min(right1.x, right2.x)
result_right.y = max(right1.y, right2.y)

area = ((result_right.x - result_left.x)
        * (result_left.y - result_right.y))
return area;
```

4. Math

18. How can you encode all possible orderings of a deck of cards using only 32 bytes (256 bits)?

A deck of cards has 52 cards. Each card has one of 4 possible symbols (diamond, clubs, heart, spades) and one of 13 possible values (Ace, 2, 3, 4, 5, 6, 7, 8, 9, 10, King, Queen, Jack). We can encode the 4 symbols using 2 bits and encode the 13 values using 4 bits. So each card needs 2+4 = 6 bits. To encode an ordering of 52 cards we need 52 * 6 = 312 bits. However we are provided only 256 bits.

To achieve this we use the following approach. As before we initially assign a 6 bit code for each card. We pick the first 20 cards in the deck and encode each card with 6 bits. So we need 20 * 6 = 120 bits. Next we are left with 32 cards remaining in the deck. Since we have already observed the first 20 cards which can no longer occur in the remaining deck, 5 bits is sufficient to encode the 32 cards in the remaining deck. So we assign a new 5 bit code for the remaining 32 cards and use 5 bits to encode the next 16 cards. We need 16 * 5 = 80 bits. Now we are left with 16 cards in the deck for which 4 bits are sufficient. We can encode the next 8 cards using 4 bits. We need 8 * 4 = 32 bits. Now we are left with 8 cards for which 3 bits are sufficient. We encode the next 4 cards with 3 bits. We need 4*3 = 12 bits. Now we are left with 4 cards for which 2 bits are sufficient. We encode the next 2 cards with 2 bits. We need 2*2 = 4 bits. Now we are left with 2 cards for which 1 bit is sufficient. We encode the next card with 1 bit. We need 1*1 = 1 bit. We are left with the last card. Since we know all the other 51 cards in the deck, we can automatically determine the last card and we don't need to encode this card.

So the total number of bits required = 120 + 80 + 32 + 12 + 4 + 1 = 249 bits which solves the problem.

The Big Book of Coding Interviews

19. Three ants are initially located at the 3 corners of an equilateral triangle. Each ant picks a direction randomly and begins to move along the edges of the triangle. All the ants move with the same speed. What is the probability that two or more ants collide with each other?

It is easier to first find out the probability that the ants don't collide with each other and then use this information to find the probability that any two ants collide.

Each ant can pick either the clock-wise direction or the anti-clock wise direction to move along the edges of the triangle. Since the ant picks the direction randomly, the probability that an ant moves in the clockwise direction is 0.5 and the probability that it moves in the anti-clockwise direction is 0.5.

The ants will not collide if all the ants decide to move in the clockwise direction or if all the ants move in the anti-clockwise direction.

The probability that all the 3 ants move in clockwise direction = 0.5 * 0.5 * 0.5 = 0.125

The probability that all the 3 ants move in anti-clockwise direction = 0.5 * 0.5 * 0.5 = 0.125

So probability that all ants move in either clockwise or anti-clockwise direction = 0.125 + 0.125 = 0.25

So the probability that no ant collides with any other ant is 0.25

The probability that two or more ants collide with each other = 1 – 0.25 = 0.75

4. Math

20. If a stick breaks randomly into three pieces, what is the probability that you can form a triangle from the pieces?

To form a triangle, the sum of any two sides should be greater than the other side.

Let the length of the stick be L. Let the stick be broken at the points X and Y. Let the 3 pieces be a, b and c.

If the cuts are formed on the same half of the stick, then one side will always be larger than the sum of the other two sides as shown in Scenario-1 and Scenario-2 below.

Scenario-1: the two cuts are present in the left half of the stick

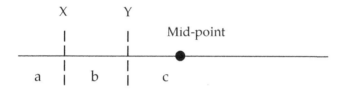

Since c > 0.5L and (a+b) < 0.5L, c > (a+b) and we can't form a triangle. The likelihood of forming the cut X on the left half of the stick = 0.5. Similarly the likelihood of forming the cut Y on the left half of stick = 0.5. So the likelihood of forming cut X and Y on the left half of the stick = 0.5 * 0.5 = 0.25

Scenario-2: the two cuts are present in the right half of the stick

Since a > 0.5L and (b+c) < 0.5L, a > (b+c) and we can't form a triangle.

Similarly the likelihood of forming cut X and Y on the right half of the stick as shown in the diagram above = 0.5 * 0.5 = 0.25

So the two cuts have to be on different halves of the stick to form a triangle.

If the cuts are formed on different halves of the stick, then if cut X is formed in the first quarter of the stick and Y is formed in the last quarter of the stick, then again we can't form a triangle as shown in the diagram.

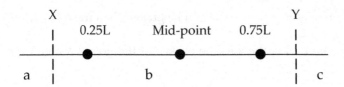

a < 0.25L, c < 0.25L. So b > 0.5L. Since b > (a+c) we can't form the triangle. The likelihood of cut X in the first quarter of the stick = 0.25. The likelihood of cut Y in the last quarter of the stick = 0.25. The likelihood of cut X in the first quarter and cut Y in the last quarter = 0.25 * 0.25 = 0.125

Similarly if cut X is formed in the last quarter and cut Y is formed in the first quarter as shown in the diagram, we can't form the triangle.

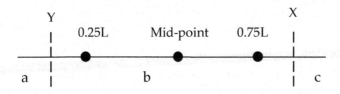

The likelihood of cut X in the last quarter and cut Y in the first quarter = 0.25 * 0.25 = 0.125

So the total likelihood that we can't form a triangle = 0.25 + 0.25 + 0.125 + 0.125 = 0.75

The likelihood that we can form a triangle = 1 - 0.75 = 0.25

5. Design

Relation between classes

The diagram below shows the classification of the relations between classes

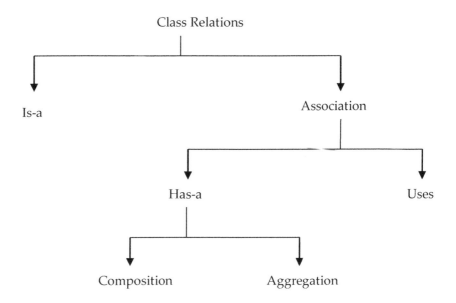

The relation between classes are broadly classified into two types:

- ✓ "Is-a": One class "is-a" kind of another class. For instance, parrot "is-a" bird. Inheritance can be used in this case.
- ✓ Association

Association has two further subtypes

- ✓ "Has-a" association: One class contains another class
- ✓ "uses" association: One class uses another class. For instance the class Car uses the class GasStation

"Has-a" has two further sub-types

- ✓ Composition – The contained class is an integral part of the containing class. For instance, tire is an integral part of a car. So a car is composed of a tire
- ✓ Aggregation – The contained class and container class can exist independently. For instance, class Car and class Passenger can exist independently. So the class Car aggregates class Passenger

Prefer Composition to inheritance

Composition is preferred to inheritance in many cases. Inheritance should be used only where there is a genuine "is-a" relationship. Let us say that the fly function is common to the class Airplane and the class Bird. The class Airplane has already implemented the fly function and the Bird class is now being developed. To reuse the fly functionality of the Airplane class, if we try to inherit the Bird class from the Airplane class it will result in a bad design because Bird is not an Airplane. A better design would be to have a separate class implement the fly functionality and let the Airplane and Bird classes contain this class that implements the fly functionality

UML Diagrams

Consider the Python class

```
class A(object):

    def __init__(self, a, b, c):
        self.x = a
        self.y = b
        self.z = c

    def f1(self):
        pass

    def f2(self):
        pass

    def f3(self):
        pass
```

5. Design

In the UML diagram as shown below, the name of the class is first mentioned, followed by the data members followed by the function members. The public members are represented with + symbol

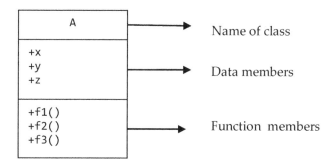

The UML diagram for class Parrot "is-a" class Bird is given below:

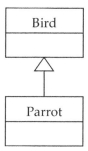

The UML diagram for class Car "has-a" class Tire (composition) is given below:

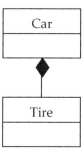

The UML diagram for class Car aggregates class Passenger (aggregation) is given below:

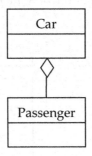

The UML diagram for class Car uses class Gas Station is given below:

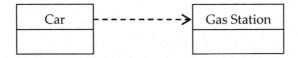

5. Design

1. Design a book library

When interviewers ask a design problem, they may be interested in the class diagram or the code or both. It is good to ask the interviewers what they are interested in and proceed along those lines. For this design problem, we will give the class diagram. For the remaining design problems we will give the code. A possible design of a book library is shown below:

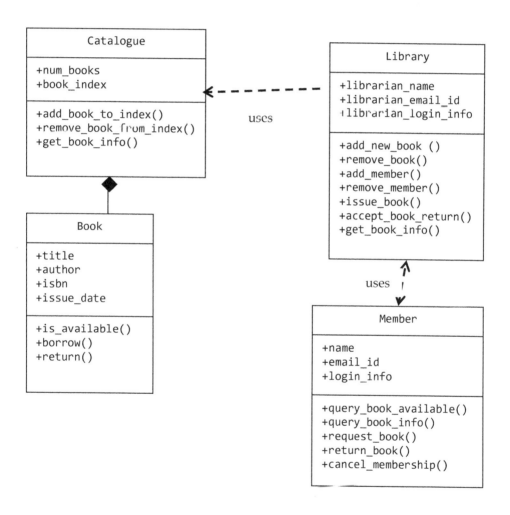

2. Design a parking lot

A parking lot consists of two main classes: the Vehicle class and the ParkingLot class.

Different types of vehicles such as Car, Truck, MotorBike etc. will be derived from the Vehicle class.

The Slot class maintains the information about every parking slot such as the location of the slot, the vehicle currently present in the slot, etc. The ParkingLot class is a composition of many objects of the Slot class.

```
class Vehicle(object):

    def __init__(self, vehicle_id, vehicle_type, size):
        self.id = vehicle_id
        self.type = vehicle_type
        self.size = size

    #Returns the registration number of the vehicle
    def get_vehicle_registration_id(self):
        pass

    #Returns the vehicle type
    def get_vehicle_type(self):
        pass

    #Returns the vehicle size
    def get_vehicle_size(self):
        pass

    #Returns if the vehicle fits in the parking slot
    def does_vehicle_fit(self, parking_slot_size):
        pass


class Car(Vehicle):

    pass
```

5. Design

```python
class Slot(object):

    def __init__(self, unique_slot_num, location, vehicle, start_time):
        self.unique_slot_num = unique_slot_num
        self.location = location
        self.vehicle = vehicle
        self.startTime = start_time


class ParkingLot(object):

    #Assigns a parking slot to the vehicle and returns the slot
    def assign_slot(self, vehicle):
        pass

    #Reserves a parking slot to the vehicle for the time specified and
    #returns the slot
    def reserve_slot(self, from_time, to_time, vehicle):
        pass

    #Computes the parking fare for a particular parking slot
    def compute_parking_fare(self, slot):
        pass

    #Vehicle has left the slot. So the slot will be freed up
    def vacate_slot(self, slot):
        pass

    #Returns the physical location of the parking slot
    def get_location(self, slot):
        pass

    #Returns the number of free parking slots available right now
    def get_num_free_slots(self):
        pass

    #Indicates whether parking lot is full or not
    def is_full(self):
        pass
```

3. Design an elevator

Each elevator maintains its current state. The state information includes the current floor in which the elevator is present, whether the door is open or shut, etc. The design for an elevator class is shown below:

```
class Elevator(object):

    #Initializes the elevator indicating how many floors
    #are in the building and the height of each floor
    def __init__(self, numFloors, floorHeight, initialState):
        self.numFloors = newFloors
        self.floorHeight = floorHeight
        self.currentState = initialState

    #Returns the data about the button the user has pressed
    def get_user_input(self):
        pass

    #Indicates if weight of all passengers in lift is within
    #the safe limits or not
    def is_weight_safe(self):
        pass

    #closes the doors of the lift
    def close_door(self):
        pass

    #Performs the actions needed to go to the floor the user has requested
    def go_to_floor(self, floorNumber):
        pass

    #Opens the door of the lift
    def open_door(self):
        pass

    #Performs the actions needed during a power failure
    def power_failure(self):
        pass

    #Performs the actions needed during an emergency
    def emergency_procedure(self):
        pass

    #Returns the current state of the lift
    def get_state(self):
        pass
```

4. Design a hotel reservation system

A hotel reservation system consists of two main classes: the Room class and the BookingSystem class.

Different types of rooms such as Normal-Room, Queen-Room, Deluxe-Room etc. will derive from the Room class.

The BookingSystem class is a composition of many objects of the Room class.

```
class Room(object):

    def __init__(self, room_type, size, room_number, num_beds):
        self.room_type = room_type
        self.size = size
        self.room_number = room_number
        self.num_beds = num_beds

    #Reserves a room for a particular customer for the indicated duration
    def reserve_room(self, from_time, to_time, customer):
        pass

    #Frees up a room and makes it available for being booked
    def free_room(self):
        pass

    #Checks if a particular room is occupied or free
    def is_occupied(self):
        pass


class NormalRoom(Room):

    pass
```

```python
class BookingSystem(object):

    def BookingSystem(self):
        pass

    #Checks if a room of the required type is available
    def check_availability(self, room_type, from_time, to_time):
        pass

    #Reserves a room of the required type and returns the reservation
    def book_room(room_type, from_time, to_time, customer):
        pass

    #Cancels a reservation
    def cancel_room(reservation):
        pass

    #Performs the actions during checkout (such as calculating the bill)
    #and then frees up the room
    def check_out(room):
        pass

    #Returns the current bill amount for the room
    def get_running_bill_amount(room):
        pass
```

5. Design

5. Design a chess game

The chess game can be implemented using the ChessPiece class and the Chess class. Each type of chess piece such as the King, Queen, Pawn, etc. will derive from the ChessPiece class. The Chess class is a composition of the chess pieces. The main function of the Chess class is to move a chess piece from one location of the board to another.

```python
class ChessPiece(object):

    def __init__(self, position):
        self.current_position = position

    #Checks if the piece can be moved to position p
    def validate_move(self, position):
        pass

    #Moves the piece to the position p
    def move(self, position):
        pass



class King(ChessPiece):

    def __init__(self, position, is_white):
        self.current_position = position
        self.is_white = is_white
        self.is_active = True

    #Checks if the piece can be moved to position p
    def validate_move(self, position):
        pass

    #Moves the piece to the position p
    def move(self, position):
        pass
```

```
class Chess(object):

    def __init__(self):
        #create the 8*8 grid for storing the chess pieces
        self.grid = [[None for x in range(0, 7)] for x in range(0, 7)]

        #Create all the pieces at their initial position
        pass

    def move(self, piece1, pos1, piece2 = None, pos2 = None):
        #Moves a chess piece to a particular position. If we castle the
        #king, we will have to move two pieces in a single move. So we
        #have another set of arguments whose default value is None
        pass


    def is_check_mate(self):
        pass
```

6. Design a vending machine

The main classes in a vending machine are the Item class and the VendingMachine class. The Item class is used for representing the items dispensed by the vending machine. Classes such as Beverage class or Candy class will inherit the Item class. The VendingMachine class is a composition of Items. A vending-code is associated with each item and corresponds to the buttons that the user has to press on the vending machine to get the item.

```
class Item(object):

    def __init__(self, product_id, vending_code, price, quantity):
        self.product_id = product_id
        self.vending_code = vending_code
        self.price = price
        self.quantity = quantity

    def set_price(new_price):
        pass

    def set_quantity(new_quantity):
        pass

    def get_price():
        pass

    def get_quantity():
        pass


class Candy(Item):

    pass
```

```python
class VendingMachine(object):

    def __init__(self):
        pass

    #Adds a new item to the vending machine
    def add_new_item(self, item, vending_code):
        pass

    #Loads a certain number of units of the item into the vending machine
    def load_machine(self, item, count):
        pass

    #Updates the price of the item
    def update_price(self, item, new_price):
        pass

    #Changes the vending code for an item
    def set_vending_code(self, item, vending_code):
        pass

    #Gets the number of units available for the item with the
    #given vendingCode
    def get_count(self, vending_code):
        pass

    #Gets the price of the item corresponding to vendingCode
    def get_price(self, vending_code):
        pass

    #Performs the actions when user presses the button to purchase
    #an item
    def purchase(self, vending_code):
        pass

    #Removes an item from the vending machine
    def remove_item(self, item):
        pass
```

6. Python

1. What values are printed when the following code is executed?

```
x = 5
def f1():
    x = 9
    print(x)

f1()
print(x)
```

The output is

9
5

Python uses the LEGB rule. Python first searches the Local namespace, then the Enclosed namespace, then the Global namespace and finally the Built-in namespace. So when function f1() is called, Python first searches if f1 has a name binding for x in it. The statement x = 9 binds the name x to an object in local scope. So f1 uses the local x and not the global x. So when x is printed in f1, 9 is printed first. After coming out of function f1, the print(x) statement refers to the global x. The global x continues to have a value of 5. So 5 is printed next.

The Big Book of Coding Interviews

2. What values are printed when the following code is executed?

```
x = [1, 2, 3, 4, 5]

def f1():
    print(x)
    x.append(6)

f1()
print(x)
```

The output is

```
[1, 2, 3, 4, 5]
[1, 2, 3, 4, 5, 6]
```

Again we apply the LEGB rule. Python first searches if the name x is bound to an object in f1(). In this case, the name x is not bound to any object in f1(). So Python then searches the enclosed scope and then the global scope. In the global scope, the statement x = [1, 2, 3, 4, 5] binds the name x to an object. So the global x is used while printing x in f1. Also the statement x.append(6) appends 6 to the global x. So after finishing executing f1, when we print x, we get the result [1, 2, 3, 4, 5, 6]

3. What happens when the following code is executed?

```
x = 1

def f1():
    print(x)
    x = 5

f1()
print(x)
```

In function f1(), Python first searches to see if the name binding for x is defined in the local scope. The statement x = 5 in f1() binds the name x to an object in the local scope. So x in f1() refers to the local x and doesn't refer to the global x. But now in function f1, the print statement is accessing the local x, even before the initialization of the local x. So when Python tries to execute the statement print(x) in f1(), it throws an error indicating that we are trying to access the local variable x in the print statement before assigning it a value.

4. What is the output of the following code?

```
def f1(x):
    x += 1
    print(x)

x = 1
f1(x)
print(x)
```

The output is

2
1

Initially when the statement x = 1 is executed, the global name x is bound to an object with a value 1. When f1 is called, a new name binding is established for the argument x in f1. This new name binding continues to bind the argument x in f1 with the original object with value 1. However on executing the statement x += 1, 1 is added to 1 and the result 2 is stored in a new object. The name x in f1() now is bound to the new object with value 2. So on printing x in f1, we get 2. Once f1 finishes executing, in the main code, we print x. In the main code the name x continues to be bound to the original object with value 1. So 1 is printed.

5. What is the output of the following code?

```
def f1(x):
    x.append(2)
    print(x)

x = [1]
f1(x)
print(x)
```

The output is

[1, 2]
[1, 2]

Initially when the statement x = [1] is executed, the global name x is bound to an object with a value [1]. When f1 is called, a new name binding is established in f1 for argument x, wherein the name x in f1 continues to be bound to the original object with value [1]. On executing the statement x.append(2), 2 is appended to the original object and the name binding for x doesn't change. So x continues to be bound to the original object. So on printing x in f1, we get [1, 2]. Once f1 finishes executing, in the main code, we print x. In the main code the name x continues to be bound to the original object with value [1, 2]. So [1, 2] is printed.

6. What is the output of the following code?

```
def f1(x):
    x = [9]
    print(x)

x = [1]
f1(x)
print(x)
```

The output is

[9]
[1]

Initially when the statement x = [1] is executed, the global name x is bound to an object with a value [1]. When f1 is called, a new name binding is established in f1 for argument x, wherein the name x in f1 continues to be bound to the original object with value [1]. However on executing the statement x = [9], a new object is created with the value [9]. The name x in f1() now is bound to the new object with value [9]. So on printing x in f1, we get [9]. Once f1 finishes executing, in the main code, we print x. In the main code the name x continues to be bound to the original object with value [1]. So [1] is printed.

6. Python

7. Print the index and value of each element in the list

The Pythonic way of doing this is to use the enumerate function. Printing the index and value of each element in a list called words is shown in the code below:

```
words = ['Apple', 'Ball', 'Cat']

for index, element in enumerate(words):
    print('{}, {}'.format(index, element))
```

8. Reverse a list

The Pythonic way of reversing a list is to use the slice operator [::-1] as shown in the code below

```
x = [1, 2, 3, 4, 5]
print(x[::-1])
```

The syntax for the slice operator is x[start:end:step]. Here step is -1. When step is negative, the default value for start is -1 (end of the list) and the default value for end is -(length of list) - 1 (i.e. beginning of the list). So in the above example, x[::-1] becomes x[-1:-6:-1] and we end up with a new list that is the reverse of the original list.

The Big Book of Coding Interviews

9. What is the output of the following code?

```
x = [1, 2, 3, 4, 5]
print(x[10:])
```

The output is

[]

We expect that Python will throw the IndexError to indicate that the index 10 is out of bounds for the list x. However the Python slice operator returns an empty list [] . This is because the result of the slice operation is always a new object. So if incorrect indexes are specified to slice a list, the output is a new empty list.

10. What is the output of the following code?

```
def f1(x = []):
    x.append(1)
    return x

result = f1()
print(result)

result = f1()
print(result)
```

The output is

[1]
[1, 1]

The reason for this behavior is that the default arguments of Python are evaluated only once when the function is defined and not every time the function is called. So the empty list is created when the function f1 is defined. Each time the function f1 is called without any arguments, 1 gets appended to the same list. So do not use mutable defaults.

The solution to the problem is to write the code as below

```
def f1(x = None):
    if (x == None):
        x = []
    x.append(1)
    return x
```

11. What is the output of the following code?

```
class A(object):
    x = 1

#B is derived from A
class B(A):
    pass

#C ALSO is derived from A
class C(A):
    pass

print A.x, B.x, C.x

B.x = 2
print A.x, B.x, C.x

A.x = 3
print A.x, B.x, C.x
```

The output is

1 1 1
1 2 1
3 2 3

In Python, class variables are internally handled as dictionaries. If the variable name is not found in the dictionary of the current class, then Python searches in the dictionaries of the classes in the class hierarchy (parent classes).

Initially only class A has the variable x in it. B and C are children of class A. So B.x and C.x refer to A.x. Initial value of A.x is 1. So 1 1 1 is printed.

Next the class variable x is added to the class B and its value is set to 2. A.x continues to be 1. Since C inherits from class A, C.x refers to A.x So the output is 1 2 1

Finally A.x is set to 3. B.x continues to be 2. Since C inherits from A, C.x refers to A.x. So the output is 3 2 3.

12. What is the difference between shallow copy and deep copy?

Consider the code below:

```
a = [1]
b = a
b[0] = 9
print(a)
```

The output of the code is [9]. This is because initially a is bound to the list [1]. When we perform b = a, b is also bound to the same list [1]. When we execute b[0] = 9, the first element in the same list will be modified to 9. Since a is still bound to the same list, when we print a, we get the result [9].

So when b is modified, a also gets modified. To overcome this problem, we should do a shallow copy. In the code below shallow copy is performed by the statement b = a[:]. So a and b are now two separate lists and each list has its own set of values. When we print a in the code below, we get the value [1] indicating that the statement b[0] = 9 did not affect the object bound to the name a.

```
a = [1]
b = a[:]
b[0] = 9
print(a)
```

6. Python

Now consider the code below where we are doing shallow copy using the statement b = a[:].

```
a = [ [1, 1]]
b = a[:]
b[0][1] = 9
print(a)
```

The output of this code is [[1, 9]]. So although a and b are separate objects, when b[0][1] is modified then a[0][1] also gets automatically modified. This is because we are storing a list within a list in a and b. So initially the reference to the inner list [1, 1] is stored in list a. Then when a shallow copy is performed using the statement b = a[:], a new object is created and bound to the name b. But b will also have the same reference to the inner list [1, 1]. So both a and b have a reference to the same inner list. Changing the inner list from b will show up when we print a.

To overcome this problem we have to do a deep copy as shown in the code below.

```
from copy import deepcopy

a = [ [1, 1]]
b = deepcopy(a)
b[0][1] = 9
print(a)
```

The output of this code is [1, 1]. So when b = deepcopy(a) is executed, then not only is a new object created for b, but new objects are recursively created for all the objects inside object a. So an object inside a could be a simple element or a list, or a list within a list or a list within a list within a list and so on.

13. What is monkey patching?

Monkey patching is a technique used in Python to change the behavior by swapping functions and methods. For instance, consider the code below. The compute method of the Numbers class performs addition. It is possible to monkey patch the compute method with the product function to now find the product of two numbers instead of the sum.

```
class Numbers(object):
    def compute(self, x, y):
        return x + y


def product(self, x, y):
    return   x * y

n = Numbers()
result = n.compute(10, 9)
print('Result = {}'.format(result)) #We will get 10 + 9 = 19

#Store the old compute method which performs add
old_compute = Numbers.compute

#Monkey patch the compute method to now return the product
Numbers.compute = product

result = n.compute(10, 9)
print('Result = {}'.format(result)) #We will now get 10 * 9 = 90

#We can restore back the old compute method that performs add
Numbers.compute = old_compute
```

Some programmers are against monkey patching since it makes the code difficult to debug. Monkey patching however can be useful while testing the code.

14. What is the difference between range and xrange?

In Python 2, range creates a list. So range (1, 1000), will create a list with 999 elements in it. In Python 2, xrange is a sequence object which can be iterated. So xrange(1, 1000) will not create 999 elements. Instead it is possible to iterate through the elements one by one as and when we need them. So xrange is much more memory efficient than a range.

In Python 3, range behaves the same way as xrange does in Python 2. So in Python 3, range is a sequence object over which we can iterate. The use of xrange has been deprecated in Python 3 and so xrange doesn't exist in Python 3.

6. Python

15. What are docstrings?

Docstrings are strings enclosed within """ characters and provide additional information about Python modules, classes, methods and functions. The main difference between docstrings and normal comments are as follows:

1. A docstring should be the first statement in the object's definition, whereas normal comments can occur anywhere

2. Docstrings can be accessed from the program using the __doc__ method whereas normal comments can't. For instance:

```
def add(x, y):
    """
    Adds x and y and returns the result
    """
    return x + y

print add.__doc__ #This will print the docstring for the add function
```

3. Docstrings are mainly used to document information useful for the user of the Python object while normal comments contain information useful for the developer of the Python object.

16. Mention some of the portability problems when migrating from Python 2 to Python 3

In Python 2.x, print is a statement whereas in Python 3.x print is a function

In Python 2.x, / performs integer division. So 3/2 is 1. In Python 3.x, / performs floating point division. So 3/2 is 1.5

In Python 2.x, range creates a list and xrange is a sequence object. In Python 3.x, range is a sequence object and xrange has been deprecated.

17. What is the use of 'from __future__ import' directive?

To overcome some of the portability problems in Python, we make use of the 'from __future__' directive. This statement indicates that the syntax or semantics of a future release of Python should be used even when running an older version of Python. For instance, suppose we are using Python 2.6 but we want the code that we write to be compatible with both Python 2.6 and Python 3.4. We know that the operator / performs integer division in Python 2.x whereas it performs floating point division in Python 3.x. To overcome this problem, we use the statement

```
from __future__ import division
```

This statement causes Python 2.x to get the meaning of / operator from the future version and so / is treated as floating point division even on Python 2.x. In this manner we keep the meaning of / the same on all versions of Python.

18. What is the use of if (__name__ == '__main__')?

Each module has the __name__ attribute. Usually __name__ stores the name of the module. However for the module that is executed in the main scope, __name__ is set to '__main__'. We can use this to run a module either as a reusable module or as a standalone program. For instance, we can have the following code

```
if (__name__ == '__main__'):
    unit_tests()
```

So in this case, if the module is executed in the main scope, we will make the module act as a standalone program and invoke the unit tests for the module.

19. What is PEP 8?

PEP-8 is the style guide for Python code. It mentions the generally followed practices for the following:

- Code layout: use 4 spaces for indentation, use spaces instead of tabs, etc.

- Naming variables: Class variables should use CamelCase (for instance LinkedList). Function names, method names and instance variables should use lowercase with words separated by underscore (for instance main_list)

20. What is the difference between a list and a tuple?

Example of list is a = [1, 2, 3]. Example of tuple is b = (1, 2, 3)

The main difference between a list and a tuple is that a list is mutable whereas a tuple is immutable. So elements in the list can be changed and elements can be added and deleted from the list. In a tuple however, it is not possible to change any element in the tuple. It is also not possible to add or delete elements from a tuple. The main advantages of a tuple over a list are

1. A tuple has a slightly better performance than a list

2. A tuple can be the key of a dictionary as it will not change. This is not possible with a list. For instance if a = [1, 2, 3], b = (1, 2, 3), then the dictionary c = {a:1} is not possible but it is possible to have a dictionary c = {b: 1}

3. When passing a tuple as an argument to a function or method, the programmer can be sure that the tuple will not get modified inside the function

The Big Book of Coding Interviews

21. What is the difference between a list and a set?

Example of list is a = ['Apple', 'Ball', 'Cat']. Example of set is b = {'Apple', 'Ball', 'Cat'}

A list is an ordered sequence of elements which can contain duplicates.

A set is an unordered collection of unique elements. So although we have specified the order of elements as 'Apple', 'Ball' and 'Cat' to the set b, the actual order in which the elements are stored will most likely be different. We can't use an index to access the elements in a set. All the elements in a set should be hashable and immutable. A set is similar to a dictionary except for the fact that a set has only keys whereas a dictionary has key-value pairs.

22. What is the difference between an instance method, a class method and a static method?

Consider the following code:

```
class A(object):
    def f1(self):
        print('Executing instance method ')

    @classmethod
    def f2(cls):
        print('Executing class method ')

    @staticmethod
    def f3():
        print('Executing static method ')

a = A()

a.f1() #calls instance method f1 with self = a

a.f2() #calls class method f2 where cls = class A
A.f2() #calls class method f2 where cls = class A

a.f3() #calls static method f3
A.f3() #calls static method f3
```

f1 is an instance method. It can be invoked only by calling it on an object of class A. So a.f1() will invoke the instance method. The object is always automatically passed to f1 through the first argument of the method (self).

f2 is a class method. It can be invoked by calling it on an object of class A or on class A itself. So a.f2() and A.f2() will invoke the class method. The class (in this case class A) is always automatically passed to f2 through the first argument of the method (cls).

f3 is a static method. It can be invoked by calling it on an object of class A or on class A itself. So a.f3() and A.f3() will invoke the static method. There is no implicit value passed automatically for the first argument. If the first argument is present, then the user has to explicitly specify it while invoking the method.

23. What is a generator?

In some cases, the entire data to be processed is not available beforehand. In other cases, the memory requirements needed to store the data are very high and it is not feasible to store all the data. In such cases, we make use of generators. A generator generates values on the fly.

For instance consider the list

```
list1 = [x for x in range(1, 101)]
```

The list has 100 elements in it and memory has to be allocated to store all 100 elements.

Instead we can make use of a generator expression as shown below:

```
gen1= (x for x in range(1, 101))
```

We use the '(' character to define the generator. The generator doesn't have a length associated with it. The elements are created one at a time and returned as and when needed. So the memory requirements for a generator are significantly smaller.

It is possible to iterate through a generator as shown in the code below

```
for element in gen1:
    print (element)
```

24. What is the use of the yield keyword in Python?

The yield statement returns the value from a function and the next time the function is called, the execution of the code starts from the line after the yield statement instead of starting from the beginning of the function. Using the yield statement, it is possible to build a generator function. For instance, consider the code below to generate the fibonacci numbers that are less than n.

```
def fibonacci(n):
    x = 1
    y = 1
    while (x < n):
        yield x
        x, y = y, x+y
```

To create the generator gen1 for the fibonacci numbers that are less than 100, we make use of the following line.

```
gen1 = fibonacci(100)
```

To obtain the fibonacci numbers on the fly, we make use of the following lines

```
for element in gen1:
    print element
```

The initial values of x and y are 1. The first time fibonacci is called, we return a value of 1. Since the yield statement has been used, the next time around the execution starts from after the line x, y = y, x + y. So the while loop continues and we get the next Fibonacci number.

It is also possible to find the values from the generator using next as shown below

```
gen2 = fibonacci(50)
result = next(gen2)
print result
```

When the generator has generated all the possible values, it will raise the StopIteration exception just like any other iterable object.

25. What is the difference between an iterator and an iterable?

An iterator is an object that supports two methods: the __iter__ method and the next method (__next__ in Python 3.x). The __iter__ method returns itself (the iterator object). The next method returns the next value each time it is called.

An iterable object is any object that can return an iterator that can be used for traversing through the elements in the object. An iterable object also implements the __iter__ method which returns the iterator for the object. A list is an iterable object. Even non-containers such as open files and open sockets are iterable objects.

In case of a list, the list is an iterable object but not an iterator (since listiterator is used to iterate through the list object). It is possible that the same object is both iterable and its own iterator.

Consider the following code

```
a = [1, 2, 3]
b = iter(a) #obtain the iterator for list a
print (next(b))
```

a is iterable whereas b is an iterator for list a

26. What is a decorator?

Suppose we want to find out the time it takes to execute function f1. We can do the following:

```
def f1():
    #Add code to find the start time

    #Perform the operations of f1

    #Add code to find the end time. end_time - start_time gives
    #the time taken by f1
```

Suppose now we have to find the time taken by some more functions. One way is to duplicate the timing code in all the functions. We can avoid having to duplicate the timing code by making use of decorators. A decorator is a function that modifies the behavior of another function.

In Python, functions themselves are first-class objects. Just like a class can have functions within it, a function too can have functions within it. The functions inside a function are called inner functions or nested functions. Using this information, we implement the decorator function find_time as shown below:

```
from datetime import datetime

def find_time(original_function):
    def inner_function(*args, **kwargs):
        start_time = datetime.now()
        result = original_function(*args, **kwargs)
        end_time = datetime.now()

        print('Time taken = {}'.format(end_time - start_time))

        return result
    return inner_function

#Decorate f1
f1 = find_time(f1)
```

Let us follow the sequence of events. In the main code, we first have the statement f1 = find_time(f1). So find_time() is called with f1 as the argument. In the function find_time, the argument original_function takes on the value of the actual f1 function. The find_time function returns the inner_function. Notice that inside the inner_function we are calling the original_function.

So in the statement f1 = find_time(f1), the f1 on the left hand side of the assignment will now take the inner_function. Subsequent calls to f1 will now call the inner_function which in turn executes the original_function and prints the time taken by it. Also note that we don't have to pass original_function when the inner_function is called. The original_function becomes available to the inner_function due to the closure property. So the inner_function wraps the original_function and decorates the original_function.

Python provides a simpler syntax to decorate a function. Instead if using the statement f1 = find_time(f1), we can add the statement @find_time before we define function f1

6. Python

27. What is map, filter, reduce? Give examples

map(f, seq) - map calls the function f on each member of the sequence seq and returns a new sequence containing the result. The original sequence is not modified. For instance, consider the following code

```
a = [1, 2, 3, 4, 5]
result = list(map( lambda x: x*x, a))
print(result)
```

result will now store [1, 4, 9, 16, 25]

filter(f, seq) - filter calls the function f on each member of the sequence seq and if the function evaluates to True, then the member is placed in the result. The original sequence is not modified. For instance, consider the following code

```
a = [10, 20, 30, 40, 50]
result = list(filter(lambda x: x < 30, a))
print(result)
```

result will now store [10, 20]

reduce(f, seq, initial_value) - reduce combines all the members in the sequence seq into a single value using the function f and initial_value. The manner in which the function is called is as follows:

```
result0 = initial_value
result1 = f(result0, first element of seq)
result2 = f(result1, second element of seq) and so on
```

For instance, consider the following code

```
a = [1, 2, 3, 4, 5]
result = reduce(lambda x, y: x*y, a, 1)
print(result)
```

The result will be 120 (1 * 2 * 3 * 4 * 5 = 120)

28. What is duck typing?

In any programming language, the compiler/interpreter should know how an object behaves. For instance, consider the statement print(a[0]). The compiler/interpreter will need to know if given the index, it can obtain a member of object a. One way of doing this is to look at the type of the object either statically (static typing) or dynamically at run time (dynamic typing). Another way of doing this is to use duck typing. In case of duck typing, the interpreter doesn't look at the type of the object. It instead looks at the methods of the object at run time to determine the behavior of the object. So if the object has the methods needed to perform a certain action, then the interpreter goes ahead and performs the action. Python uses duck typing. The popular saying is that "If it quacks like a duck and swims like a duck, then it is a duck."

So to determine if a[0] can be performed, Python doesn't check the type of object a. It instead checks if the method __getitem__ can be invoked on the object. If __getitem__ is available, then it simply invokes the method and returns the result.

29. What is a metaclass?

In Python, a class is also an object. Since the class is an object, the class too has to be an instance of something. In this case, a class is an instance of a metaclass. So we can treat metaclass as the class of a class. The metaclass defines the behavior of a class.

The default metaclass for a class is type. We can define our own metaclass for a class. One of the uses of a metaclass is that it can serve as a class factory.

6. Python

29. What is pickling?

Pickling is the process by which an object is serialized (converted to byte code). Unpickling is the reverse process by which an object is deserialized (object is reconstructed from byte code). The pickle module implements pickling in Python.

30. Is it possible to maintain order of elements in a dictionary?

Python provides the OrderedDict class where the information about the order in which entries are added to the dictionary is preserved. While iterating through the ordered dictionary the elements are returned in the order in which they were inserted. The OrderedDict makes use of a dictionary and an auxiliary list. The order information is maintained in the auxiliary list

31. What are the disadvantages of Python?

Python is an interpreted language. So its performance is definitely slower than C++

Python is not suited for memory intensive tasks

The lack of pointers in Python limits the use of Python in pure system programming tasks.

32. What is Python Global Interpreter Lock (GIL)?

The most popular Python interpreter is CPython. The memory management performed by CPython is not thread-safe. To overcome this problem, CPython makes use of the Global Interpreter Lock. The Global Interpreter Lock is a mutex used to prevent multiple bytecode threads from running concurrently. Due to the presence of the Global Interpreter Lock, it is not possible to fully utilize a multi-processor or multi-core system and the performance is considerably reduced.

33. How is garbage collection performed in Python?

The garbage collector maintains a reference count for each object. For instance, if objects A, B, C have a reference to object D, then the reference count for object D is 3. Each object is also assigned a generation value to indicate how recently the object was created. When the number of objects for a particular generation exceeds a threshold value, the garbage collection is triggered for objects of that generation. During garbage collection, the memory for all unreachable objects whose reference count is 0 is freed. There can be reference cycles. For instance, object A can refer to object B and object B can refer back to object A. The garbage collector will try to detect these reference cycles and free up these objects as well.

7. Computer Science Concepts

Scheduling

The scheduler decides which thread to execute. The different types of scheduling are first come first serve, round-robin, priority based, etc. When the scheduler picks a new thread to execute, a context switch is performed. Context switch involves the following actions

- ✓ save the context (register values, etc.) of the currently executing thread
- ✓ place the current thread in the queue
- ✓ pick the next thread to execute from the queue
- ✓ load the context of the new thread and execute it

Inter-Process Communication

Processes can communicate with one another using the following

- ✓ Pipes: one-way channel of communication between processes mainly used to connect the output of one process to the input of another process
- ✓ Message queues: queue for storing messages sent to a process or thread
- ✓ Semaphores: synchronization element that is mainly used for controlling access to a shared resource by multiple threads or processes
- ✓ Shared memory: memory that can be accessed by multiple processes
- ✓ Signals: an asynchronous notification about an event sent to a process or a thread
- ✓ Sockets: end-points in a computer network that are used for communicating across the network

Deadlocks

A deadlock occurs when two or more sequences of code execution are waiting for each other to finish. The necessary conditions for a deadlock are

- ✓ At least one resource can't be shared by all the processes

- ✓ At least one process has acquired some resources and is waiting to acquire a resource
- ✓ Resources can't be preempted
- ✓ The processes are circularly waiting for resources (example: Process P0 is waiting for resources of process P1 and P1 is waiting for resources of P0)

Deadlock prevention schemes try to make sure that at least one of these necessary conditions doesn't hold good.

Segmentation

In segmentation, the logical memory is partitioned into segments that have variable lengths. To access a particular address, the user specifies the segment number and the offset within the segment.

Paging

In paging, the logical memory is broken into fixed sized blocks called pages. The physical memory is also partitioned into fixed sized frames. Page tables maintain the mapping between the logical memory and physical memory. TLB (Translation Lookaside Buffer) is a cache that stores the page table.

Virtual Memory

Virtual memory is a technique which enables execution of processes that can't be completely be stored in physical memory. Logical memory is divided into pages. The pages that are currently in use are stored in physical memory. The unused pages that can't fit into physical memory are stored on the disk. When a page that is not present in physical memory is accessed (a page fault), an unused page is swapped out from physical memory to the disk and the page stored on the disk is swapped into physical memory.

Belady's anomaly states that the number of page faults can increase with increase in number of pages stored in physical memory

Least Recently Used (LRU) is one of the most commonly used page replacement algorithm, where-in the least recently used page is replaced to make space for the incoming page.

7. Computer Science Concepts

Thrashing occurs when too many page faults occur and the process spends more time on paging than actually executing

<u>Miscellaneous</u>

Watch dog timers are used to detect if a system has become unresponsive. Watchdog timer is initialized to a value and allowed to count down to zero. If the system is operating correctly, then watch dog timer is reinitialized before the timer reaches 0. If the system becomes unresponsive due to a deadlock, then the watchdog timer doesn't get reinitialized and eventually the timer becomes 0. When a watchdog timer reaches 0, the typical action taken is to reboot the system

DMA (Direct Memory Access) allows hardware to directly access physical memory without the intervention of the processor

Interrupt is an asynchronous signal to the processor that an important event has occurred. The processor suspends the current activity, executes the appropriate interrupt service routine and then resumes the suspended activity.

1. What are the differences between a process and a thread?

Process and thread are sequences of code execution. A process can consist of one or more threads. Different threads in a process share the same address space whereas different processes running on a system have separate address spaces.

2. What are the differences between a mutex and a semaphore?

The primary function of a mutex is mutual exclusion. The mutex allows only a single thread to access a resource at a given time. A mutex has only two states - locked state and unlocked state.

The primary function of a semaphore is signaling. For instance, a thread can signal to another thread that a particular activity is complete using a semaphore. Semaphores are not restricted to just two states and have a count associated with them.

All the actions of a mutex can be performed using a semaphore but the reverse is not true.

3. What is the difference between a reentrant function and a thread safe function?

A reentrant function can be interrupted in the middle of its execution and then be safely resumed from its previous state. The interruption is usually caused by an interrupt service routine or a function call. The conditions for a function to be reentrant are

- A reentrant function should not have global data or static data
- A reentrant function should not modify its own code
- A reentrant function should not call non-reentrant functions

7. Computer Science Concepts

A thread-safe function can be called safely by multiple threads and maintains data concurrency even when accessed simultaneously by multiple threads.

A function can be thread-safe and still non-reentrant. For instance, consider a function that uses a lock on the critical section to ensure that it is thread-safe. Now suppose this function is used as an interrupt service routine. When the function is executing the critical section, another interrupt occurs and invokes the same function. The first instance of the function is suspended and the second instance of the function is invoked. However the second instance of the function can't complete as it can't enter the critical section since the first instance of the function has already acquired a lock on it. So this function is thread-safe but non-reentrant.

4. What are the main differences between kernel mode and user mode?

In the kernel mode, the code that is executed has complete and unrestricted access to CPU instructions, memory locations and underlying hardware. There is no protection offered in the kernel mode. So crashes in the kernel mode are catastrophic and will halt the entire system. Only the most basic functions of the OS which need to be carefully executed and the drivers which directly interact with the hardware are run in the kernel mode.

In the user mode, the code that is executed cannot directly access the underlying hardware. The code also can't access unallocated memory. Protection is offered in the user mode. So if a crash occurs in the user mode, then the system terminates execution of the offending process and recovers so that other user-mode processes can continue to be executed. Most of the programs developed by users run in user mode.

The Big Book of Coding Interviews

5. What are the main differences between a real time OS and a non-real time OS?

The primary goal of a real time OS is to provide deterministic execution time guarantees and to run fast. So the following differences are observed between a real time and non-real time OS

- a real time OS generally has no virtual memory
- a real time OS generally has no memory protection (mechanism to prevent a thread or task from accessing unallocated memory) and there is only a single mode in which the OS runs. A non-real time OS has memory protection and has a separate user mode and kernel mode.
- a real time OS generally has no dynamic linking

6. When are spin locks used?

When a thread uses a spin lock, it waits in a while loop until the lock is acquired. The thread does not go to a sleep state if the lock is currently unavailable. So the thread uses up CPU cycles as it waits on the lock. So this waiting is also called busy waiting.

Spin locks are efficient if the time needed to execute the critical section is smaller than the time taken to switch the context.

Consider a multi-core system where thread-A is executing on core-1 and thread-B is executing on core-2. Thread-A has successfully acquired the lock, while thread-B is waiting on the same lock. Let us say that the context switching time is 50 micro seconds and the time to execute the critical section is 20 micro seconds. If a normal lock was used, thread-B would be pre-empted and some other thread-C would be executed on core-2 after 50 micro seconds since the OS has to switch the context from thread-B to thread-C. However if a spin lock is used, after 20 micro seconds, thread-B can start executing on core-2 thereby saving 30 micro seconds.

Spin locks are also used in interrupt service routines since interrupt service routines can't go to a wait state (ISRs have to be processed immediately).

7. What is Priority Inversion?

Priority inversion is the scenario where a lower priority task is processed even though a higher priority task is waiting to be executed, thereby indirectly inverting the priorities of the tasks.

Consider 3 tasks L, M and H. L has lowest priority, M has medium priority and H has highest priority. Tasks L and H need to access a common resource R.

Initially task L is executing and locks the resource R. Then task H starts and tries to acquire R. Since L has already acquired the resource, H has to wait. Then task M starts. Since task M has higher priority than L, it pre-empts L. Now task M will continue until it is finished even though there is a higher priority task H. This is because task H can't run until L releases the resource and L can't run until M finishes. If the task H is starved due to priority inversion, then it can result in a serious system malfunction. This is what happened on the Mars Pathfinder. The high priority task was starved, causing the watch dog timer to reset the entire system.

To solve this issue, priority inheritance is used. When a high priority task waits on a resource held by a low priority task, the low priority task is temporarily assigned the priority of the high priority task until it releases the resource.

So in the example above if we used priority inversion, task L will get the priority of task H until it releases the resource. So task M can't pre-empt task L. Once task L releases the resource, it will get back its original priority. Then since task H is the highest priority task and it can acquire the resource released by L, task H will be scheduled next.

8. What is a race condition?

Race condition is a condition where the output of a system depends on the order in which events occur in the system. If the sequence in which the events occur is not how the programmer intended them to occur, then it can result in a bug. The problem with race conditions is that they are hard to reproduce and debug.

For instance, consider a multi-threaded system in which there are two threads and each thread tries to read the same shared variable, and then increments the value by 1.

If the order in which the events occur is as shown in the table below, then there is no problem

Thread-1	Thread-2	Value of shared variable
Read		1
Increment and write		1 + 1 = 2
	Read	2
	Increment and write	2 + 1 = 3

However if the order of execution of the two threads is as shown below, then there is a clear problem since the increment of the shared variable does not occur correctly.

Thread-1	Thread-2	Value of shared variable
Read		1
	Read	1
Increment and write		1 + 1 = 2
	Increment and write	1 + 1 = 2

To prevent race conditions from occurring, the critical section where a shared variable is operated upon should be protected using a synchronization construct such as a mutex or a semaphore, so that only one thread can be active in the critical section.

7. Computer Science Concepts

9. What is the difference between a DBMS (Database Management System) and a Relational DBMS?

In a DBMS, data is generally stored in files. It is not possible to apply normalization on the database. Example of a DBMS is an xml file.

In a Relational DBMS, the data is stored in a tabular form using the relational model. Since data is stored as tables, it is possible to apply normalization to the relational database. Example of a relational DBMS is mysql.

10. Describe the ACID properties in a database management system?

Each transaction in a database management system should follow the ACID properties: Atomicity, Consistency, Isolation and Durability

Atomicity: Each transaction may involve multiple operations in it. Atomicity indicates that every transaction should be treated as an atomic unit. Either all the operations in the transaction are completed or none of the operations are performed. For instance, if A wants to transfer $50 to B, then this transaction has two operations: debit A's account by $50 and credit B's account by $50. Atomicity indicates that we are not allowed to do only one operation. Either both the operations are done or none of them are done.

Consistency: If the database is consistent before the transaction, then it should remain consistent after the transaction is complete. For instance, suppose there is a request for buying 2 books but there is only one book in the warehouse, then the number of books in the database should not become negative.

Isolation: When there are concurrent transactions taking place in a database management system, the transactions should be isolated from one another. Each transaction is unaware of the other concurrent transactions.

Durability: Once a transaction is complete and the user has been notified about the success of the transaction, then the result of the transaction should persist and should not be lost. For instance, if a transaction is complete but before writing the result to the disk if the power is lost, then the results should be written to the disk once the power is back.

11. In SQL, what is the difference between inner join and outer join?

The join operation combines two tables into a single table. One of the fields in one table is used to find matching records in the other table. For instance, consider the Price table and the Quantity table below

ID	Price
A	$5
B	$2
C	$8

ID	Quantity
B	3
C	7
D	6

The join operation will be based on the key field ID which is common to both tables

Inner join will select the records where the joined keys are present in both the tables. So we get

ID	Price	Quantity
B	$2	3
C	$8	7

Left outer join will select all the records from the first table and those records from the second table that match the joined key. So we get

ID	Price	Quantity
A	$5	NULL
B	$2	3
C	$8	7

Right outer join will select all the records from the second table and those records from the first table that match the joined key. So we get

ID	Price	Quantity
B	$2	3
C	$8	7
D	NULL	6

Full outer join will select all the records from the first table and the second table.

ID	Price	Quantity
A	$5	NULL
B	$2	3
C	$8	7
D	NULL	6

12. What is denormalization?

Data normalization is the process of removing redundancy in a relational database. Denormalization is the opposite process wherein redundancy is introduced into a database in order to improve its performance.

When data normalization is done, the database is divided into multiple tables. When a query on the database is issued, data from two or more tables may have to be joined to get the result. This can slow down the performance. There are two ways in which redundancy can be introduced to speed up the performance:

1. Store multiple copies of each table on the disk - This keeps the design of the table free from redundancy. The database management system has to ensure that multiple copies are kept consistent

2. Have redundancy in the logical data design – This complicates the database design.

the Big Book of Coding Interviews

13. Differentiate between OSI model and TCP/IP model?

OSI is a theoretical model proposed by the International Organization for Standardization (ISO). It consists of 7 layers. The interfaces and services in the model are clearly defined.

TCP/IP is the protocol suite which is practically used for communicating on the internet. It consists of 4 layers. The interfaces and services are not clearly separated in TCP/IP.

The layers of OSI and TCP/IP are given below

OSI
Application
Presentation
Session
Transport
Network
Data link
Physical

TCP/IP
Application
Transport
Network
Network interface

13. What is circuit switching and packet switching?

In circuit switching, a static communication channel is established between the sender and the receiver. The communication channel is a dedicated channel that is used exclusively by the sender and receiver. The order of intermediate nodes in the communication channel is pre-established and doesn't change. The advantage of circuit switching is reliability while the disadvantage is low utilization of the communication channel.

In packet switching, the data to be transferred is divided into packets and sent across the network. The exact route which the packets will take is determined dynamically. Each packet can take a different path and the packets can arrive out of order. The advantage of packet switching is that the effective utilization of the communication channel increases.

15. Describe the TCP 3-way handshake?

If A wants to establish a TCP connection with B, then A first sends a TCP packet with the SYN (Synchronize) bit set to 1 in the TCP header. Let the sequence number in the TCP header of this packet be X.

When B receives the packet, B sends a response with SYN and ACK (Acknowledgement) bits set to 1. The sequence number in this packet is initialized to Y and the acknowledgement number is set to X+1.

On receiving the packet sent by B, A sends the response with ACK bit set to 1. The sequence number of this packet will be X+1 and the acknowledgement number will be Y+1.

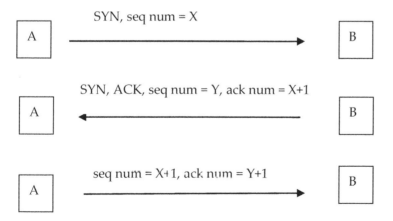

16. What is the difference between TCP and UDP?

The differences between TCP and UDP are

1. Connection: TCP is a connection oriented protocol that first establishes a connection between sender and receiver. UDP is a connectionless protocol where the packet is sent across the network without first establishing a connection

2. Reliability: As long as the connection is active, it is the responsibility of TCP to make sure that a transmitted packet is received by the receiver. If a packet is lost and the sender doesn't get back an acknowledgement for a packet, then the sender resends the packet. In UDP, since there is no acknowledgement sent for a received packet, the sender has no information if the packet was received at the destination

3. Ordering of packets: The TCP header consists of sequence numbers. So if the packets arrive out of order, TCP can rearrange the data packets so that the upper layer receives packets in the order in which they were sent. The UDP header doesn't consist of sequence numbers. So UDP can't guarantee that the data packets will be delivered in the order in which they were sent. If ordering of data packets is needed, then the application layer should take care of it.

4. Flow control: Flow control is performed in TCP. If the sender is fast and the receiver is slow, then flow control limits the rate at which data is sent by the sender. UDP has no flow control.

So UDP is a light weight protocol compared to TCP. Example of protocols that use TCP are HTTP, FTP and SMTP. Examples of protocols that use UDP are DNS (Domain Name System) and TFTP (Trivial File Transfer Protocol)

17. What is the difference between IPv4 and IPv6?

The differences between IPv4 and IPv6 are:

1. Address: An IPv4 address is 32 bit long whereas an IPv6 address is 128 bit long

7. Computer Science Concepts

2. Header length: The IPv4 header is 20 bytes long whereas an IPv6 header is 40 bytes long

3. Checksum: Checksum is present in the IPv4 header whereas the checksum is absent in the IPv6 header

4. Internet Protocol Security (IPsec): IPsec is optional in IPv4 whereas it is mandatory in IPv6

5. Fragmentation: Fragmentation is done by the host and routers in IPv4 whereas fragmentation is done only by the host in IPv6.

18. What are the sequence of events that occur when you type a URL in a browser?

The URL is first sent to a Domain Name Server. The DNS lookup happens over UDP. The DNS server returns the IP address corresponding to the URL.

The browser then makes a HTTP request to the server to get the web page. The HTTP request is sent via TCP. The IP address returned by the DNS server is filled into the destination address of the IP header. TCP will establish a 3 way handshake with the webserver. The webserver will then respond to the HTTP request with a HTTP response. The browser will parse the information sent by the web server and display it. Unless the connection is a persistent one, the webserver will close the HTTP session. The TCP connection between the browser and the webserver is closed using the four way handshake.

8. Puzzles

In most interviews, the interviewer asks puzzles to get an idea of the general problem solving skills of the candidate.

In this section, we will cover the following topics

1. Arithmetic puzzles
2. Measurement puzzles
3. Probability puzzles
4. Lateral thinking puzzles
5. Logic puzzles
6. Classic puzzles

8.1 Arithmetic Puzzles

1. In a certain type of sugar syrup, 99% of the weight of the sugar syrup is made of water while the remaining 1% is made of sugar. 100 pounds of sugar syrup is exposed to the sun and some of the water evaporates. The sugar syrup is now composed of 98% water. How much of water has evaporated?

It looks like 1 pound of water has evaporated, but this is not the right answer.

Initially we have 99 pounds of water and 1 pound of sugar in the sugar syrup. After the water evaporates, there is 98% of water and 2% of sugar. The amount of sugar remains constant after evaporation. So even after evaporation, there is still 1 pound of sugar in the sugar syrup.

Now 1 pound is 2% of the sugar syrup

So how many pounds (x) is 100% of sugar syrup

x = 100/2 = 50 pounds

So the final weight of the sugar syrup is 50 pounds. Of this, 1 pound is sugar. So only 49 pounds of water is present after evaporation. Before evaporation, we had 99 pounds of water. So the amount of water that has evaporated is 99 - 49 = **50 pounds**.

2. A car travels a distance of 60 miles from city A to city B at an average speed of 30 mph. How fast should the car travel on the return leg from city B back to city A so that the average speed for the entire journey is 60 mph?

At first glance it looks as if the car should be driven at a speed of 90 mph on the return journey so that the average speed for the entire journey is 60 mph. However this is not the case.

In the first leg of the journey, the car travels 60 miles at 30 mph. So the total time taken for the first leg of the journey = 60/30 = 2 hours.

For the return leg of the journey, the car travels 60 miles. Let the speed in the return journey be S and the time taken be T.

For the entire journey (from A to B and then back from B to A), the total distance covered = 60 + 60 = 120 miles. The total time for the entire journey = 2 + T

Average speed = total distance / total time

So average speed for entire journey = 120 / (2 + T)

Since average speed for entire journey must be 60 mph, 60 = 120 / (2+T)

If we solve this equation, we get T = 0. This means that the car should travel the 60 miles on the return leg within 0 time which implies that the car should travel at infinite speed! This is obviously not possible. So **it is not possible to achieve an average speed of 60 mph on the return journey.**

3. How many squares are there in a chessboard?

A chess board has 8 rows and 8 columns. Starting at any row and column we can form a square of size 1*1. Since there are 8 rows and 8 columns, the number of squares of size 1 are 8 * 8 = 64.

To form a square of size 2*2, we can't start from the last row and last column. For instance a 2*2 square can start in row 7 and extend into row 8, but it can't start at row 8 itself. So the number of 2*2 squares we can form = 7 * 7 = 49.

Similarly to form a square of size 3*3, we can't start from the last two rows and last two columns. So the number of 3*3 squares we can form = 6 * 6 = 36.

8.1 Arithmetic Puzzles

Using this reasoning, we can compute the total number of squares on the board as (8*8) + (7*7) + (6*6) + (5*5) + (4*4) + (3*3) + (2*2) + (1*1) = 64 + 49 + 36 + 25 + 16 + 9 + 4 + 1 = **204**

4. How many rectangles are there in a chessboard?

A chess board has 8 rows and 8 columns. To have 8 rows, there should be 9 horizontal lines (H1 to H9) and to have 8 columns, there should be 9 vertical lines (V1 to V9).

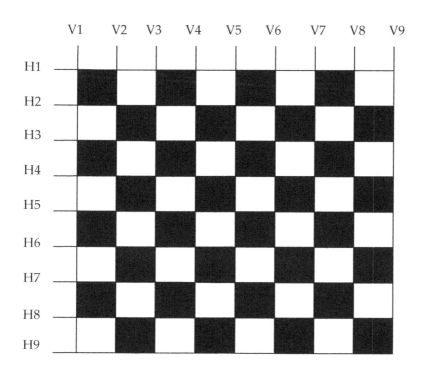

To form a unique rectangle, we can pick any 2 horizontal lines and any 2 vertical lines. For instance the intersection of the lines H1, H2, V3, and V7 forms one unique rectangle. The number of ways in which we can pick 2 horizontal lines out of 9 lines is $^9C_2$. The number of ways in which we can pick 2 vertical lines out of 9 lines is $^9C_2$. So the total number of rectangles = $^9C_2 * {}^9C_2$ = 36 * 36 = **1296**.

The Big Book of Coding Interviews

5. A small cube measures 1 * 1 * 1. 1000 such small cubes are used to make a single large cube that measures 10 * 10 * 10. The large cube is completely dipped in blue paint. How many of the small cubes have paint on them?

Each face of the cube measures 10 * 10. So there are 100 smaller cubes on each face. When a face is dipped in paint all the 100 smaller cubes get painted. Since there are 6 faces on a cube it looks like 6 * 100 = 600 cubes are painted. However this is not the correct answer since some of the cubes have been counted multiple times and have to be subtracted to arrive at the correct answer.

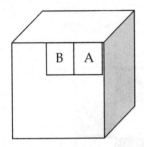

Consider the small cube (labeled A in the diagram) at the corner of the large cube. It gets counted 3 times since it is common to 3 faces. Ideally we should count it only once. So we should subtract 2 cubes for every corner cube. There are totally 8 corners in a cube. So we should subtract 2 * 8 = 16 cubes.

Consider the small non-corner cubes (labeled B in the diagram) that are at an edge of the large cube. There are 8 such small cubes at each edge (10 cubes along edge – 2 corner cubes = 8). These cubes are counted twice but they should have been counted only once. So we should subtract 8 cubes for each edge. There are totally 12 edges in a cube. So we should subtract 12 * 8 = 96 cubes.

So the total number of cubes that are painted = 600 - (16 + 96) = **488**

In general, if we have an N * N * N cube, then the number of non-unique smaller cubes = $6N^2$

Number of cubes to be subtracted at the corners = 8 corners * 2 per corner = 16 (this is independent of N). Number of cubes to be subtracted at the edges other than corners = 12 edges * (N-2) per edge = 12 * (N-2)

So the number of unique cubes that are painted = $6N^2 - (12(N-2) + 16) = 6N^2 - 12N + 8$

8.1 Arithmetic Puzzles

6. Find the angle between the hour hand and minute hand in a clock at any given time

---

Let the angles of the hour and minute hands be calculated from the 12 o' clock position.

The minute hand moves 360° in 60 minutes. So the number of degrees it moves in 1 minute = 360/60 = 6°. If the time is M minutes in the clock, then the angle made by the minute hand from the 12 o' clock position is $\theta_M = 6 * M$

The hour hand moves 360° in 12 hours. So the number of degrees the hour hand moves in 1 hour = 360/12 = 30°. The number of minutes in 12 hours = 60*12 = 720. So the hour hand moves 360° in 720 minutes. So the number of degrees it moves in 1 minute is 360/720 = 0.5° per minutes. If the time is H hours and M minutes in the clock, then the angle made by the hour hand from the 12 o' clock position is $\theta_H = 30H + 0.5M$

The absolute difference between θ_H and θ_M will give the angle between the hour hand and minute hand

= absolute_value(30H + 0.5M - 6M) = **absolute_value(30H - 5.5M)**

So if the time is 3:30, then the angle between the two hands = absolute_value(30*3 - 5.5 * 30) = 75°.

7. How many times will the hour hand and minute hand of a clock be exactly aligned in a day?

The minute hand is faster than the hour hand. The minute hand overtakes the hour hand many times in a day. Each time the minute hand overtakes the hour hand, the angle between them will be zero (0° and 360° are equivalent) and they will be exactly aligned. So to solve the problem, we need to find the number of times the minute hand overtakes the hour hand.

For each hour, the hour hand moves 360/12 = 30° whereas the minute hand moves 360°. So for each hour, the minute hand is ahead of the hour hand by 360 - 30 = 330°.

Over a 24 hour period, the minute hand will be ahead of the hour hand by 330 * 24 = 7920°

If the angle between the hour hand and minute hand is 360° - then there is 1 overtake

If the angle between hour hand and minute hand is 7920°- then how many overtakes (x)?

x = 7920 / 360 = 22

So the minute hand overtakes the hour hand 22 times in a day. So the hour hand and minute hand will be exactly aligned **22 times** in a day.

To calculate the exact time when the hour hand and minute hand are aligned, we use the formula derived in the previous problem: the angle between the hour hand and the minute hand = absolute_value(30H - 5.5M).

When the hour and minute hand are exactly aligned, the angle between them will be zero. So 30H - 5.5M = 0

M = 30 H / 5.5

Using this formula, for a particular hour H, we can calculate the minute M when the hands are exactly aligned as shown in the table below

Hour	Minute
0	0
1	5.45
2	10.91
3	16.36
4	21.82
5	27.27
6	32.73
7	38.18
8	43.64
9	49.09
10	54.54
11	60

Note that 11:60 is the same as 0:0

8.1 Arithmetic Puzzles

8. There are 100 players in a knockout tennis tournament where each loser is immediately eliminated and the winner advances to the next round. How many matches should be played to determine the final winner?

The easy way to solve the problem is to use the following argument: at the end of the tournament there will be only 1 winner and the remaining 99 players have to be eliminated. In each match, exactly 1 player is eliminated. So **99 matches** have to be played to eliminate 99 players and determine the final winner. In general if there are N players, then N-1 matches will be needed

9. There is a rectangular floor with size m*n. Square tiles have to be laid on the floor without breaking any tile so that the entire floor is covered. Find the maximum size of the square tile with which this is possible.

The total area of the floor is m*n. Let the length of one side of the square tile be k. Then the area of a single tile is k^2.

Let the number of tiles needed to fill the room be t.

Then, $t * k^2 = m * n$. So $t = m * n / k^2 = m * n / (k * k)$

Since the tiles should not be broken, the number of tiles t should be an integer. This implies that k should be a factor of m and k should also be a factor of n. So **the maximum possible size of the square tile is equal to the greatest common factor of m and n.**

We have already mentioned the procedure to calculate the greatest common factor in page 304.

10.

There are N people in a room. Two people shake hands only if they know each other. Prove that there are at least two people with the same number of handshakes

If a person does not know anyone then he will make no handshakes. If a person knows everyone else in the room then he will make N-1 handshakes. So the number of handshakes that a person can make is in the range 0 to N-1. So there are a total of N possibilities.

Now, if a person does not shake hands with anybody, then no person can shake hands with everybody in the room since one person didn't participate in the handshakes at all.

Similarly if a person shakes hands with everybody in the room, then no person can have 0 handshakes since everybody has participated in at least one hand shake.

So 0 handshakes and N-1 handshakes are mutually exclusive. Only one of them can occur and never both. So the number of possible handshakes a person can make is either in the range (1, N-1) or in the range (0, N-2). So that is a total of N-1 possibilities in either case.

There are N people and N-1 possible number of handshakes. So there are more people than the possible number of handshakes. Using the pigeon-hole principle, we infer that at least two of the people should have the same number of handshakes.

8.2 Measurement Puzzles

1. How will you get 4 gallons of water using a 3 gallon jug and a 5 gallon jug?

Fill the 3 gallon jug completely

Pour water from the 3 gallon jug completely into the 5 gallon jug. The 5 gallon jug now has 3 gallons of water.

Fill the 3 gallon jug completely

Pour water from the 3 gallon jug into the 5 gallon jug until the 5 gallon jug is full. So the 3 gallon jug now has 1 gallon of water.

Empty the 5 gallon jug completely

Pour the 1 gallon of water from the 3 gallon jug to the 5 gallon jug. The 5 gallon jug now has 1 gallon of water

Fill the 3 gallon jug completely

Pour the water completely from 3 gallon jug into the 5 gallon jug. The 5 gallon jug now has 4 gallons of water.

2. How will you get 6 gallons of water using a 7 gallon jug and a 4 gallon jug?

Fill the 7 gallon jug completely.

Fill the 4 gallon jug completely from 7 gallon jug. The 7 gallon jug now has 3 gallons of water.

Empty the 4 gallon jug

Fill the 4 gallon jug using the remaining 3 gallons of water in the 7 gallon jug. The 4 gallon jug now has 3 gallons and the 7 gallon jug is empty.

Fill up the 7 gallon jug completely.

Pour the water from the 7 gallon jug into the 4 gallon jug until the 4 gallon jug fills up. The 4 gallon jug already had 3 gallons in it and so it can only accept another one gallon. So 6 gallons remain in the 7 gallon jug.

3. How will you get 6 gallons of water using a 4 gallon jug and a 9 gallon jug?

Fill the 9 gallon jug completely.

Fill the 4 gallon jug completely from 9 gallon jug. The 9 gallon jug now has 5 gallons of water.

Empty the 4 gallon jug

Fill the 4 gallon jug completely using the remaining 5 gallons of water in the 9 gallon jug. The 9 gallon jug now has 1 gallon of water in it.

Empty the 4 gallon jug

Fill the 4 gallon jug using the remaining 1 gallon of water in the 9 gallon jug. The 4 gallon jug now has 1 gallon and the 9 gallon jug is empty.

Fill up the 9 gallon jug completely.

8.2 Measurement Puzzles

Pour the water from the 9 gallon jug to the 4 gallon jug until the 4 gallon jug fills up. The 4 gallon jug already had 1 gallon in it and so it can accept another 3 gallons. So 6 gallons remain in the 9 gallon jug.

4. There is a small jug with capacity x gallons and another bigger jug with capacity y gallons. x and y are co-prime. How will you get exactly 1 gallon of water using these two jugs?

Two numbers are co-primes if the only common factor between the two numbers is 1. For instance, 3 and 8 are co-prime.

If two numbers x and y are co-prime, we are guaranteed that there is some multiple of x which when divided by y leaves a remainder of 1 (this is called the multiplicative inverse property of co-primes under modulo operation). For instance, consider 33 which is a multiple of three. 33 on dividing by 8 gives a remainder of 1.

So to measure 1 gallon, we have to use the following technique

- Find the multiple M of x which when divided by y leaves a remainder of 1.

- Transfer a total of M gallons of water from the small jug to the big jug, x gallons at a time. If the big jug becomes full at any point, then discard the water in the big jug and keep continuing.

At the end, 1 gallon of water will be left in the large jug.

The Big Book of Coding Interviews

5. There are two sandglasses: one measuring 7 minutes and the other measuring 11 minutes. An egg needs 15 minutes to boil. Using just these two sandglasses, accurately measure 15 minutes and boil the egg.

First start the 7 minute sandglass and the 11 minute sandglass simultaneously.

When the 7 minute sandglass runs out, start boiling the egg.

When the 11 minute sandglass runs out, the egg would have boiled for 11-7 = 4 minutes.

Reverse the 11 minute sandglass and start it. When the 11 minute sandglass runs out, stop boiling the egg. The egg would have boiled for a total of 4+11 minutes = 15 minutes.

6. Using a 7 minute sandglass and a 4 minute sandglass, how can you measure 9 minutes?

First start the 7 minute sandglass and the 4 minute sandglass simultaneously. The measurement of 9 minutes duration starts as soon as both sandglasses are started

At 4 minutes, the 4 minute sandglass runs out. So reverse the 4 minute sandglass.

At 7 minutes, the 7 minute sandglass runs out. So reverse the 7 minute sandglass.

At 8 minutes, the 4 minute sandglass runs out again. Now 1 minute has passed since the 7 minute sandglass has been reversed. Reverse the 7 minute sandglass.

At 9 minutes, the 7 minute sandglass runs out since it had only 1 minute of sand left in it.

So this way 9 minutes can be measured using the 7 minute and 4 minute sandglasses.

8.2 Measurement Puzzles

7. There are two ropes. Each rope takes one hour to burn completely. The ropes burn non-uniformly. So the length of the ropes burnt can't be used to find the time elapsed. How will you time 45 minutes using the two ropes?

Start burning the first rope by lighting a fire at both ends of the first rope. At the same time, light a fire at one end of the second rope.

Since the fire is started from both ends of the first rope, the two flames will meet after 30 minutes (note that the point where the flames meet need not be the center of the rope as the ropes burn non-uniformly).

When the two flames in the first rope meet, the first rope will be completely burnt. The second rope will still need another 30 minutes to burn completely. Now start a flame at the other end of the second rope. The two flames on the second rope will meet after 15 minutes.

When the two flames on the second rope meet, a total of 30 + 15 = 45 minutes would have elapsed.

8. There are 8 marbles. One of the marbles weighs heavier than the other marbles. All the remaining 7 marbles have the same weight. You are given a weighing pan balance. Find the heavier marble using minimum number of weighings

We need only 2 steps to find the heavier marble.

Step 1: Place 3 marbles on the left side of the scale and 3 marbles on the right side of the scale.

If the scale indicates that the marbles on one of the side are heavier, then

> Step 2: Discard the 3 marbles from the lighter side of the scale and pick the 3 marbles from the heavier side of the scale. Reinitialize the scale. Place one of the marbles on the left side of the scale and another marble on the right side. If the scale indicates that one of them is heavier, then this is the heaviest marble. If the scale indicates that both are of the same weight, then the third marble which has not been used is the heaviest marble.

The Big Book of Coding Interviews

If the scale indicates that marbles on both sides are of the same weight, then

> Step 2: Discard all the 6 marbles from the scale. Reinitialize the scale. Two marbles remain. Place one of the marbles on the left pan and the other on the right pan. The scale will indicate the heaviest marble.

9. There are 10 boxes of oranges. Each box can contain either all good oranges or all bad oranges. One of the boxes contains bad oranges. The remaining 9 boxes contain good oranges. Each good orange weighs 1 pound while a bad orange weighs 0.9 pounds. You are given a digital weighing machine. How will you find the box which has bad oranges with just a single weighing?

It is possible to find the box with bad oranges using the digital weighing machine only once. Pick one orange from the first box, two oranges from the second box, ... n oranges from the nth box. Place all of them on the weighing machine and find the weight W.

There are a total of 1+2+3 ... +10 = 55 oranges. If all oranges were good the total weight should be 55 pounds. However since one of the boxes has bad oranges that are lighter, the weight will be less than 55 pounds.

If the weight W is 54.9, then there is exactly one bad orange in 55 oranges because a bad orange is lighter by 0.1 pound. Since the only box from which we picked only a single orange is the first box, the first box must have the bad orange.

Similarly if the weight is 54.8, then there are exactly two bad oranges in the 55 oranges. Since the box from which we picked exactly two oranges is the second box, the second box must have the bad oranges.

Using this reasoning we have the results below

Weight	Bad orange box number
54.9	1
54.8	2
54.7	3
54.6	4
54.5	5
54.4	6
54.3	7

8.2 Measurement Puzzles

54.2	8
54.1	9
54	10

10. There are 3 boxes of oranges. Each box can contain either all good oranges or all bad oranges. Any of the boxes can contain bad oranges. So the number of boxes that contain bad oranges can be 0 or 1 or 2 or 3. A good orange weighs 1 pound while a bad orange weighs 0.9 pounds. You are given a digital weighing machine. How will you find which boxes have bad oranges with just a single weighing?

It is possible to find the boxes with bad oranges using the digital weighing machine only once. Pick one orange from the first box, two oranges from the second box and four oranges from the third box (in general 2^{n-1} oranges from the nth box). Place the chosen oranges on the weighing machine and find the weight.

Based on the weight obtained, we can make the following inference

Weight	Inference
7	All the boxes have good oranges (1*1 + 2*1 + 4*1).
6.9	1st box has bad oranges (1*0.9 + 2*1 + 4*1).
6.8	2nd box has bad oranges (1*1 + 2*0.9 + 4*1).
6.7	1st and 2nd box have bad oranges (1*0.9 + 2*0.9 + 4*1)
6.6	3rd box has the bad oranges (1*1 + 2*1 + 4*0.9)
6.5	3rd box and 1st box have bad oranges (1*0.9 + 2*1 + 4*0.9)
6.4	3rd box and 2nd box have bad oranges (1*1 + 2*0.9 + 4*0.9)
6.3	All boxes have bad oranges (1*0.9 + 2*0.9 + 4*0.9)

The Big Book of Coding Interviews

11. A company has to sort boxes into the following four weight categories: 1-25 pounds, 26-50 pounds, 51-75 pounds and 76-100 pounds. A scale will be provided to weigh a box. If the weight of the box is within the range of the scale, then a bulb will glow otherwise the bulb will not glow. You can choose the range of the scale. For instance if you choose a scale 20-40 and weight of the box is 38, then the light will glow. Each scale is expensive. What is the minimum number of scales that you will need to sort the boxes?

The minimum number of scales required is **2**. The range of weights of the scales will be 1-50 pounds and 26-75 pounds. Weigh each box in both the scales and do the following:

If the 1-50 pound scale glows and the 26-75 pound scale is off, then the weight of the box is 1-25 pounds

If the 1-50 pound scale glows and the 26-75 pound scale glows, then the weight of the box is 26-50 pounds

If the 1-50 pound scale is off and the 26-75 pound scale glows, then the weight of the box is 51-75 pounds

If the 1-50 pound scale is off and the 26-75 pound scale is off, then the weight of the box is 76-100 pounds

12. You are given a weighing pan balance and asked to purchase weights to measure any whole number up to 100 pounds. What is the least number of weights that you need to purchase?

The answer that an interview candidate is most likely to give is that 7 weights are needed, the weights being: 1 pound, 2 pounds, 4 pounds, 8 pounds, 16 pounds, 32 pounds and 64 pounds. However this answer is wrong.

The least number of weights required is **5**, the weights are: 1 pound, 3 pounds, 9 pounds, 27 pounds and 81 pounds (powers of 3). Any number from 1 to 100 can be represented using a combination of addition and subtraction of these weights. For instance, the number 25 can be represented as 27 + 1 - 3. So to measure if an object weighs 25 pounds,

8.2 Measurement Puzzles

27 pounds and 1 pound is placed in one pan while the object and 3 pounds is placed in the other pan.

8.3 Probability Puzzles

1. It is night and the lights are not working in your room. The drawer has socks of three different colors - black, white and grey. How many socks do you have to remove from the drawers to be absolutely sure that you have a matching pair of socks?

Let us say that you remove two socks from the drawers. In the worst case both socks can be of different colors and you can't be sure of having a matching pair.

Let us say that you remove three socks from the drawers. In the worst case, all the three socks have different colors and you can't be sure of having a matching pair of socks. So in the worst case you will have 1 black socks, 1 white socks and 1 grey socks. Now when you pick up the fourth socks from the drawer, its color is either black or white or grey. So it has to match with any one of the socks that you already have. So to be absolutely sure that you have a matching socks pair, the least number of socks to pick up is **4**.

In general, the problem can be solved using the pigeon hole principle. If there are N unique item types, and N+1 items are chosen, then there will be at least one type which has two chosen items. For instance if a bag contains 50 red balls, 25 green balls, 34 blue balls and 48 yellow balls then there are 4 unique item types (red, green, blue and yellow). So to be absolutely sure to pick two balls of the same color, N+1 = 4+1 = 5 balls have to be picked.

8.3 Probability Puzzles

2. A bag contains a single marble that is either white or black. A new white marble is added to the bag and the bag is shaken. Then a marble is removed from the bag and it happens to be white. What is the probability that the remaining marble in the bag is also white?

It may initially look as though the answer is 0.5, but this answer is not correct.

Let marble P be inside the bag. Its color may be black or white. Let the white marble Q be added to the bag. A white marble is removed from the bag. So there are a total of three possibilities by which a white marble can be removed from the bag as shown in the diagrams below

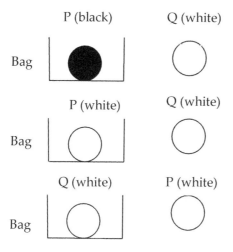

Out of these 3 possibilities, the bag has a white marble in two of the scenarios. So the probability of having a white marble in the bag is **2/3**.

3. Initially bag A has 10 red marbles and bag B has 10 blue marbles. Three marbles are randomly picked from bag A and added to bag B. Then 3 marbles are randomly picked from bag B and added to bag A. Which bag contains more marbles of the other color (which of the two is greater - the number of blue marbles in bag A OR the number of red marbles in bag B)?

Initially 3 red marbles are removed from bag A and added to bag B. Bag A now has 7 red marbles. Bag B now has 10 blue marbles and 3 red marbles.

Now 3 marbles are removed from bag B and added to A. The manner in which this can be done and the effect on the bags is shown in the table

Action	Effect on bag A	Effect on bag B
Remove 3 blue marbles from B and add to A	7 red, 3 blue	7 blue, 3 red
Remove 2 blue marbles and 1 red marble from B and add to A	8 red, 2 blue	8 blue, 2 red
Remove 1 blue marble and 2 red marbles from B and add to A	9 red, 1 blue	9 blue, 1 red
Remove 3 red marbles from B and add to A	10 red	10 blue

So there are four possibilities and in each of the four possibilities, the number of blue marbles in bag A is equal to the number of red marbles in bag B. So at the end, both bags contain the same number of marbles of the other color.

8.3 Probability Puzzles

4. There are 50 red marbles and 50 blue marbles. You are allowed to place all the marbles in two jars in whatever manner you want. One of the jars will then be randomly selected and given to you from which you have to pick a marble randomly. If you pick a blue marble you win. How should you arrange the marbles in the jars to maximize your chances of winning?

To maximize the chances of winning, place 1 blue marble in the first jar and place the remaining marbles (49 blue marbles and 50 red marbles) in the second jar.

The likelihood of selecting the first jar is 0.5. Once the first jar is selected, the likelihood of choosing a blue marble is 1 since there is only a single blue marble in the jar. So the likelihood of selecting the first jar and choosing the blue marble = 0.5 * 1 = 0.5

The likelihood of selecting the second jar is 0.5. Once the second jar is selected, the likelihood of choosing a blue marble = number of blue marbles / total number of marbles = 49 / (49+50) = 49/99. The likelihood of selecting the second jar and choosing the blue marble = 0.5 * 49 / 99 = 0.247

The overall likelihood of choosing the blue marble = 0.5 + 0.247 = **0.747**

5. You are given two dice. The first dice is a normal dice while the second dice has no numbers on it. How will you mark numbers on the second dice so that when both dice are thrown, the sum of the results of the two dice is uniformly distributed between 1 and 12?

Suppose we get a six on the second dice, then when the first dice generates numbers from 1 to 6, the sum of the results of the first two dice will be in the range 7 to 12.

Suppose we get a zero on the second dice, then when the first dice generates numbers from 1 to 6, the sum of the results of the first two dice will be in the range 1 to 6.

To ensure that there is an equal likelihood of generating numbers from 1 to 12, the second dice should have an equal number of zeroes and sixes. So three faces of the second dice should be marked with 0 and the remaining three faces of the second dice should be marked with 6.

6. You are participating in a game show where you are shown 3 doors. Behind one of the doors is a treasure. When you have decided which door to pick, the game show host opens another door which you have not chosen and shows that there is nothing behind. Now there are two doors left and behind one of them is a treasure - either the one you have picked or the one you haven't picked. You are allowed to change your original decision. What should you do?

The answer to this problem is counter-intuitive. It looks as though there is an equal likelihood that the treasure is behind any of the two doors. But this is not the case.

To have a deeper understanding, let us first modify the problem. Suppose there are 100 doors shown and there is treasure only behind one of the doors. When you choose a door there is a 1/100 chance that the treasure is behind that door. There is 99/100 chance that the treasure is behind some other door.

Now the game show host opens 98 of the doors and shows you that there is no treasure behind any of the 98 doors. Now the probability that there is treasure behind the door you have chosen continues to be 1/100. The probability that the treasure is present in the remaining doors continues to be 99/100. But only one of the remaining doors is unopened. So the probability of the treasure in the remaining unopened door which you didn't choose is 99/100. So if you are allowed to switch the doors, you should.

Similarly, when there are 3 doors and you choose 1 of the doors, the probability of treasure behind the door is 1/3. When the game show host opens one of the doors, then the probability that the treasure is behind the unopened door which you have not chosen is 2/3. So if you are allowed to switch the doors, you should.

7. There are 50 people in a room. Your friend offers a bet. If all persons in the room have different birthdays, then your friend will pay you $100. If any two people in the room share the same birthday, then you have to pay your friend $100. Will you accept the bet?

The likelihood that any two persons share the same birthday is 1/365. The likelihood that any two people have different birthdays is 364/365.

In the room of 50 people, the number of pairs of people present is $^{50}C_2 = 1225$.

8.3 Probability Puzzles

The probability that a pair of people have different birthdays is 364/365

So the probability that all the 1225 pairs have different birthdays is $(364/365)^{1225} = 0.035$.

So the probability that any of the 1225 pairs have the same birthday = 1 - 0.035 = 0.965.

So there is a very high likelihood that any two people share the same birthday. So **you should not take the bet**.

If the number of persons in the room is 23, then the likelihood of two people sharing the same birthday is 0.4995. If there are more than 23 people, then the likelihood of two people sharing the same birthday increases to more than 0.5. So you can accept the bet only if there are up to 23 people in the room.

8. In a particular country, people only want boy children. So if a family gets a boy child, the family stops having kids. If they get a girl child, then they continue to have kids until they get a boy. What is the ratio of boys to girls in this country? Assume that there is an equal likelihood of getting a boy or a girl.

Surprisingly the ratio of number of boys to number of girls is equal (1:1) in that country.

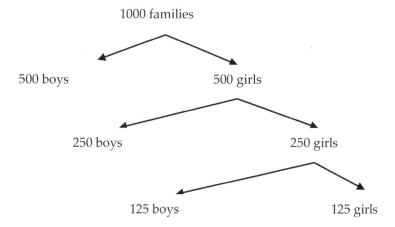

Let us say that there are 1000 families in the country. 500 of the families will have the first kid as a boy and 500 of them will have the first kid as a girl. So at this stage there are 500 boys and 500 girls. So the number of boys and girls are equal.

The Big Book of Coding Interviews

Next the 500 families that had a girl child will have a second child. In 250 of the families the second child will be a boy and in 250 of the families the second child will be a girl. This is shown in the diagram. So at this stage there are 500 + 250 = 750 boys. The number of girls = 500 + 250 = 750. So there are equal number of boys and girls.

Next the 250 families that had two girl children will have a third child. In 125 of the families, the third child will be a boy and in 125 of the families the third child will be a girl. This is shown in the diagram below.

So at this stage there are 500 + 250 + 125 = 875 boys. The number of girls = 500 + 250 + 125 = 875. So there are equal number of boys and girls.

We observe that at each stage, there are equal number of boys and girls and this will continue in further stages. So **the proportion of boys to girls will be 1:1**.

9. 100 airline travelers are waiting in line to board a plane that has 100 seats. Each traveler has been assigned a specific seat number on the plane. The first traveler in the line has lost his boarding pass and will pick one of the 100 seats at random to sit. The remaining travelers will sit in the seat assigned to them if it is free. But if the seat assigned to them is already occupied, then they will choose a random free seat. What is the probability that the last traveler to board the plane will sit in his proper seat?

Let the travelers in the line be labeled from T1 to T100. Let the probability that the traveler Ti will **not** sit in his seat be P(i).

The first traveler T1 has lost his boarding pass and will choose a seat at random.

The next passenger T2 will not sit in his seat, if T1 sits in T2's seat. T1 has a 1/100 chance of choosing T2's seat. So

P(2) = 1/100

T3 will not sit in his seat, if T1 sits in T3's seat or if T2 sits in T3's seat. T1 has a 1/100 chance of choosing T3's seat.

P(3) = 1/100 + probability that T2 sits in T3's seat.

8.3 Probability Puzzles

P(3) = 1/100 + probability that T2 doesn't sit on his seat * probability that T2 chooses seat of T3

By definition, probability that T2 doesn't sit on his seat is P(2). When T2 chooses, there are 99 seats available. So the probability that T2 chooses the seat of T3 is 1/99.

P(3) = 1/100 + P(2) * (1/99)

P(3) = 1/100 + (1/100) * (1/99)

P(3) = 1/100 (1 + 1/99)

P(3) = 1/99

T4 will not sit in his seat, if T1 sits in T4's seat or if T2 sits in T4's seat or if T3 sits on T4's seat. T1 has a 1/100 chance of choosing T4's seat.

P(4) = 1/100 + probability that T2 sits in T4's seat + probability that T3 sits in T4's seat

P(3) = 1/100 + (probability that T2 doesn't sit on his seat * probability that T2 chooses seat of T3) + (probability that T3 doesn't sit on his seat * probability that T3 chooses seat of T4)

By definition, probability that T2 doesn't sit on his seat is P(2). When T2 chooses, there are 99 seats available. So the probability that T2 chooses the seat of T4 is 1/99.

By definition, probability that T3 doesn't sit on his seat is P(3). When T3 chooses, there are 98 seats available. So the probability that T3 chooses the seat of T4 is 1/98.

P(4) = 1/100 + P(2) * (1/99) + P(3) * (1/98)

P(4) = 1/100 + (1/100) * (1/99) + (1/99) * (1/98)

P(4) = 1/98

We observe that P(2) is 1/100. P(3) is 1/99. P(4) is 1/98. Extending this we get P(100) = 1/2

So the probability that the 100th traveler does **not** sit on the seat assigned to him is 1/2.

So the probability that the 100th traveler sits on the seat assigned to him = 1 - 1/2 = 1/2

The Big Book of Coding Interviews

10. What is the probability that two dogs in the world have the same number of hair?

To solve the problem, we can use the pigeon hole principle which states that if n items have to be put into m pigeon holes and n > m, then at least one pigeon hole will have more than one item.

Let the number of dogs in the world be N. Let the maximum number of hair that a dog can have be H. If the number of dogs in the world is greater than the maximum number of hair on a dog, then applying the pigeon hole principle we are guaranteed to have two dogs with the same number of hair. The problem does not indicate the values for N and H. So we will have to guess here if N > H or not.

If we do some searching on the internet for the values for N and H, some sources indicate that the number of dogs is about 400 million and the average number of hair on a dog is about 1.5 million. So N > H and applying the pigeon hole principle the probability that two dogs share the same number of hair is **1**.

8.4 Lateral Thinking Puzzles

1. Cut a round cake into 8 equal pieces with three knife cuts

There are two ways to do it.

First method: Cut the cake into 4 equal parts with two cuts as indicated by the dashed lines in the diagram. Then make the third cut horizontally along the middle of the height of the cake so that the cake is divided into 4 pieces above and 4 pieces below.

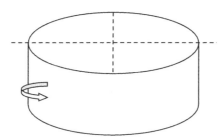

Second method: Cut the cake into 4 equal parts with two cuts. Then stack all the 4 pieces on top of each other and make the 3rd cut so that the 4 pieces get cut into 8 pieces.

The Big Book of Coding Interviews

2. Given a crescent moon shape, cut it into 6 parts using 2 straight lines

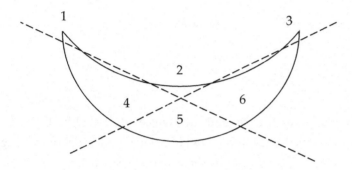

3. There are two cubes on a person's desk using which the person shows the current day of the month from 01 to 31. What numbers are present on the faces on the cubes?

We will have to represent the dates 11 and 22. So both cubes must have a 1 and a 2 on them.

We will also have to represent the dates 01 to 09. So 0 has to be paired with nine numbers. If we put 0 on one of the cubes, then we can pair this 0 with six numbers on the other cube. However we want 0 to be paired with nine numbers. This is possible only if 0 is present on both the cubes.

Let the two cubes be A and B. We have the following

A - 0, 1, 2

B - 0, 1, 2

8.4 Lateral Thinking Puzzles

There are a total of six positions still available - 3 on each cube. But we have to represent seven numbers still (3, 4, 5, 6, 7, 8, 9). To achieve this we have to do a little out of the box thinking and use the fact that 6 can be converted to 9 by inverting the cube. So it is sufficient to represent only one of them. So the cubes will be as follows:

A - 0, 1, 2, 3, 4, 5

B - 0, 1, 2, 6, 7, 8

4. There are 10 trees. How do you arrange them in a garden so that there are 5 rows, each row having 4 trees?

The trees should be placed on the dots shown in the diagram below. In this way we end up with 5 rows (ACFH, ADGJ, BCDE, BFIJ, EGIH), each having 4 trees

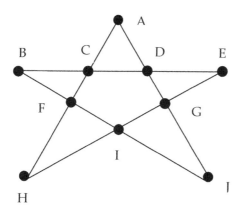

The Big Book of Coding Interviews

5. Arrange 9 trees in a garden so that there are 10 rows, each row having 3 trees

---

The trees are placed at the dotted points A, B, C, D, E, F, G, H and I as shown in the diagram below

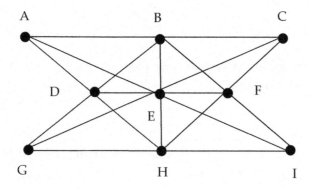

The 10 rows of trees are ABC, DEF, GHI, ADH, BDG, BFI, CFH, BEH, AEI and CEG

---

6. Can 4 trees on a farm be equidistant from each other?

If the farm is completely flat then this is not possible. However this is possible in 3 dimensions - the trees should be at the corners of a regular tetrahedron. So 3 trees on the farm form an equilateral triangle on the flat portion of the farm and the 4th tree is on an elevated portion at the middle of the equilateral triangle.

8.4 Lateral Thinking Puzzles

7. An ant is sitting at one corner of the cube and wants to go to the opposite corner of the cube. What is the shortest path that the ant can take?

The first answer that comes to mind is to take the diagonal path from A to C (or to F or to H) and then reach G from there. However this is not the correct answer. Let us say that the size of one edge of the cube is x. The ant is sitting at the corner A and wants to move to corner G. The shortest path for the ant is to take the path from A to P (P is the midpoint of BC) and then move from P to G.

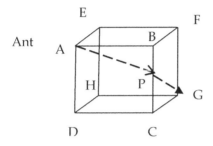

Using Pythagoras theorem, length of $AP^2 = AB^2 + BP^2$ (AB = x, BP = x/2)

So length of $AP = \sqrt{x^2 + \frac{x^2}{4}} = 1.12\,x$

Similarly the length of $PG^2 = CG^2 + PC^2$ (CG = x, PC = x/2)

So length of $PG = \sqrt{x^2 + \frac{x^2}{4}} = 1.12\,x$

So the total length of the shortest path = length of AP + length of PG = 1.12x + 1.12x = **2.24x**

8. An old man has three daughters. One day his intelligent friend visited him and asked the ages of his daughters. The old man replied that the product of their ages is 36. The friend couldn't figure out the ages and asked the old man for another clue. The old man replied that the sum of their ages was equal to his door number. The friend couldn't still figure out the ages and asked for another clue. The old man replied that only his youngest daughter had blue eyes. The friend immediately gave the correct answer. What are the ages of the old man's daughters?

Initially it looks like we can't figure out the ages of the daughters. The actual door number is not indicated in the problem. There are 3 unknown ages and we can construct only a single equation out of them. However if we consider all possible solutions to the problem and then go on filtering them out based on the old man's clues we can arrive at the correct answer.

The first clue indicates that the product of the ages of the 3 daughters is equal to 36. So let us find all possible groups of 3 numbers which when multiplied give 36. These are given below

Possible ages
(1, 1, 36)
(1, 2, 18)
(1, 3, 12)
(1, 4, 9)
(1, 6, 6)
(2, 2, 9)
(2, 3, 6)
(3, 3, 4)

The second clue indicates the sum of the ages. So let us find the sum of all the groups

Possible ages	Sum
(1, 1, 36)	38
(1, 2, 18)	21
(1, 3, 12)	16
(1, 4, 9)	14
(1, 6, 6)	13
(2, 2, 9)	13
(2, 3, 6)	11
(3, 3, 4)	10

Now in 6 of the cases the sum is unique. So if it was any of the 6 cases, then when the old man indicated the sum of the ages, the friend would have immediately been able to tell the ages of the daughters. But the friend couldn't find the ages based on the second clue. So this means that the door number had multiple answers associated with it. The only

8.4 Lateral Thinking Puzzles

sum that has multiple answers is 13. So the door number must have been 13. So the ages of the daughters may be (1, 6, 6) or (2, 2, 9).

The third clue indicates that only his youngest daughter has blue eyes. The possible answers are (1, 6, 6) and (2, 2, 9). We have to assume here that if two daughters are of the same age, then they are twins. So if only the youngest daughter has blue eyes, then the youngest daughter and second youngest daughter are not twins and so they should have different ages. The only solution that satisfies this is (1, 6, 6). So the ages of the old man's daughters are 1, 6 and 6.

9. There are 3 light bulbs inside a room. Outside the room there are 3 switches to those bulbs. The room is locked and has no windows. You are allowed to manipulate the switches before entering the room. Once you enter the room, you can't manipulate the switches. How will you find the switch for each bulb?

Put on the first switch for a few minutes. Then turn off the first switch and turn on the middle switch and go into the room. The middle switch is for the bulb which is glowing. Touch the remaining two bulbs and identify the bulb which is hot. The first switch is for the bulb which is hot but not glowing. The last switch is for the bulb which is neither hot nor glowing.

10. A sheikh tells his sons to race their camels to a distant city. The one whose camel is slower wins the race and inherits the fortune of the sheikh. The two brothers wander aimlessly in the desert until they reach an old man whom they ask for guidance. Upon hearing the advice of the old man, the two brothers run towards the camels and race to the city. What does the old man tell them?

The old man asks the two brothers to switch their camels. So now brother A has brother B's camel and vice versa. If A rides as fast as he can on B's camel and reaches the city first, then A's own camel will reach the city in second place and A will inherit the fortune. So the two brothers race the swapped camels and try to reach the city as soon as possible.

8.5 Logic Puzzles

1. There are three boxes, one containing only oranges, one containing only apples, and one containing both apples and oranges. However, EVERY box has been incorrectly labeled. You are allowed to pick only one fruit from any one of the boxes and then correctly label all the boxes. How will you do it?

Pick a fruit from the box labeled as Apples + Oranges. Since EVERY box is incorrectly labeled, the box labeled Apples + Oranges can't have both apples and oranges. It can have either apples or oranges.

Suppose the fruit that we picked from the box labeled Apples + Oranges is an apple, then

- the box labeled Apples + Oranges contains only apples
- the box labeled Oranges can't contain only oranges since each box is labeled incorrectly. It can't contain only apples since we have already found the box having only apples. So box labeled Oranges contains apples and oranges.
- the box labeled Apples should then be containing only oranges

Suppose the fruit that we picked from the box labeled Apples + Oranges is an orange, then

- the box labeled Apples + Oranges contains only oranges
- the box labeled Apples can't contain only apples since each box is labeled incorrectly. It can't contain only oranges since we have already found the box having only oranges. So box labeled Apples contains apples and oranges.
- the box labeled Oranges should then be containing only apples

The Big Book of Coding Interviews

2. There are two chests, a gold chest and a silver chest. Only one of the two chests has a treasure in it while the other chest is empty. The silver chest has the following inscription: "This chest is empty". The gold chest has the following inscription: "Only one of the two inscriptions is true". You are allowed to open only one chest. Which chest would you open?

Suppose the statement on the gold chest is correct, then the statement on the silver chest should be false since the gold chest states that only one of the inscriptions is true. So the silver chest is not empty and contains the treasure.

Suppose the statement on the gold chest is false, then there are two possibilities.

1. The statements on both the chests are false. So the silver chest is not empty and contains the treasure.

2. The statements on both the chests are true. However this is a contradiction, since we initially assumed that the statement on the gold chest is false and ended up with the conclusion that the statement on the gold chest is true. So we can discard this scenario.

So in all the valid scenarios, the silver chest has the treasure. So we can conclude that the silver chest has the treasure.

3. There are 3 chests - a silver chest, a gold chest and a bronze chest. The silver chest has the inscription "Treasure is in this Chest". The gold chest has the inscription "Treasure is not in this Chest". The bronze chest has the inscription "Treasure is not in the Gold Chest".

At least one of the inscriptions is true, and at least one of the inscriptions is false. You can open only one chest. Which one will you open?

We first note that the statements on the gold chest and the bronze chest are identical and just worded differently. So either the gold chest and bronze chest statements are both true or the gold chest and bronze chest statements are both false. We can't have gold chest statement true and bronze chest statement false since this will lead to a

8.5 Logic Puzzles

contradiction. Similarly we can't have the gold chest statement false and bronze chest statement true.

To solve this problem, let us form a truth table with all possibilities.

Silver chest	Gold chest	Bronze chest	Inference
T	T	T	not possible since the problem states at least one statement is false but here all statements are true
T	T	F	not possible since there is a contradiction between gold chest and bronze chest
T	F	T	not possible since there is a contradiction between gold chest and bronze chest
T	F	F	this indicates treasure is in the silver chest and that treasure is in the gold chest. But only one chest has the treasure. So this is not possible
F	T	T	**possible.** this indicates the treasure is in bronze chest
F	T	F	not possible since there is a contradiction between gold chest and bronze chest
F	F	T	not possible since there is a contradiction between gold chest and bronze chest
F	F	F	not possible since the problem states at least one statement is true but here all statements are false

So the treasure is in the bronze chest.

The Big Book of Coding Interviews

4. There are 100 statements written on a sheet of paper. The first statement says "At most 0 of these 100 statements are true". The second statement says "At most 1 of these statements are true". The nth statement says "At most (n-1) of these statements are true." The last statement says "At most 99 of these statements are true". So how many of these 100 statements are actually true?

Let us first look at a smaller case where there are 4 statements. Let the exact number of true statements be N.

Statement A: "At most 0 of the 4 statements are true" (indicates $N \leq 0$)

Statement B: "At most 1 of the 4 statements are true" (indicates $N \leq 1$)

Statement C: "At most 2 of the 4 statements are true" (indicates $N \leq 2$)

Statement D: "At most 3 of the 4 statements are true" (indicates $N \leq 3$)

Number of true statements (N)	True statements	Inference
N = 0	A ($N \leq 0$), B ($N \leq 1$), C ($N \leq 2$), D ($N \leq 3$)	4 statements – A, B, C, D are true. But we assumed that 0 statements are true. So this is a contradiction
N = 1	B ($N \leq 1$), C ($N \leq 2$), D ($N \leq 3$)	3 statements - B, C, D are true. But we assumed that exactly 1 statement is true. So this is a contradiction
N = 2	C ($N \leq 2$), D ($N \leq 3$)	2 statements – C and D are true. We also assumed that exactly 2 statements are true. So this is **possible**
N = 3	D ($N \leq 3$)	1 statement – D is true. But we assumed that exactly 3 statements are true. So this is a contradiction
N = 4	N > 3	All the 4 statements – A, B, C and D are false. But we assumed that all 4 statements are true. So this is a contradiction

8.5 Logic Puzzles

So the only possible scenario when there is no contradiction is when exactly 2 out of the 4 statements are true. So if we have 4 statements, then exactly half of them (the last two statements) can be true. Extending this to 100 statements, exactly 50 statements (the last 50 statements) can be true without any contradictions.

5. Bob is lost in a forest and comes across a fork in the path: one way leads to a safe village while the other leads to hungry cannibals. There are two brothers present at that location. One of the brothers is always honest and the other always lies. Bob doesn't know which brother is honest and which brother lies. Bob can only ask a single question. What question should Bob ask?

Suppose Bob asks the question "which is the safe path?", the honest brother will point to the safe path while the lying brother will point to the cannibals. Since the two answers are different and since Bob does not know who the honest brother is, Bob has no way of figuring out the correct path. To solve this problem, Bob should ask a question so that both brothers give the same answer. One way to do this is to ask the honest brother what answer the lying brother will give and ask the lying brother what answer the honest brother will give. So Bob should ask the question "According to your brother, which path leads to the cannibals?".

If the question "which path leads to the cannibals?" is asked to the lying brother, the lying brother will indicate the safe path. So if Bob asks the honest brother "According to your brother, which path leads to the cannibals?", the honest brother will indicate the safe path.

If the question "which path leads to the cannibals?" is asked to the honest brother, the honest brother will indicate the path to the cannibals. So if Bob asks the lying brother "According to your brother, which path leads to the cannibals", the lying brother has to give the answer opposite to that of the honest brother. So the lying brother also indicates the safe path. So both brothers indicate the safe path and Bob can safely proceed in that direction.

The Big Book of Coding Interviews

6. Bob is lost in a forest and comes across a fork in the path: one way leads to a safe village while the other leads to hungry cannibals. There is a man present at that location but Bob doesn't know if he is honest or if he lies. Bob can only ask a single question. What question should Bob ask?

Since Bob doesn't know if the man is honest or if he always lies, Bob should ask a question for which an honest man and a lying man will give the same answer. To achieve this Bob should make use of the fact that lying on a lie will result in the truth. So Bob should ask the question "If I were to ask you which is the safe path, what would you indicate?"

Suppose the man is honest. The honest man will indicate the safe path when asked the question.

Suppose the man lies. If Bob asks the lying man the question "which is the safe path?", then the lying man would indicate the path to the cannibals. So if the man lies, the truthful answer to the question "If I were to ask you which is the safe path, what would you indicate?" is "the path to the cannibals". However the lying person always gives false answers. So when the lying man is asked "If I were to ask you which is the safe path, what would you indicate?" the lying man will indicate the opposite path – the safe path. So this way the lying person is forced to lie on a lie resulting him answering truthfully and indicating the safe path.

In both cases, if a man is honest or if he is lying, the safe path is always indicated. So Bob can safely take the direction indicated by the man

7. A box contains 3 black hats and 2 white hats. Three men A, B, and C pick one hat each from the box and place it on their heads. Each person does not know the color of the hat he is wearing. A can see the hats worn by B and C. B can see the hat worn by C. C can't see any hats. A is asked if he knows the color of the hat he is wearing. A replies no. B is asked if he knows the color of the hat he is wearing. B replies no. C is asked if he knows the color of the hat he is wearing, C replies yes and correctly tells the color of his hat. What is the color of C's hat?

8.5 Logic Puzzles

Suppose B and C are wearing white hats. Since there are only two white hats, A will know that he is wearing a black hat. But A does not know the color of the hat he is wearing. So B and C should be wearing one of the following combinations

B	C
Black	White
White	Black
Black	Black

Now there are 3 possibilities. Consider the first possibility. Suppose C is wearing a white hat, then B can only be wearing a black hat. So when B sees C wearing a white hat, B will know for sure that B is wearing a black hat. However, B does not know the color of the hat that B is wearing. So this rules out the first possibility.

In the second and third possibilities, C wears a black hat and B could be wearing a white or black hat. Both the possibilities fit with the case where B knows the color of C's hat but can't figure out the color of B's own hat. In both possibilities C is wearing a black hat. So C should be wearing a black hat.

8.6 Classic Puzzles

1. Four men want to cross a bridge at night. Since it is night, the men need to carry a flashlight while crossing the bridge but there is only one flashlight. The bridge is strong enough only for 2 men to cross at a time. If 2 men simultaneously cross the bridge, they will move at the speed of the slower man. The first person takes 1 minute to cross the bridge, the second person takes 2 minutes, the third person takes 5 minutes and the fourth person takes 10 minutes. What is the least time that they need to cross the bridge?

Let the persons be labeled A (1 minute), B (2 minutes), C (5 minutes) and D (10 minutes)

Since there is only one flashlight, after two men cross the bridge, one of the men has to return back with the flashlight. One strategy is to make the fastest man A to return with the flashlight each time. With this approach, we can do the following:

A and B cross the bridge in 2 minutes

A returns back in 1 minute

A and C cross the bridge in 5 minutes

A returns back in 1 minute

A and D cross the bridge in 10 minutes

So the total time taken is 2 + 1 + 5 + 1 + 10 = 19 minutes

However there is a better strategy which can reduce the time to 17 minutes. The idea is to make the slowest two persons cross the bridge together and on the return journey have a faster person return. With this approach we can do the following:

8.6 Classic Puzzles

A and B cross the bridge in 2 minutes

A returns back in 1 minute

C and D cross the bridge in 10 minutes (the two slowest persons are grouped together)

B returns back in 2 minutes (B who is already at the other end of the bridge is faster than C and D and returns back)

A and B cross the bridge in 2 minutes

The total time taken is 2 + 1 + 10 + 2 + 2 = 17 minutes

So the shortest time taken is **17 minutes**

2. There are 3 missionaries and 3 cannibals who want to cross the river using a boat. The boat can carry a maximum of 2 people. If the cannibals outnumber the missionaries, then the cannibals will eat the missionaries. How will the missionaries cross the river without being eaten by the cannibals?

Let M represent a missionary and C represent a cannibal. The missionaries and cannibals have to move from bank A to bank B. Then the sequence of actions that should be taken are shown in the table

Trip Nr	Travel	Starting Bank (A)	Ending Bank (B)
Initial		3M, 3C	
1	1M, 1C move from A to B	2M, 2C	1M, 1C
2	1M moves from B to A	3M, 2C	1C
3	2C move from A to B	3M	3C
4	1C moves from B to A	3M, 1C	2C
5	2M move from A to B	1M, 1C	2M, 2C

6	1M, 1C move from B to A	2M, 2C	1M, 1C
7	2M move from A to B	2C	3M, 1C
8	1C move from B to A	3C	3M
9	2C move from A to B	1C	3M, 2C
10	1C moves from B to A	2C	3M, 1C
11	2C move from A to B		3M, 3C

So finally the 3 missionaries and the 3 cannibals are present on bank B.

3. How will three people find their average salary without revealing their individual salaries to each other?

Let the 3 persons be A, B and C.

A first picks a random number which is known only to A.

A then adds his salary to the random number and passes on the result to B (C should not get to know the value passed on from A to B).

B then adds his salary and passes on the result only to C (A should not get to know the value passed on from B to C)

C then adds his salary and passes on the result back to A. (B should not get to know the value passed from C to A)

A then subtracts the random number from the result to get the sum of the salaries of the 3 people. Dividing the sum of salaries by 3 will give the average salary.

8.6 Classic Puzzles

4. A king has organized a party in 24 hours. 13 barrels of wine are going to be used for the party. However the king has come to know that one of the 13 barrels contains a poison. Consuming even a drop of wine from the poisoned barrel can make a person very sick. It takes about 24 hours for the poison to act. The king decides to use the prisoners to taste the wine and determine which barrel contains the poison. What is the least number of prisoners required?

The least number of prisoners required is **4**.

Let the Barrels be labeled B1 to B13. Let P1, P2, P3 and P4 be the four prisoners. The table below gives the barrels from which each prisoner will drink

	P1	P2	P3	P4
B1	0	0	0	0
B2	0	0	0	1
B3	0	0	1	0
B4	0	0	1	1
B5	0	1	0	0
B6	0	1	0	1
B7	0	1	1	0
B8	0	1	1	1
B9	1	0	0	0
B10	1	0	0	1
B11	1	0	1	0
B12	1	0	1	1
B13	1	1	0	0

None of the prisoners drink from barrel B1. So if none of the prisoners fall sick, then the poison is in B1

Only prisoner P4 drinks from barrel B2. So if only P4 falls sick, then the poison is in B2.

Only prisoner P3 drinks from barrel B3. So if only P3 falls sick, then the poison is in B3.

Only prisoners P3 and P4 drink from barrel B4. If only P3 and P4 fall sick, then the poison is in B4.

This technique can be extended to all the barrels.

5.

A worker is going to work under you for 7 days. Each day the worker should be paid 1/7th portion of a silver bar. How will you pay the worker if you are allowed to cut the silver bar at two places only?

If we were permitted to cut the silver bar at 6 places, then we could have got 7 equal pieces. Each day we could pay one piece to the worker. However we are allowed to cut the silver bar at two places only.

To solve the problem, cut the silver bar at two places so that we have 3 pieces with lengths 1/7, 2/7 and 4/7. On the first day, give the worker the 1/7 piece. So the worker now has 1/7 portion of the silver bar.

On the second day, take back the 1/7 piece from the worker and give him the 2/7 piece. So the worker now has 2/7 portion of the silver bar

On the third day, give the worker the 1/7 piece. So worker now has 2/7 + 1/7 = 3/7 portion of the silver bar

On the fourth day, take back the 1/7 and 2/7 pieces from the worker and give him the 4/7 piece. So the worker now has 4/7 portion of the silver bar.

On the fifth day, give the worker the 1/7 piece. So the worker now has 4/7 + 1/7 = 5/7 portion of the silver bar.

On the sixth day, take back the 1/7 piece from the worker and give him the 2/7 piece. So the worker now has 4/7 + 2/7 = 6/7 portion of the silver bar.

On the seventh day, give the 1/7 piece to the worker. Now the worker has the entire silver bar with him.

8.6 Classic Puzzles

6. There are many coins on the table of which 10 of the coins have heads facing up while the remaining have tails facing up. A blindfolded person has to split the coins into two groups such that each group has the same number of coins with heads facing up. The person does not know the total number of coins present and the person has no way of finding out which side of the coin is facing up. How can this be done?

Pick any 10 coins and form one group. The remaining coins form the other group. In the group having 10 coins, flip all the 10 coins to the opposite side. Now the number of heads is equal in both the groups.

To see how this solution works let us first take a specific case of 50 coins where 10 coins have heads facing up and 40 coins have tails facing up. Now pick any 10 coins and form a group. Let us say that there are 4 heads in this group. The remaining group will have 40 coins out of which there are 10 - 4 = 6 heads (since the total number of coins with heads facing up = 10)

	G1	G2
Heads	4	6
Tails	6	34

When we flip all the coins in the first group to the opposite side, we get the following

	G1	G2
Heads	6	6
Tails	4	34

So there are equal number of heads in both groups.

To see that this solution works in general, let the total number of coins be N with 10 coins having heads facing up. We form a group of 10 coins of which let us say x coins have heads. The remaining $10-x$ coins will have tails.

The total number of coins in the second group is $N - 10$ since the first group has 10 coins. The number of coins with heads in the second group will be $10-x$ since the total number of heads is 10 of which x heads are in the first group. The number of tails in the second group = total number of coins in second group - number of heads in second group = $(N - 10) - (10-x) = N-20+x$

The Big Book of Coding Interviews

	G1	G2
Heads	x	10-x
Tails	10-x	N-20+x

When we flip the coins in the first group, we get the following

	G1	G2
Heads	10-x	10-x
Tails	x	N-20+x

So the number of heads is the same in the two groups.

7. Alice has to take exactly one pill of type A and one pill of type B every day. On one day, Alice opens the A pill container and drops one pill on her hand. Then she opens the B pill container and accidentally drops two pills on her hand. The A pill and B pill look exactly identical and their weight is also the same. Now Alice doesn't know which pill on her hand is the type A pill and which pill is the type B pill. How will Alice ensure that she takes the correct dosage of the pills without wasting any pills?

Alice has two pills of type B and one pill of type A but she doesn't know which is which. To solve the problem, Alice drops one more pill of type A onto her hand. She now has 2 pills of type A and 2 pills of type B. She then breaks each pill into exactly two halves. The upper half of each pill is collected into one group and the lower half of each pill is collected into another group.

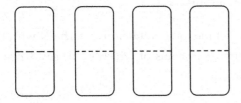

The upper half group will have some permutation of 0.5A, 0.5A, 0.5B and 0.5B. So totally we have 1 pill of type A and 1 pill of type B in the group. Alice can take the pills in

the upper half group today. Similarly the lower half group will also totally have 1 pill of type A and 1 pill of type B. She can take the pills in the lower half group tomorrow.

8. Consider a game where coins have to be placed on a circular table. All coins are of the same size. There are two players: you and your friend. Each person takes turns placing a coin on the table. The last person to place a coin on the table wins. What strategy would you use to always win the game?

To always win the game, you should play first and place the coin at the center of the circular table. From then on, whenever your friend places a coin on the table, you should choose the diametrically opposite position to place your coin as shown in the diagram. If your friend has found a position, you are assured to find the position diametrically opposite to it to be vacant. So you will always place the last coin on the table

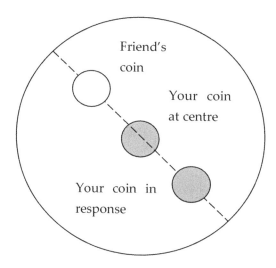

The Big Book of Coding Interviews

9. You and your friend play a game of calling out numbers with the following rules: A player starts the game by calling out a number between 1 and 10. The next player should then call out a number that exceeds the previous player's number by at least 1 and no more than 10. The first person to call out 50 is the winner. What strategy would you use to win the game?

Generalize the strategy for any value N that the winner calls out in the end.

To solve this problem, let us work backwards. Suppose you call 39, then your friend is forced to choose a number between 40 and 49. You can then choose 50 and win. So your friend has no chance to win the game if you choose 39.

If you choose 28, then your friend is forced to choose a number from 29 to 38 and you can choose 39 which will result in you winning the game. So you can always win if you choose 28.

If you choose 17, then your friend is forced to choose a number from 18 to 27 and you can choose 28 which will result in you winning the game. So you can always win if you choose 17.

If you choose 6, then your friend is forced to choose a number from 7 to 16 and you can choose 17 which will result in you winning the game. So you can always win if you choose 6.

So to win the game you should be the first person to call out the number and you should call out 6.

The key to this game is that if you have chosen the number X, and your friend chooses X+A, then you can choose the number X+A+B where B is 11 - A. So if you chose X previously, then no matter what your friend chooses, you can always choose X+11 in your next turn.

Suppose we have to develop a general strategy for any value of N that the winner calls out in the end. Then we have to do the following:

> Find the remainder when N is divided by 11

> If the remainder is non-zero, then your strategy is to start first and pick the remainder of N /11 as your first number (So if N is 50, the remainder of 50/11 is 6.

So you should pick 6 as the starting number). Then when it is your turn to pick a number, you have to add 11 to your previous number (So the next numbers you will choose are 6+11 = 17, 17+11 = 28 and so on).

> If the remainder is 0, then your strategy is to allow your friend to start first. Then for each of your turn, you should choose the next multiple of 11. (So first pick 11, then 22 and so on)

10. To share a cake fairly between two people, one person cuts the cake and the other chooses. Three people want to fairly share a cake using this principle. How can they do it?

Let us say that three people A, B and C want to fairly share the cake using this principle. Then they have to do the following:

- A and B divide the cake equally amongst themselves where one of them cuts the cake and the other chooses. A now has half the cake and B has the other half of the cake.

- A then divides his share of the cake into three pieces and C chooses one piece. A is forced to cut fairly so that the three pieces are equal otherwise C will choose the larger piece.

- B also divides his share into three pieces and C chooses one piece. B is also forced to cut fairly so that the three pieces are equal otherwise C will choose the larger piece.

So A, B and C each now have 2 out of 6 equal pieces. So each has 1/3rd of the cake.

The Big Book of Coding Interviews

11. There is a cuboid cake from which someone has already cut out a small cuboid cake piece. How will you divide the remaining cake into two equal portions?

To solve this problem, the main idea we have to use is that any line passing through the center of a rectangle divides the rectangle into two portions of equal area. For instance in the diagram below, the line through the center divides the rectangle into two portions of equal area

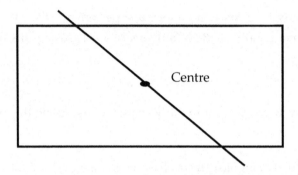

Now let us assume that the cake is flat and rectangular. Suppose a small rectangular portion is cut out of the cake and is missing from the cake and we have to divide the remaining cake into two equal partitions. We can achieve this if we can divide the original rectangular cake into two equal parts and the missing rectangular portion into two equal parts simultaneously. This way the missing portion and the remaining portion of the cake are equally shared by the two equal partitions.

Any line passing through the center of the original cake will divide the original cake into 2 equal parts. Any line passing through the center of the cut out rectangular portion will divide the missing portion into two equal parts. So to simultaneously achieve both, we need to pick the line that passes through the center of the original rectangle C1 and center of the cut out rectangle C2 as shown in the diagram below.

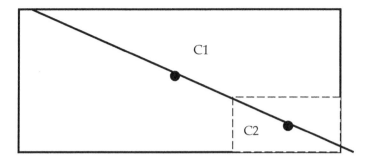

The same idea can be extended to 3 dimensions. So to divide the remaining cuboid cake into two equal parts, cut along the line joining the center of original cuboid cake and the center of the missing cuboid piece.

12. There are 25 racehorses and 5 race tracks. What is the least number of races needed to find out the top three fastest horses? Watches are not allowed to measure the time taken by the horses.

We can find out the fastest 3 horses in 7 races as described below.

Divide the horses into 5 groups, A, B, C, D and E. Each group has 5 horses. If a horse's rank in group A is N, then it is denoted as A-N. So the fastest horse in group A is represented as A-1.

Race each group of 5 horses. This requires 5 races. We then retain the 3 fastest horses in each race and discard the remaining horses. So we are left with A-1, B-1, C-1, D-1, E-1, A-2, B-2, C-2, D-2, E-2, A-3, B-3, C-3, D-3 and E-3.

In the 6th race, pick the fastest horse in each group and race them. So we will race A-1, B-1, C-1, D-1 and E-1. The horse that comes first in the race is the fastest horse among all the 25 horses.

For ease of understanding, let us assume that in the 6th race, A-1 comes first, B-1 comes second, C-1 comes third, D-1 comes fourth and E-1 comes fifth in the race. Then D-1 and E1 can be eliminated. Since D-2 and D-3 are slower than D1, D2 and D3 can also be eliminated. Since E-2 and E-3 are also slower than E1, E2 and E3 can also be removed.

Since A-1 is the fastest horse, only B-1 and B-2 may be present in the top 3. B-3 will definitely not be present in the top 3. So B-3 can be removed.

Similarly since A-1 is fastest and B-1 is second fastest, only C-1 may be present in the top 3. C-2 and C-3 will definitely not be present in the top 3. So C-2 and C-3 can be removed.

Now we are left with A-1, A-2, A-3, B-1, B-2 and C-1. We know that A-1 is the fastest. So in the 7th race, we race A-2, A-3, B-1, B-2 and C-1. The fastest horse in the 7th race will be the second fastest in the group of 25 horses. The second fastest horse in the 7th race will be the third fastest in the group of 25 horses.

13. There are 100 people stranded on an island. A ship reaches the island and the captain of the ship decides to play a game. Each person will be made to wear a hat which is either red or blue. Each person does not know the color of the hat he is wearing. All the people are then made to stand in a line. A person can see the color of all the hats of the persons in front of him. The captain then will start asking each person to identify the color of his own hat starting from the person at the back of the line. If the person guesses the color correctly he will be saved otherwise he will have to stay on the island. What strategy can be used to save the maximum number of people?

The last person in the line counts the number of blue hats in front of him.

Scenario-1: If there are odd number of blue hats on the 99 people ahead of the last person, the last person shouts blue. Now the 99th person counts the number of blue hats on the 98 people ahead of him. After counting the blue hats, the table below can be used to find the color of the 99th person's hat.

Number of blue hats in the first 99 people	Number of blue hats in the first 98 people	Inference
Odd	Odd	99th person must be wearing red since the number of blue hats in the first 99 people should be odd
Odd	Even	99th person must be wearing blue since number of blue hats in the first 99 people should be odd

8.6 Classic Puzzles

Scenario-2: If there are even number of blue hats on the 99 people ahead of the last person, the last person shouts red. Now the 99th person counts the number of blue hats on the 98 persons ahead of him. After counting the blue hats, the table below can be used to find the color of the 99th person's hat.

Number of blue hats in the first 99 people	Number of blue hats in the first 98 people	Inference
Even	Odd	99th person must be wearing blue since the number of blue hats in the first 99 people should be even
Even	Even	99th person must be wearing red since the number of blue hats in the first 99 people should be even

Now the remaining persons in the line can use similar logic to find the color of his hat using the table below. A = B + C + 1 if person X wears a blue hat. A = B + C if X wears a red hat

A: Number of blue hats in first 99 persons as indicated by 100th person	B: Number of blue hats called out from the previous persons, excluding 100th person	C: Number of blue hats in front of person X (excluding X)	The color of hat of person X
odd	odd	odd	B+C is even, A is odd. So X = blue
odd	odd	even	B+C is odd, A is odd. So X = red
odd	even	odd	B+C is odd, A is odd. So X = red
odd	even	even	B+C is even, A is odd. So X = blue
even	odd	odd	B+C is even, A is even. So X = red
even	odd	even	B+C is odd, A is even. So X = blue
even	even	odd	B+C is odd, A is even. So X = blue
even	even	even	B+C is even, A is even. So X = red

Using this strategy it is possible to definitely save the first 99 people in the line. The last person in the line has a 50% chance of correctly guessing the color of his hat.

14. A warden gives a challenge to 23 prisoners. Each day a random prisoner is chosen and brought to a room that has two switches. The prisoner has to choose one of the switches and then toggle the chosen switch. The prisoners will be kept isolated from each other at all times and so they can't communicate with each other. If a prisoner can correctly guess when all the prisoners have visited the switch room at least once, then they win their freedom. How can the prisoners achieve this?

Let the two switches in the room be called switch A and switch B. The prisoners will choose one of the prisoners to be the leader. The remaining 22 prisoners are referred to as helper prisoners.

Any helper prisoner can turn on switch A only once. Helper prisoners are never allowed to turn off switch A. Only the leader is allowed to turn off switch A. All the prisoners including the leader are allowed to turn on and turn off switch B any number of times. The strategy that the prisoners can use is as follows:

When a helper prisoner enters the room, if switch A is off and switch A has never been turned on by the prisoner, then he turns on switch A. Otherwise he presses switch B and toggles it.

When the leader prisoner enters the room, if switch A is on, he turns off switch A and keeps a track of the number of times he has turned off switch A. Otherwise he presses switch B and toggles it.

This way, for each helper prisoner, switch A is turned on exactly once and turned off exactly once. So when the leader has turned off switch A 22 times, once for each helper prisoner, then all prisoners have been to the switch room at least once.

15. A room has 100 doors. Initially all the doors are closed. The first person enters the room and toggles all the doors (toggling a door means that a closed door is opened and vice versa). Then a second person enters and toggles every 2nd door. Then a third person enters the room and toggles every 3rd door and so on. Find the

8.6 Classic Puzzles

final state of all the doors after 100 people enter the room.

The state of a door can be found based on the number of factors of the door number. If there are odd number of factors for the door number, the door will be open (opposite state of initial state). If there are even number of factors for the door number, the door will be closed (same state as initial state).

For instance, door 9 has three factors - 1, 3, 9. So the final state of door 9 will be open (opposite state of initial state). Door 10 has four factors - 1, 2, 5 and 10. So the final state of door 10 will be closed (same as initial state).

Only perfect squares like 1, 4, 9, etc. will have odd number of factors. The rest of the numbers will have even number of factors.

So at the end the doors 1, 4, 9, 16, 25, 36, 49, 64, 81 and 100 will be open. The rest of the doors will be closed.

9. Personality

The HR round will consist of questions to check if the personality of the candidate and the attitude of the candidate are in line with the expectations of the company. Some of the frequently asked questions are listed below. For each of these questions, you will have to prepare your own answer based on your experiences at college and in the industry. It will be good if you can cite an example in your life while answering these questions.

1. Why should we hire you?

2. What is the most challenging task that you have done so far?

3. What was the most critical situation that you faced in any project and how did you handle it?

4. What are you most proud of yourself?

5. What are your strengths and weaknesses? How have you tried to overcome your weaknesses?

6. Give an instance where you were given negative feedback. How did you handle the situation?

7. How will you manage conflict with your manager or your colleague?

8. What are you not happy with in your current company? What did you do about it?

9. Explain the latest project that you are working on.

10. What software development model do you follow in your project? What are its pros and cons? Which software development model do you like and why?

11. Where do you see yourself in the organization a few years from now?

9. Personality

There are three more questions you should be prepared for. These require more careful thought.

1. Why are you leaving your current organization?

It is better not to talk about any personal disputes or differences of opinion you had with your colleagues or your manager. You can mention that you are looking for better career opportunities and that the skills that you possess would suit the role for which you are being interviewed for

2. Why have you been changing jobs frequently?

It is better not to change jobs too frequently. Each recruiting manager has his or her own criteria to decide on this issue. In case you have changed jobs too frequently you should prepare an answer for this. Again please be diplomatic while answering this question

3. What salary do you expect?

It is better to let the employer first make an offer and then you can negotiate. Sometimes employers will not make the offer. They may insist the candidate on indicating his or her expectation. In this case, do find out the average and maximum hike offered in the industry for your experience level. Mention that the market value of hike offered is x % and that you are willing to negotiate at the end of the technical rounds. Once you are through with all the rounds, if you have performed very well in the interview rounds, you can bargain hard and say that the hike you are asking for is worth it!

I hope you enjoyed reading the book. **If you liked the book, I request you to please give your review comments on Amazon.** All the best for your interviews!

Made in the USA
Middletown, DE
15 May 2019